CASH MANAGEMENT FOR SMALL GOVERNMENTS

Ian J. Allan, editor

Government Finance Research Center
of the
Government Finance Officers Association

180 N. Michigan Avenue
Suite 800
Chicago, IL 60601-7476

Library of Congress catalog card number 89-84639

ISBN 0-89125-135-9

Printed in the United States of America

First printing, June 1989
Second printing, June 1993

CONTENTS

FOREWORD

The last decade has witnessed dramatic changes in the field of public cash management. The opportunity to earn additional revenues for government through improvements in the cash management process has prompted state and local governments to modernize the cash management function. Many have begun to take advantage of the rapid advances in computer technology to improve the efficiency of their operations. Others have joined the growing ranks of governments that have updated their investment statutes to reflect the reality of today's financial climate and market opportunities. These changes are taking place in an environment which places increased emphasis on investment safety and protection of the public money.

This book provides practical advice and encouragement to small local governments interested in improving their cash management operations. *Cash Management for Small Governments,* providing a comprehensive look at concepts and practices in cash management in local government, is more than just a synthesis of prior material. It contains new and useful information, particularly in the areas of computer technology, accounting and financial reporting, and performance evaluation. It is a welcome addition to the growing number of professional publications in the area of public cash management that the Government Finance Officers Association has produced in recent years.

As with other GFOA publications, *Cash Management for Small Governments* is the result of the efforts of many individuals. The authors are to be congratulated for their contribution to the field. Thanks are also due Ian J. Allan, a Manager with the GFOA's Government Finance Research Center in Washington, D.C., and editor of this volume, for his efforts in developing this project and bringing it to completion. Also assisting in the process were members of the GFOA's Committee on Cash Management and staff of the GFOA's Government Finance Research Center and Federal Liaison Center. Finally, I would like to thank Rebecca Russum and the staff of the GFOA's Publications Center for their work in producing the final product.

Jeffrey L. Esser
Executive Director
Government Finance Officers Association
May 1989

PREFACE

The idea for this book grew out of the success of a seminar on cash management for small governments held at the annual conference of the Government Finance Officers Association (GFOA) in Washington, D.C., in June of 1987. The level of interest in the subject matter made it apparent that a need existed for information on cash management concepts and practices that addressed the concerns of finance officers in smaller local governments. Given the rapidly changing environment of public cash management in the 1980s, it was decided that the publication of a book on the subject was an appropriate means to accomplish this. *Cash Management for Small Governments* is the result.

In consultation with members of the GFOA's Committee on Cash Management, a decision was made to focus the book on local governments serving populations of 50,000 or less. Not everyone agreed with this definition of small government, however. Some felt that small governments serve populations of 25,000 and under. Still others, from organizations that served much larger populations, believed that their governments should be considered small because they acted like, or had the characteristics of, a small government. Our decision to define small governments as those which serve populations of under 50,000 persons, although somewhat arbitrary, was intended to make certain that we addressed not only the needs of the smallest organization, but also those that served larger populations that considered themselves to be small. While the book is written for governments in this size range, it contains practical and useful information that will be of value to finance officers in any size government.

Cash Management for Small Governments takes a comprehensive look at cash management in smaller local governments. It was designed to provide finance officers with practical and useful information to enable them to improve the cash management function in their jurisdictions. Its twelve chapters examine different aspects of the topic. Chapter 1 provides the framework for the book through a description of a typical cash management program and the players involved, and a discussion of the steps necessary for establishing and maintaining such a program. Chapter 2 discusses cash control and reporting systems, and their importance to small governments. Chapter 3 examines the impact of GASB Statement No. 3 on accounting and financial reporting for deposits and investments. Chapter 4 evaluates the options available to cash managers for improving the efficiency of the collections and disbursements process. Chapter 5 discusses the establishment of a banking relations policy and the types of bank services available to local governments. Chapter 6 provides tips on negotiating with banks for their services and on how to evaluate proposals for such services, and the services themselves. Chapter 7 discusses the development of a cash forecasting capacity. Chapter 8 provides practical advice on how small governments can develop an investment policy for use in their jurisdictions. Chapter 9 examines the tools and techniques available to cash managers for investing public funds. The appendix to the chapter provides useful information on investing bond proceeds in the aftermath of the Tax Reform Act of 1986. Chapter 10 discusses the importance of performance evaluation and reporting to an effective cash management program. Chapter 11 examines the options available to cash managers in need of short-term financing to cover temporary cash flow deficits. Chapter 12 discusses the role of technology in the dynamic and constantly changing field of cash management.

The authors are to be congratulated for their contributions to this book and to the field of public cash management. While the primary credit for this book is theirs, there were many others who contributed to its completion.

Several members of the GFOA Committee on Cash Management and other individuals played an important role in reviewing various parts of the book. They are: John Bilafer, Treasurer, Town of Arlington, Massachusetts; Michael Chu, CPA, Lance, Soll & Lunghard; Lisa Cole, Cole & Associates; Andrea Daroca, Director of Finance, City of Santa Clarita, California; Charles Darth, Intergovernmental Relations Director, City of Brooklyn Park, Minnesota; Paul Glick, Senior Financial Management Associate, Carl Vinson Institute of Government and the Georgia Center for Continuing Education, University of Georgia; Lloyd Hara, Treasurer, City of Seattle, Washington; Tony Logalbo, Finance Director, Town of Concord, Massachusetts; Lawrence McNerney, Director of Finance, City of Pompano Beach, Florida; Girard Miller, Vice President/Government Markets, Fidelity Investments; J. Virgil Moon, Director of Finance, Cobb County, Georgia; George Nielsen, Vice President, Prudential Bache Securities; Dan Parker, Assistant City Manager, City of Richardson, Texas; Kent Rock, Treasurer, Boise City, Idaho; Henry Sciortino, Deputy State Treasurer, Commonwealth of Pennsylvania; Larry Williamson, Prudential Bache Securities; and, Roberta Wilson, Director of Finance, Denver Board of Water Commissioners, Denver, Colorado.

Two others reviewed the entire book: Greg Aikman, Associate, W.H. Mell & Company; and, Jay Dutcher, Assistant to the Chief for Strategic Planning, Office of the Secretary of Defense.

In addition, several staff members of the GFOA's Government Finance Research Center and Federal Liaison Center assisted in the production or review of the book. Barbara Weiss and Andria Brummitt deserve special recognition for their assistance in editing the text, along with Benjamin Mays for graphics. In addition, I would like to thank the following staff members for their assistance in the production or review of portions of the book: Paul Zorn, Paul Shinn, Joni Leithe, George Valais, Tom McLoughlin, Catherine Holstein, Joe Osha, Sue Robinson, Jim Mallory, William Graham, Percy Aguila, Suzette Randolph, Cathy Spain, and Cathie Eitelberg. I would also like to thank the Senior Director of the Government Finance Research Center, John E. Petersen, for his support of the project.

Finally, thanks are due Rebecca Russum, Director of the GFOA's Publications Center, and to Sharon Fucone, Publications Center Secretary, for their assistance with the production of the book.

Ian J. Allan
Manager
Government Finance Research Center
Government Finance Officers Association
April 1989

1

AN OVERVIEW OF CASH MANAGEMENT

by Paul L. Shinn

Cash management has grown in importance to governments of all sizes and purposes over the past ten to fifteen years. External factors such as rising interest rates, tax limitations, and increasingly competitive financial markets have combined with the growing professionalism of the finance office and the availability of low-cost computer technology to revolutionize the field. The rise of cash management as a discipline has presented finance officers with both new opportunities and greater risks. This book is designed to help cash managers in small governments recognize those opportunities and risks and provide a set of tools to improve cash management techniques.

This chapter provides the basic framework for those chapters that follow. It summarizes the planning and operation of a cash management program, including the objectives of the program, the players it involves, and the steps for establishing and maintaining a cash management system. Most of the concepts and practices examined in this chapter are discussed in greater detail in later chapters. The goal of this chapter is to relate these concepts to each other and to the larger environment of local government finance and management.

The Rise of Cash Management

Until the late 1970s, cash management was a somewhat neglected facet of financial management, especially in smaller governments where staffing limitations outweighed the relatively limited earnings to be gained from more effective cash management practices. In the past ten years, however, a number of events coincided to make cash management much more important. First, interest rates rose abruptly (see Exhibit 1-1). Second, a recession that was severe in some parts of the country reduced growth in the tax base, bringing on budget crises for many state and local governments. Third, the "taxpayers' revolt" forced governments to look elsewhere for revenue to supplement or supplant tax revenues. Fourth, deregulation of the financial markets made cash management both more lucra-

Exhibit 1-1
Annual Rates for 3-Month Treasury Bills
1960-1987

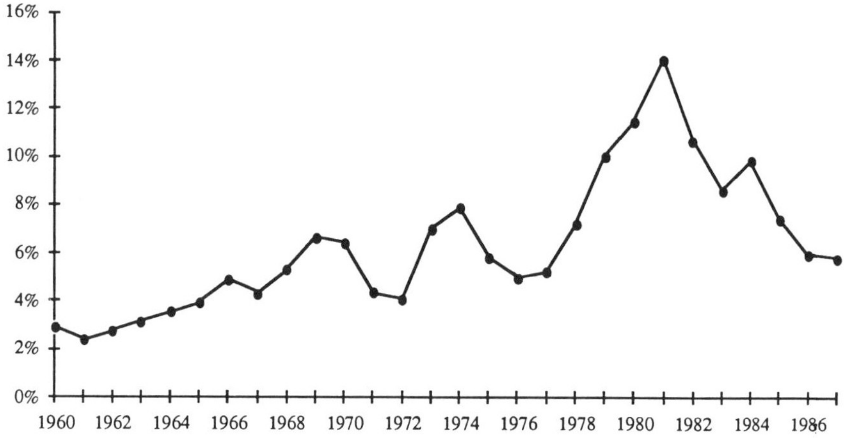

Source: *Economic Report of the President*, (Washington, D.C.: U.S. Government Printing Office, February 1988), Table B-71, pp. 330-1.

tive and more complex. Banks and other institutions offered additional services, disclosed and constantly revised their fees for services, and attempted to compete for public-sector business.

All four events combined to bring cash management to the attention of elected officials, managers, and finance officers. Interest earnings suddenly grew, often partially or wholly making up losses in tax revenue due to limitations or recession. New investment instruments appeared and banks marketed services to governments that they had traditionally limited to large private-sector customers. At the same time, increasing professionalism in the finance office opened the door to better cash management. Large and small jurisdictions alike took steps to collect revenues more quickly and completely and to time expenditures more carefully. They took greater interest in banking services and demanded more cost-effective service and better support from banks. Most importantly, they invested more aggressively both by increasing investable balances and seeking higher yields. Never again would cash management be the neglected stepchild in the finance office.

In the 1980s, cash management experienced somewhat of a backlash against the early rush to maximize yield. A string of defaults by securities dealers, wild fluctuations in the financial markets that stuck some local governments with serious liquidity problems, and increasing suspicions regarding the banking and savings and loan industries made many cash managers sit back and reexamine their cash management programs. At the same time, some states reacted to these problems by placing more restrictions on the options available to the cash manager. The result has been a return to a balanced outlook. The goals of maximizing availability and yield remain, but they are now balanced by a healthy respect for the risks involved and the need to subordinate cash management goals to overall organizational goals.

Objectives of the Cash Management System

Cash management may be defined as all activities undertaken to insure maximum cash availability and maximum investment yield on a government's idle cash. Cash management is concerned with the efficient management of cash from the time revenue is earned to the time an expenditure payment clears the bank. The overriding goals of the cash management system are to maximize availability and to maximize yield. The first goal is met by decreasing time lags from the earning of revenue to its conversion into cash and by timing expenditures to be made on their due dates, not before or after. The second goal is achieved by maximizing investment yield on cash between its collection and disbursement.

To reduce cash management to the twin goals of maximizing available cash and maximizing yield, however, is to oversimplify. The constraints under which the cash manager operates and the inherent conflicts between investment yield and risk dictate that the cash manager strive toward a number of subsidiary objectives as well. These objectives are discussed below and illustrated in Exhibit 1-2 on the next page.

The Cash Management System Should Support the Operations of the Government, Not the Other Way Around

The recent focus on cash management can give the impression that governments are in the business of making money through aggressive investing. This is of course not the case, but it can be difficult to maintain perspective. The cash manager should bear in mind that the government exists to provide services to its citizens and that it must collect tax and fee revenue in order to do so. Effective cash management operates within the constraints dictated by the purpose of government, rather than working consciously or unconsciously to subvert that purpose. Cash should not be maximized at the expense of paying vendors late or alienating taxpayers with intimidating collection procedures. Similarly, yield should not be maximized at the expense of other goals. Where conflicts exist between the two primary goals of cash management, the government should put a higher priority on cash availability than on yield. The cash management system should, above all else, ensure that cash is available to support operations.

The Cash Management System Must Meet all Legal Obligations and Constraints Placed Upon It

Cash management systems do not operate within a legal vacuum. Every state regulates the cash management activities of its local governments to some extent. Revenue collection activities, for example, may be constrained by state legis-

Exhibit 1-2
Cash Management Objectives

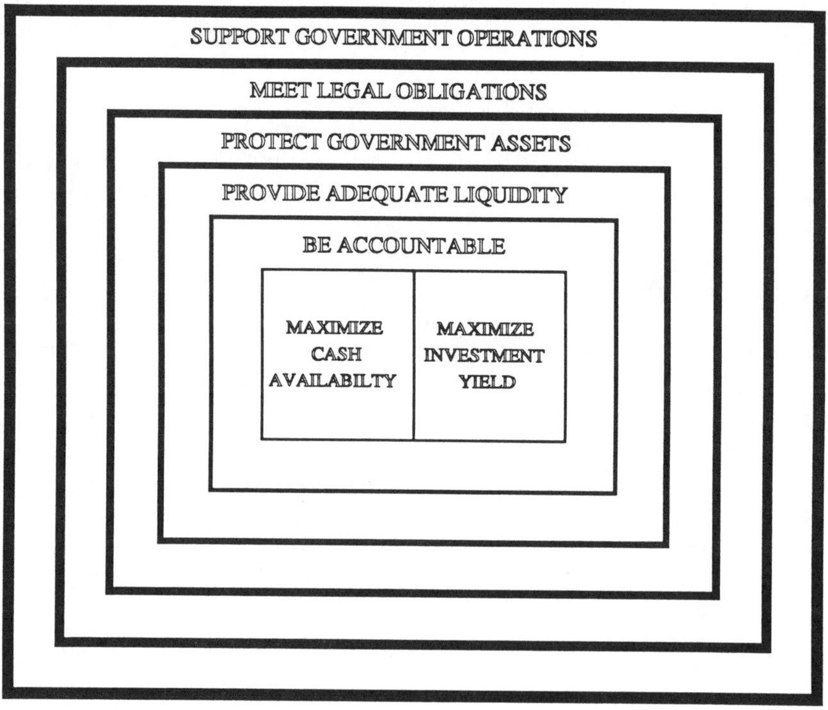

lation specifying the payment schedule and collection process for property and other taxes, and for fees. Expenditure timing may be affected by laws regarding timely payments and interest charges on overdue bills. State laws may restrict the type of financial institutions in which local governments may deposit funds and specify the methods that municipalities may use for selecting banks and securities dealers.

It is in the area of investments, however, that state law plays the greatest role in the cash management system. Many states require that local governments adopt investment policies. Some states also specify maximum investment terms, diversity requirements, and how interest earnings must be apportioned. Most importantly, every state has some legal restrictions on what investment instruments local governments may use. While there is great variation between these statutory limitations, they generally restrict investments to federal, state and local obligations and only low-risk private-sector instruments.

In some states (e.g., Florida), home rule statutes provide certain local governments with more latitude in cash management than otherwise allowed by state law. Regardless of how broad the coverage of the state law, however, its limitations rarely inflict serious damage on a responsible cash management program. Indeed, many small governments may find that an effective cash management program does not have to make use of all of the options available under state law.

The Cash Management Program Must Protect the Assets of the Government at All Times

Cash management is really another form of risk management. Any time that a government earns revenue, makes an investment, or commits to an expenditure, it incurs a certain amount of risk. The cash manager must recognize and minimize the government's exposure to five distinct types of risk, as discussed below.

Default Risk. Default risk applies mainly to investments, but could also come into play with simple checking accounts. Default risk is the risk that some or all of the principal amount of an investment or account will not be available due to default by the issuer, securities dealer or broker, bank or other financial institution. Default risk is best avoided by carefully screening investment dealers and banks for potential default problems, by limiting investments to those instruments which are least likely to result in default, and by insisting upon holding good collateral against all investments. Once a default occurs, the government may have some recourse through the deposit insurance, regulatory, and legal systems. Unfortunately, this will occur only after the government's ability to meet its obligations has been jeopardized, its reputation has been damaged, and its cash manager has spent many sleepless nights.

Market Risk. Market risk is the risk that, while the local government holds an investment instrument, changes in the financial markets reduce the value of the investment. In extreme cases (usually periods of rapidly rising interest rates), the market value of an instrument may fall below the principal amount invested by the government. If the cash manager sells the investment before it matures, part of the principal will be lost. The investor's only recourse is to hold the security until either the market rebounds or it matures, repaying both the face value and interest. The cash manager can protect against market risk by avoiding instruments that are traditionally subject to rapid market swings and by investing with the intent of holding all instruments to maturity. This latter technique makes the government immune to market risk, but may significantly reduce both the investment options available and investment yield. In practice, most governments balance the need to avoid market risk with the desire to maximize yield, always placing the highest priority on reducing market risk.

Reputational Risk. An offshoot of the other forms of risk discussed in this section, reputational risk is simply the risk that the government will lose stature by making a cash management mistake. Few events are more damaging to a government's prestige and potential than a well-publicized investment loss. While the most common cause is loss of principal due to default, the government's reputation may also be damaged by overzealous collection processes or by late payment of expenditures. Reputational risk may cause long-term harm to the government as citizens question the management capability of both elected officials and the professional staff. A poor reputation might also discourage vendors and potential new businesses and residents from working with or locating in the jurisdiction.

Safekeeping Risk. The rise of electronic funds transfers and creative investment instruments has spawned a whole new process of investing, in which many cash managers never see the instrument in which they are investing, if the instrument even exists in tangible form. Many banks, brokers, and dealers prefer to issue a safekeeping certificate or use another simple method to evidence receipt of the principal. The most common use of safekeeping certificates is in repurchase agreements, in which the government purchases certain securities and the broker agrees to repurchase them with interest at a later date. The broker often issues a certificate that the securities are on hand and being held against the investment. This practice makes it difficult for the government to insure that its investment is actually protected in the form of the underlying (or "collateral") securities. Many governments protect against this "external" safekeeping risk by insisting that the collateral securities be physically delivered to the government as a condition of making the investment. This practice may reduce yields, but provides an important form of protection.[1]

Practically speaking, safekeeping risk occurs any time that cash or investment assets are being held or transferred. There is risk that the government will lose cash when it is collected at the finance office, when it is held pending deposit, or when it is being transported for deposit. The more points of cash collection and disbursement the government has, the greater the risk of loss. Governments should develop a practical system of internal controls to minimize "internal" safekeeping risk.[2]

Collection Risk. There can be a significant difference between revenue earned and revenue collected. Nonpayment of taxes, fees, and fines poses a risk that resources budgeted and treated in the accounting system as if received never actually appear. There is also a strong word-of-mouth factor. If a few people seem to get away without paying large amounts in parking fines, many others will try this technique. The government must protect itself against collection risk by adopting and implementing aggressive collection policies.

The Cash Management System Must Provide Adequate Liquidity to Meet All Expected and Unexpected Obligations

Idle cash is only idle and available to invest until it is needed to pay employees or invoices.[3] An important objective of an effective cash management program is to time investments so that they mature at the same time they are needed to meet these obligations. If they mature too early, the government is losing interest earnings. If they mature too late, the government risks a potentially damaging problem of illiquidity, or not having cash available to meet obligations due. The

[1] See Chapter 9 for more information on investment safekeeping.
[2] Chapter 2 provides additional information on internal controls.
[3] Cash is never truly idle; if not invested by the government it is invested by the bank.

cash manager should strive to guarantee liquidity by carefully forecasting expenditures; determining if each upcoming expenditure obligation is "covered" by cash on hand, incoming revenue, or maturing investments; and timing investments to meet the next "uncovered" obligation. The effective cash manager will also allow a margin for unexpected expenditures.

The Cash Management System Must be Well-Documented and Accountable

Because of the risks inherent in cash management, it is essential that the cash management system include a strong accounting and reporting element. The cash manager, outside auditor, elected officials, and citizens must be guaranteed that all receipts are properly recorded and credited, that expenditures are properly charged, and that investments are tracked and earnings properly prorated among funds that provided the principal for the investment. Recently, however, accountability has gone beyond simple cash accounting to embrace management accounting as well. Cash management systems are now expected to be able to document compliance with all state laws and local policies and to report and explain investment earnings.

Cash management must do more than simply maximize cash availability and maximize investment yield. It must support the overall goals of the government rather than detracting from them, satisfy all legal requirements placed upon it, protect assets throughout the process, meet all expenditure obligations, and maintain accountability. As if these qualifiers were not enough to make cash management a challenge, it must be accomplished in an environment of many players both internal and external to the government.

Players in the Process

Cash managers must carry out their duties in an environment of diverse groups and individuals with often conflicting interests. These may be actors within the structure of government or external players. Exhibit 1-3 lists the players affecting the cash management program.

Internal Players

Within the government, players ranging from elected officials and the chief administrative officer through the finance office and line departments have an effect on the cash management program. The cash manager must balance the concerns of each of these players and maintain communication to insure that the cash management system is coordinated with other operations.

Elected officials and the chief administrative officer are not likely to be concerned with cash management on a regular basis. More likely, they will express interest when some external factor arises, perhaps a newspaper article on a default affecting another government or a call from a local banker. The elected body will also be involved periodically in considering policies regarding collections, disbursements, and investments, and, in many cities, in reviewing performance reports.

Exhibit 1-3
Players in the Cash Management Process

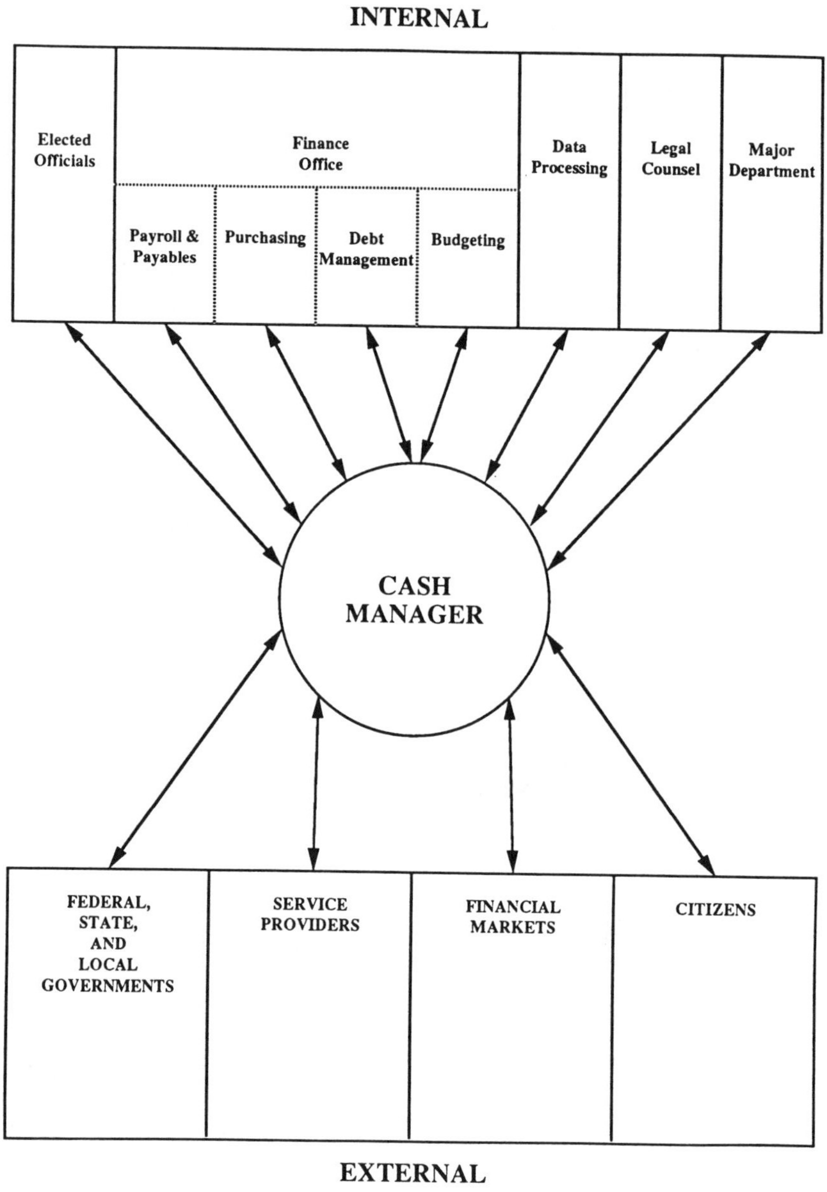

Most activities that affect the cash management program take place within the finance office itself. Small governments may actually have an advantage over larger governments in this regard; there are fewer people to coordinate. The arrangement of financial management activities varies among states and often within a given state. In some instances, cash management may be one activity included within the umbrella of a unified finance office. In others, cash management may be the responsibility of a treasurer, while budgeting and accounting duties are within the purview of a finance director. In still other instances, duties will be split differently. The discussion that follows attempts to minimize the confusion resulting from different organizational arrangements by discussing the functions within the realm of financial management that affect the cash management program. In many small governments, one person will be responsible for more than one function.

The **revenue collection** function has a profound impact on the cash management program. The timing and amount of revenue received are the primary drivers in determining how much cash is available for investing. The cash manager should work closely with the person(s) responsible for collections in order to anticipate when large inflows will be available for investment or disbursement.

The **payroll and payables accounting** functions provide the other side of the equation by defining when cash must be on hand to meet obligations. A large share of expenditures is predictable, both in amount and timing. The cash manager can work with the payroll and payables functions to make regular expenditure projections and to "fine tune" earlier projections as staffing and compensation levels change and as payments to vendors fluctuate.

Similarly, the **purchasing** function can provide valuable advance information on expenditures. Significant changes in the volume of purchase requisitions can be expected to have an impact on expenditures later in the accounting cycle. The cash manager can anticipate these changes in timing investments.

Under the Tax Reform Act of 1986, the connection between the **debt management** function and cash management is growing. The Tax Reform Act places new requirements on governments to track investment earnings on bond proceeds.[4] Meeting these requirements will require careful coordination with the debt management function and often the assistance of an outside expert.

Information must flow both ways between the **budgeting** function and the cash management program. The cash manager uses the budget as a basic background document in preparing cash flow forecasts. He or she will also use budget reports to adjust the forecasts as the fiscal year proceeds. At the same time, the cash manager's projections of interest earnings and available fund balances are integral ingredients in the development of the budget for the following year.

The cash management program is also affected by actions within operating departments other than the finance office. Two departments that provide important support services are **data processing and legal counsel.** Where cash accounting is accomplished in a centralized data processing environment, the cash manager

---

[4]See Chapter 9 for more information on investing bond proceeds.

must work with the data processing department to specify data elements, processing routines, and reporting needs. Once the system is running, the cash manager must be assured that it is properly tracking cash and investments. The government's legal counsel, whether in-house or outside, plays a key role in reviewing policies and contracts with banks, brokers, or dealers, and in assisting in monitoring compliance with state and local laws and ordinances. It is important to keep legal counsel informed of all changes in cash management policies and procedures and to enlist counsel's support in collection efforts and in dealing with investment disputes.

Operating departments with major capital outlays or other fluctuating expenditures have a profound effect on the cash management program. The cash manager should work closely with these departments (perhaps through bimonthly or quarterly meetings) to review recent expenditure history and expected changes. The same applies to departments with significant revenue collection responsibilities (e.g., the tax collector, utilities, and programs with grant funding).

The final internal player is the **rank-and-file employee.** Government is a labor-intensive industry, meaning that payroll activities play a major part in cash availability. Employee demands for more frequent paydays and direct deposit of paychecks can result in significant reductions in cash availability. When analyzing these demands, the cash manager and other officials must balance the competing goals of maximizing available cash and maintaining or improving employee morale.

External Players

External players who may affect the cash management program include other levels of government, providers of cash management services, and two rather amorphous groups of individuals and/or firms, "the financial market" and "the citizens."

Cash management operates in an arena that is dominated by the **federal government.** The Federal Reserve System controls automated payments and regulates much of the banking industry. Other federal involvement includes regulation of thrift institutions, securities dealers and brokers, private issuers of bonds and commercial paper, and insurance on bank and thrift deposits. For the cash manager, the challenge is to understand the role of the federal government, follow its activities, and operate the cash management program within the system that it establishes. The effective cash manager is aware of federal regulations for liquidity, capitalization, and reporting by banks and dealer/brokers. Similarly, the cash manager should be aware of the benefits and potential drawbacks of using the Federal Reserve's electronic transfer capabilities.[5]

The role of the **state government** in regulating investments has been discussed. The state also regulates state-chartered financial institutions. The cash manager

---

[5]See Chapters 4 and 5 for more information on electronic fund transfers.

should use these regulations, reports required to be filed under those regulations, and the state's annual report on banking to evaluate the strength of state-chartered banks.

Many states offer an investment alternative in the form of a local government investment pool. The pool allows local governments to invest excess cash and then pools these investments to purchase securities that are legal for local investing under state laws. The pool offers the advantages of reduced time in seeking yield quotes and in administering investments and may relieve governments of concerns about safekeeping. Investment policies, safekeeping practices, and interest distribution procedures of pools vary, however, and should be carefully monitored and compared to other investment options available.[6] Cash managers should regularly track state pool interest rates. Pool rates are often most competitive in periods of declining interest rates, since pool rates tend to lag behind other interest rates.

Increasingly, groups of **local governments** are forming their own investment pools. These can be advantageous to small governments because they spread both risk and administrative costs. As with state pools, the cash manager should be assured that the management and operation of the pool are sound before relinquishing control over investment decisions to the pool manager.

Contiguous or overlapping local governments may also affect the cash management program in instances where an agency relationship exists. In some states, local governments collect taxes, pay bonded debt, or perform other financial management functions for surrounding jurisdictions. If a government holds agency funds for other jurisdictions, the cash manager should solicit those jurisdictions' input into the investment decision-making process and should provide full disclosure of all cash management activities relating to their funds. In instances where a government's funds are collected or held by another jurisdiction, the cash manager should likewise expect full disclosure and take other steps to insure that the government is enjoying market yields and investment security on its funds.

The dominant external players in the cash management field are private entities providing cash management services. These include banks, thrifts, securities dealers and brokers, issuers of commercial paper, and vendors of computer software.

The cash manager's approach to **providers of financial services** should be similar to the government's approach to vendors of other services. The government must clearly communicate its needs and expectations up front to get the services it wants. It should encourage competition to the extent feasible. It must demand full disclosure of fees, procedures, and contractual requirements. It should demand regular reporting in detail sufficient to make a determination as to whether its assets are safeguarded. This approach, carried out consistently over time,

---

[6]Yields of three state pools are reported regularly in *Public Investor,* published monthly by the Government Finance Officers Association. These yield statistics are useful not only for comparison with other investment opportunities, but for contrasting yield figures resulting from different investment policies.

will earn the vendors' respect and maintain the government's best interest as well.

That collection of individuals, firms, and invisible hands that constitutes **the financial market** also affects the cash management program. It is beyond the cash manager's capability to change the market; however, it must be understood. An effective cash manager monitors interest rate trends, compares the relative yields of different instruments, and reads various economic forecasts. This information can then be used to make informed investment decisions. A word of caution is in order, however: not every new investment instrument will meet the needs of the government and today's high-yield investment may fall out of sight tomorrow. Too much knowledge is not dangerous, but it should be somewhat intimidating.

Finally, **citizens** are affected by the cash management program and may have an effect on it as well. The effects of reputational risk have already been discussed. The cash manager should bear in mind that collection procedures are used in connection with citizens (who are usually both taxpayers and voters) and that overly aggressive collection efforts may backfire in the form of citizen hostility. Similarly, many expenditures are made to local firms or individuals. Delaying payments to them will not improve their view of their local government. Finally, as alluded to already, many cash management service providers are local firms. The goals of competition and cost-effective service often must be balanced against this political reality.

While the foregoing discussion of players in the cash management game could serve to intimidate the cash manager, that is not its purpose. Its purpose, rather, is both to remind the cash manager of the complexity of the task faced in balancing the competing needs of these players and to offer suggestions for managing the cash management program in such a way as to successfully balance those needs. The following section and the remaining chapters of this book offer more detailed guidance in this regard.

Elements of the Cash Management System

The cash management system is cyclical in nature, with each government finding itself at multiple points in the various cycles of activity at any given time. A government may be revising its investment policy and selecting a bank, for instance, at the same time that it is collecting, disbursing, and investing funds under its existing system. It may be easier to think of the cash management system as two cycles that operate simultaneously. This section discusses the system in terms of the systems cycle, which consists of the occasional policy and contractual decisions to be made by the cash manager, and the operating cycle, which comprises the monthly, daily, even hourly actions taken to operate the existing system. Exhibit 1-4 shows how the two cycles relate.

The Systems Cycle

The systems cycle consists of actions that need only be taken, evaluated, and revised occasionally. These actions form the framework in which daily cash management activities are undertaken. There are five key elements within the systems cycle. They are evaluating needs, establishing policies, establishing annual objectives, establishing relationships with financial institutions, and establishing accounting systems. A government cannot realistically expect to undertake these activities sequentially. In reality, they are simultaneous and, in an effective system, ongoing.

Evaluating Needs. This phase consists of two major elements. First, the cash manager should clearly state the objectives of the cash management program. Objectives should define the priority among the often conflicting goals of cash management and government operations, discussed earlier in this chapter. Later, these objectives should be incorporated into policies to be adopted by the governing body.

Second, the cash manager should define the long-term (three to five year) cash flow pattern that the government can expect. This is not the detailed cash flow forecast used in making investments, but the financial plan that must be considered before policies are adopted. It should identify the general trend in revenues and expenditures, the relative weight of predictable and unforeseen expenditures, whether significant revenue items are subject to fluctuations, and what long-term demands will be placed on the system by capital expenditures, debt issuance, and debt repayment. With this general plan in hand, the cash manager may propose policies that closely match the government's long-term financial expectations.

Establishing Policies. Both the governing body and the cash manager will be more comfortable when the government operates under a set of adopted cash management policies than when major policy decisions are made as and when needed. Sound cash management policies improve consistency, create accountability, help insure that laws and ordinances are followed, and create goals by which to measure performance.

The most common cash management policy is the investment policy.[7] It should clearly state the objectives of the investment activity, assign responsibility, establish internal controls, define safekeeping and collateral procedures, and establish a system of monitoring and reporting performance. Investment policies usually establish limits on the maximum maturity for investments and guidelines for diversification of maturity schedules. They also define the instruments in which the government may invest and requirements for diversifying the portfolio between these different instruments and among financial institutions. Many investment policies set standards for selecting and monitoring securities dealers and brokers and guidelines for making individual investment decisions. Like all effective policies, an investment policy should provide for regular review and amendment where necessary.

Cash availability policies are less common than investment policies, but no less important. Governments may wish to have two policies, one addressing revenue collection, and the other, expenditures. The collection policy should state the

[7]See Chapter 8 for a discussion of steps leading to the development of an investment policy.

Exhibit 1-4
The Cash Management Process

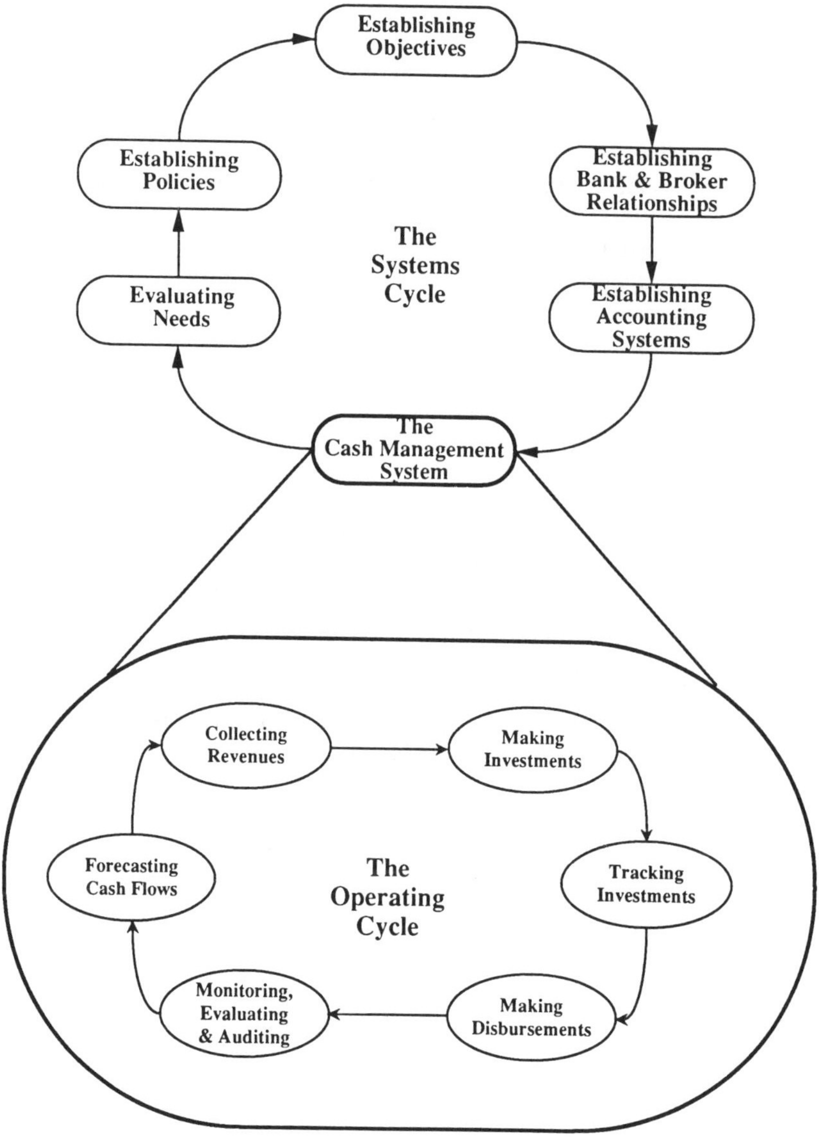

methods to be used to collect revenues (e.g., using lockbox services, offering early payment discounts) and establish procedures for collecting overdue accounts. It should also discuss use of multiple payment points, grace periods, and other amenities which may improve public perceptions of the government but restrict cash availability. An expenditures policy should establish regular payroll and expenditure payment dates, define the cost and inconvenience that the government is willing to undergo in order to more carefully match payment dates to due dates, and define exceptions policies for responding to common requests such as payroll draws and payments to capital project contractors. Like the investment policy, availability policies should provide for assignment of responsibilities, progress reporting, and regular evaluation.

Establishing Annual Objectives. The cash manager should implement the adopted policies by setting more specific objectives. This is best done on an annual basis. Objectives should cover four measures of performance: availability, yield, dollar return, and program efficiency. An availability objective is difficult to set, but can be based on simple rules of thumb such as maintaining an excess cash balance equal to one week's expenditures. A yield objective can be stated either as an absolute percentage or as an amount above or below an index rate.[8] A dollar return objective combines measures of cash availability and investment yield to set a target for total interest earnings for the year. An efficiency objective should state the percentage of idle cash that the cash manager hopes to keep invested during the year. The objectives, once set, should be compared to actual performance and reset annually.

Establishing Relationships With Financial Institutions. The government will in all likelihood work on a daily basis with at least one bank or thrift institution and one or more securities dealers and brokers. It will undoubtedly hear from others who are interested in doing business. While it is not necessarily a good idea to restrict institutions to those selected on an annual basis, it is also harmful to select these key vendors on an ad hoc basis.

The investment policy may state minimum financial requirements for brokers and dealers. The policy should similarly establish minimum requirements for banks and other depositories. The government should be quite confident that its deposits and investments are held by institutions that will be in business both tomorrow and next year.

Practices for selecting a bank vary widely. All governments should recognize that there is a political element involved regardless of the selection process. Nonetheless, the government will be best served by encouraging some level of competition among institutions through a formal or informal selection process. The government should clearly state its minimum financial standards for banks, the services it expects, the expected volume of business, and performance standards, as well as its preferred method for paying fees.[9]

Selecting investment brokers and dealers is usually less formal than selecting

---

[8] Chapter 10 contains additional information on objectives related to investment performance.

[9] See Chapter 6 for more information on selecting banks.

banks because most governments maintain relationships with multiple dealers and because investments are generally of a short-term nature when compared to full-service banking. Still, many of the same concepts apply; competition is to be encouraged and objectives and expectations should be clearly stated. Many governments develop a list of qualified investment dealers, from which they seek competitive quotes on individual investments.

Once the government has selected its financial institutions, it should maintain clear lines of communication and provide regular feedback to the service provider. Further, given the instability in financial organizations, the cash manager must be prepared to modify or sever relationships in the event of downturns in an institution's financial health or its acquisition by an unknown firm. Governments should require that all banks, dealers, and brokers provide regular financial and organizational disclosures.

Establishing Accounting Systems. The government cannot maintain daily operations, much less monitor and improve performance, without adequate accounting systems. Four systems are of importance to the cash manager: the cash accounting system, the investment tracking system, the receivables system, and the payables system.[10]

The cash accounting system tracks all cash entering and leaving government accounts. It must assign all cash transactions to the proper fund and bank account and it must provide summary and detailed information on cash balances on a daily basis. It should also be easily reconcilable to other accounting systems and to bank statements. These items should be reconciled regularly and promptly. If they are not, the cash manager has no way of knowing whether he or she is dealing with accurate information in making investment decisions.

The investment accounting system should provide a record of all investments made by amount, fund, investment institution and type, maturity, and yield. It should provide for simple, automatic apportioning of interest between funds, and should provide summary information regarding average maturity, average yield, and diversity measures. In short, the investment accounting system should provide reports that match the requirements of the investment policy and annual objectives.

Receivables and payables accounting systems can help the cash manager prepare accurate cash flow forecasts and make informed decisions regarding investment maturities. These systems may be relatively informal and may not be automated. This is fine as long as they answer the cash manager's basic questions. For the receivables system, these questions address the amount and type of receivables outstanding, the breakdown of receivables by age, and actions that the government has taken to collect the receivables. The payables system should generate an estimate of amounts and dates of future payments to employees and vendors and an estimate of encumbered amounts remaining obligated but not yet due for payment.

Accounting systems should capture all relevant transactions accurately and

---

[10]Additional information on accounting systems can be found in Chapter 2.

provide accurate and timely information in a useful format. The cash manager should work with those in the finance office, data processing department, and outside vendors who have responsibility for establishing and maintaining accounting systems, striving at all times for system improvements that make monitoring and projecting cash availability, investment status, and investment yield easier. At the same time, the cash manager should supplement the formal accounting system by building an informal network of relationships to obtain supplemental information for use in making operating decisions.

The Operating Cycle

The operating cycle is the series of regular, repetitive actions taken to manage cash. There are six major steps within the operating cycle, each of which is repeated during the year. They are: forecasting cash flows; collecting revenues; making investments; tracking investments; making disbursements; and monitoring, evaluating, and auditing. Each of these activities is discussed in detail in later chapters of this book. This section merely describes the major features and concerns regarding each of the six steps.

Forecasting Cash Flows. The cash manager needs a plan for investing funds. A cash flow forecast comprises such a plan. The goal of preparing a cash flow forecast is to identify revenue and expenditure streams over a given period in the future (usually six months to one year) in order to estimate available cash balances at all times during the forecast period. The forecast cash balances are used to select investment amounts and maturities. The cash manager should use information from the budget and purchasing functions, discussions with major departments, and historical data to prepare the cash flow forecast. The forecast should be updated regularly based on new information and a new month or quarter should be added to the end of the forecast period as each month or quarter ends.[11]

Collecting Revenues. Revenue collection is one of the more routine processes facing the cash manager, but also one with great potential for monetary loss. A government needs to develop systems that will ensure revenues are received in a timely manner, credited to the proper fund, and deposited into the correct bank account as quickly as possible. The cash manager should limit the number of offices that collect and deposit revenue and implement procedures that result in the efficient handling of cash. Finally, the government must establish and follow an aggressive program of collecting all amounts due through a combination of techniques, including the use of follow-up letters and, if necessary, legal action.

Making Investments. Making investments is the most complex and risky step in the cash management process. It requires that the cash manager use judgment in determining the amount, mix of funds, maturity, type of investment, and financial institution. These judgment calls are repeated daily, and usually more often than that. The cash manager must rely on experience as well as the information available from internal and external sources, the cash flow forecast, and the

---

[11]See Chapter 7 for more information on cash forecasting.

accounting system in making investment decisions. The cash manager will normally solicit and evaluate quotations and select the investment with the highest yield that meets all legal, safety, and liquidity requirements.[12]

Tracking Investments. Cash managers must keep track of all outstanding investments. The cash manager must know the amount of money invested, the source of funds, the maturity schedule, and the yield on the investment. For investments that are collateralized, the cash manager should regularly verify that the market value of the collateral exceeds the amount invested. This must be done on a daily basis, since market changes may have a major effect on collateral value. It is also important to track maturity dates carefully to verify that principal and interest are received from the investment institution when due. It is equally important to verify that interest is paid accurately and at the quoted rate. Finally, interest must be allocated to the contributing funds based on methods defined in the investment policy. Departments responsible for managing the funds will expect a clear statement of investment activity on a monthly basis.[13]

The cash manager relies on the investment accounting system for much of the information needed to complete this step. If the investment accounting system is inadequate, tracking investments is difficult and chancy.[14]

Making Disbursements. This step is repeated thousands of times each year. The cash manager's involvement is fairly small. The cash manager must be able to anticipate upcoming expenditures by working with the payroll and payables staff and accounting systems. Effective cash managers consider not only the amount and date of payments, but the amount and timing of disbursement float, which is the time between the day a check is written and the time funds leave the government's bank account to pay the check. The cash manager should constantly monitor the relative levels of float and cash balances in the bank accounts so that investments can be timed to mature when government checks clear the bank, not when they are written. The cash manager should also make decisions regarding payment-related issues such as when to take advantage of early payment discounts, when to pay through wire transfer, and whether to use zero-balance accounts for disbursements. Because the disbursement pattern is the driving force that determines liquidity requirements, it is well worth the cash manager's close attention.[15]

Monitoring, Evaluating, and Auditing. The cash management system must be monitored on a daily basis. Monitoring normally consists of a check on receipts, cash balances, investment balances, and disbursements each day. The cash manager will usually compare these values to the values that yesterday's investment decisions were based on to determine the validity of those decisions. System performance is monitored again at the end of each month. Accounting reports on collections, disbursements, dollars invested and average yields may be com-

---

[12]See Chapter 9 for more information on investing public funds.

[13]Additional information on tracking investments can be found in Chapter 10.

[14]See Chapters 2 and 3 for more information on this subject.

[15]Chapters 4 and 5 contain additional information on disbursements.

pared to target levels and to comparable indicators for the previous month and for the same month in the prior fiscal year. These comparisons are used to prepare performance reports for elected officials and managers, and to fine-tune forecasts for upcoming periods. Monthly data are usually combined to prepare annual reports, which are used in setting the next year's objectives and forecasts. The program is usually audited annually as part of the government's financial audit. At this time, the independent auditor will evaluate and report on internal controls, the ability of the accounting system to capture data on every transaction, and compliance with legal and policy requirements. The cash manager can also use information from the audit in preparing future policies and objectives and in completing individual transactions. The process of monitoring, evaluating, and auditing performance thus completes and ties together both the systems cycle and the operating cycle.[16]

Summary

Cash management has grown in importance to all governments, even the smallest, over the past decade, and is now considered a key element of the financial management program. The cash manager must balance often conflicting goals in an environment with many players. Establishing and maintaining a cash management system that maximizes availability of cash and maximizes investment yield is a task that will challenge the most creative and capable financial manager. This book helps meet that challenge by providing detailed guidance on current concepts and practices in small government cash management.

[16]Several of the following chapters provide information on monitoring, evaluating, and auditing a government's cash management system.

2

CASH CONTROLS AND REPORTING SYSTEMS

by Andrea Daroca and Frank P. Daroca

This chapter examines one of the most essential aspects of controlling day-to-day operations for any government, the cash control and reporting system. The cash control and reporting system is the mechanism that expedites the machinery of government by allowing managers to understand the impact of their decisions. The system permits them to plan, direct and control operations in a more effective manner, for without the data provided by the system, management would have no way of knowing where it is, much less where it wants to be.

Cash control and reporting systems, vital to the operations of all cash management programs, have three objectives:

- to assure the recording of cash receipts and disbursements on a timely basis;
- to assure that sufficient funds are on hand to meet operational and capital expenditure needs; and
- to facilitate the investment of idle cash to maximize revenues, thus permitting an increase in the level of service provided by the city or the setting aside of funds in reserve for future needs.

Accurate information is the key to accomplishing these objectives. By accurately reporting cash on hand and facilitating the forecasting of cash flows, cash control and reporting systems can help to identify investable cash and potentially boost investment earnings.

It is sometimes observed that only large governments can afford to establish and maintain an effective cash control and reporting system, but this notion is entirely mistaken. While larger governments must have a control and reporting system to simply account for their greater resources, smaller governments have an even more critical need since they lack the margin of safety and greater tolerance of error of bigger organizations. An overlooked investment opportunity, while unfortunate for a large government, may be disastrous for a smaller government because of its relatively greater dependence on each resource.

The balance of this chapter is devoted to a discussion of effective cash control and reporting systems, and their usefulness to small governments.

Cash Controls For Small Governments[1]

Because of the risk inherent in handling cash and investments, internal control is an important consideration, especially for smaller governments with fewer personnel. Independent auditors consider an adequate internal control environment essential for the reliability of financial statements. Furthermore, good internal control procedures can help to reduce audit fees by allowing the auditors to rely on those controls, thereby permitting a reduction in the extent of their audit tests.

Internal control is established by governments to help them meet their goals. While the configuration of an internal control environment varies widely, internal controls are established to meet five objectives:

- To provide reliable data for management. Transactions that represent economic events are recorded in accordance with prescribed procedures in the right accounts in the correct amounts on a timely basis.
- To safeguard assets and records. Access to assets and related documentation is restricted to authorized personnel. Furthermore, the accounting records are maintained so that they continue to reflect the operations of the government.
- To establish accountability for assets, with timely verification and appropriate follow-up.
- To promote operational efficiency, reduce unnecessary duplication of effort, and deter inefficient use of government resources.
- To assure that transactions are recorded to permit preparation of financial statements in conformity with generally accepted accounting principles (GAAP).

Although these purposes are ideal, they must be implemented within the confines of sound financial management. Thus, internal controls need only provide reasonable, not absolute, assurance that these objectives will be accomplished. Guaranteed achievement of these goals is probably impossible, and is usually financially unsound in smaller cities since they may lack the resources to provide for the necessary increased division of responsibilities among staff. Augmented internal controls generally come at a cost, and that cost should not exceed the benefits expected to be derived.

The control environment in a city permeates all aspects of operations, not just the finance function, and extends from the management philosophy and operating style of the legislative body to external influences affecting the staff. One of the most important elements of the control environment is personnel policies and procedures. To ensure a good internal control system, management must hire competent personnel with integrity and then train them so that they understand their duties.

---

[1]The American Institute of Certified Public Accountants has promulgated important pronouncements regarding internal control. This chapter has borrowed freely from its Statement on Auditing Standards No. 55, *Consideration of the Internal Control Structure in a Financial Statement Audit,* which becomes effective January 1, 1990, and replaces Statement on Auditing Standards No. 1, Section 320, *The Auditor's Study and Evaluation of Internal Control,* which is currently in effect.

Internal control does not function with people working in a vacuum, but rather in cooperation with others. Thus, the *segregation* of functions is one of the most powerful aspects of internal control. The overriding principle is: no one person should ever be placed in a situation to carry out or conceal an error or irregularity without timely detection by others in the normal course of carrying out their responsibilities.

In general, functions should be fixed and separated for three different types of activities:

- authorization of transactions;
- recording transactions; and
- maintaining custody of assets.

For example, if purchase authorization and recording were not segregated, controls would not prevent the recording of unauthorized purchases. Likewise, if recording cash receipts were not separate from maintaining custody of cash, the possibility of concealment of theft would be enhanced.

Often, operating efficiency dictates that tasks be broken into smaller functions; it is generally easier to train one person to do one thing than it is to have one person handle several tasks. However, because of the risk inherent in handling cash, segregation of functions rather than efficiency should be the guiding principle. Thus, by separating cash receipts from record keeping, collusion among employees would be required in order to conceal defalcation. In larger organizations, the segregation of functions is a common practice; recording transactions is usually the responsibility of the controller's department (responsible for general accounting, payroll, billing, receivables and payables and the general ledger), while maintaining cash comes within the scope of the treasurer's office (responsible for handling cash receipts and disbursements as well as investments). In smaller governments the separation is often less distinct since both activities are generally housed within the same department, thereby reducing the effectiveness of internal control.

Exhibits 2-1 and 2-2 are lists that independent auditors like to review with responsible officials to help them determine the control environment in a city. A "Yes" answer to each question is viewed by auditors as an indication of good internal control.

Internal Auditing. While most internal auditing functions are beyond the wherewithal of small governments that lack the financial resources to support the necessary staff, a technique used by internal auditors could easily be incorporated into the activity of even the smallest organization: periodic surprise cash counts of cash drawers and petty cash. This technique has been shown to be a powerful deterrent against petty theft. Tact must be used to prevent offending staff with control over these assets. Preferably, use of this procedure should be discussed with staff at recruiting so as not to cast aspersion on individuals.

Exhibit 2-1
Internal Control Features Concerning Cash Receipts

1. Are bank accounts properly authorized by the treasurer?
2. Is the mail opened by a person who does not prepare the deposit?
3. Is the mail opened by a person who does not have access to the accounts receivable ledger?
4. Does the employee who opens the mail list the receipts in detail?
5. Are the listed mail receipts compared with the cashier's records by an independent person?
6. Are cash receipts deposited intact daily?
7. Are cash receipts journalized and posted when received?
8. Are miscellaneous cash receipts independently controlled?
9. Is the cash deposited by someone other than the person who prepares the bank deposit?
10. Does the person who deposits the cash *not* have access to the accounts receivable ledger?
11. Is the duplicate deposit ticket, stamped by the bank, returned to a person other than the one who prepares the deposit?
12. Are bank-stamped duplicate deposit tickets compared with the cash receipts book?
13. Are persons who handle cash bonded?
14. Are post-dated checks reported when received?
15. Are post-dated checks held in safekeeping?
16. Are returned customer checks delivered to a person other than the one who prepared the bank deposit?
17. Are returned customer checks ever redeemed by an employee?
18. If the answer to Question 17 is "yes", does the employee making the redemption *not* have access to cash receipts, the accounts receivable ledger, or customer statements?
19. Is physical control of negotiable securities held for safekeeping with an independent third party?
20. Do people in the cashier's department *not*:
    a. Have any collection duties?
    b. Prepare, sign, or mail checks?
21. Are vacations mandatory?
22. Is a system of dual cash or investment controls in place?
23. Is a surety bond required for employees handling cash?

Cash Reporting Systems for Small Governments

The ability to maintain an adequate cash flow and properly invest surplus cash is the most important function of a treasurer. Cash reporting systems facilitate the performance of this function, and have the following components, each of which interacts and relies on the other:

- a cash accounting system;
- an investment and interest apportionment accounting system; and
- a reconciliation reporting system of cash and investments consisting of bank reconciliations and treasurer's reports.

The Cash Accounting System

The cash accounting system is required to maintain the daily receipts and disbursements that occur in all jurisdictions. These activities are maintained by fund and account designation, and the resulting data are used to provide information for management to help achieve the organizational goals discussed earlier. The cash accounting system is the basis upon which all other systems are built.

Exhibit 2-2
Internal Control Features Concerning Cash Disbursements

1. Are all checks prenumbered by the printer and accounted for?
2. Are spoiled or voided checks mutilated, retained, and properly filed to prevent reuse?
3. Is there a policy against making checks payable to "Cash", "Bearer", "Currency", etc.?
4. Is a check protector used?
5. Are unused checks properly controlled?
6. Are persons who sign checks other than those who:
   a. Handle petty cash?
   b. Approve disbursements?
   c. Record cash receipts?
   d. Post to the ledger accounts?
7. Are persons indicated in Question 6 forbidden to mail checks?
8. Are persons who sign checks designated by the City Council?
9. If signature facsimiles are used, is the signature machine properly controlled?
10. Have banks been instructed to cash no checks payable to the order of the City?
11. Is the signing of blank checks in advance forbidden?
12. Are checks countersigned?
13. When checks are presented for signatures, are invoices and supporting documentation also presented?
14. Are invoices and supporting documentation mutilated or stamped "Paid" at the time of payment?
15. Are the preparation of checks and approval of invoices separated?
16. Are bank accounts reconciled monthly?
17. Is the treasurer's report prepared monthly?
18. Is the treasurer's investment portfolio prepared monthly for presentation to the City Council?
19. Are bank statements and paid checks delivered directly to the person preparing the reconciliation?
20. Do the duties of the person preparing the bank reconciliation exclude:
    a. Signing the checks?
    b. Recording cash transactions?
    c. Handling cash?
21. Does the person who reconciles the bank account:
    a. Account for all check numbers?
    b. Examine signatures?
    c. Examine endorsements?
    d. Examine payee's name?
    e. Examine dates?
22. Are transfers of funds from one bank account to another promptly recorded?
23. Is authority for bank transfers limited to the treasurer?
24. Are checks bearing improper endorsements returned to the bank for correction?
25. Are long-outstanding checks properly followed and controlled?
26. Are stop-payment notices on outstanding checks properly controlled?
27. Are the responsibilities of those investing funds separated from those:
    a. Recording investments?
    b. Preparing confirmation of purchases?
    c. Matching securities purchases with confirmation from brokers, dealers or institutions?
    d. Preparing bank reconciliation and treasurer's reports?
28. Are vacations mandatory?
29. Is a surety bond required for employees disbursing cash?

Essentials. A good cash accounting system contains five essentials:

- it provides accurate and current data, resulting in improved control over cash invested and balances in bank accounts;
- it allows interest to be allocated based on daily cash balances by fund;
- it permits comparison of budgeted with actual cash on hand;
- it provides some of the information needed to perform reconciliations; and
- it supplies the cash balance information required to invest idle cash in compliance with city, state and federal investment guidelines.

Problems. A description of the basics of cash receipts and disbursements is an accounting topic and, therefore, outside the scope of this book. However, two problems that can occur with a cash accounting system should be discussed.

Although many small governments combine the treasurer's function with that of the finance director, others do not. While merging these functions causes internal control difficulties as noted earlier, separation of these duties can lead to coordination problems between the finance director and treasurer and resultant lack of timely reporting.

In governments that separate the two functions, the cash received, disbursed, and invested in a bank must be maintained by the government's reporting system under the supervision of the finance director. This often led to a second separate system maintained by the treasurer, where the potential for misunderstanding and conflict was manifest. Today, with the advent of computers and interactive software, the interface between the two functions can be easily managed by allowing the treasurer to access cash information with the use of passwords. It is imperative that the finance director and treasurer communicate and have access to the same information to facilitate expenditures and investments.

A second problem that causes conflict is the lack of timely reporting of information. Historical information is valuable, but only if it is prompt. Investments, expenditures and future planning all depend on up-to-date balances; therefore, all transactions affecting cash should be recorded as soon as possible to assure proper reporting. Examples of such reports include daily printouts of total cash balances by fund and total cash needs to cover disbursements as they become known. This latter requirement involves a proactive strategy to assure adequate funds to meet the needs of operations and investing.

One method of accomplishing this is to use a demand register, which is a listing of planned cash disbursements by date. This document should be prepared regularly by the finance department and sent to the treasurer to aid in monitoring future cash outflows.

Creating a demand register for operating expenditures is relatively simple since they tend to be easily predictable. However, capital expenditures usually call for more long-range planning because of their irregular pattern. One method of avoiding unexpected demands on cash because of unplanned capital expenditures is a monthly listing of planned capital acquisitions by dates and amounts. This document should be circulated among department heads requesting their reconfirmation of previous planned commitments and requesting updates as plans change.

To be of maximum budgeting benefit, the listing should cover a reasonable time horizon—six to twelve months—and should be a rolling report, one that continually adds a new month as the current month is completed.

Accounting for Investments and Interest

In fund accounting, each fund has its own cash account. Thus, accountants have traditionally maintained separate checking accounts that corresponded with these separate cash fund balances. However, this method can be very cumbersome. For example, a temporary overdraft in one account would have to be covered by a transfer from another account with excess funds. Moreover, with several accounts, bank service fees could be higher because of a city's difficulty in maintaining a minimum compensating balance in each of its accounts.

A more modern approach is to pool all bank accounts, regardless of fund classification, into one bank account. Not only does this reduce the likelihood of excessive bank service charges, it also facilitates the investing of idle cash funds by centralizing all banking activity into one account, enabling the treasurer to more easily identify cash resources and match them with current and anticipated demands on cash.[2]

Apportionment of Interest. Pooling should have no effect on the segregation of cash by fund for accounting purposes, interest allocation and reporting. Of course, the pooling of cash in this manner makes reconciling the bank balance more difficult when compared to the individual account approach, but this inconvenience is more than offset by the aforementioned gains.

The pooling method produces a complication, however, in that interest earned is no longer income to a particular fund but rather results from the pooling of cash of all funds. Thus, an interest allocation system must be established to properly credit individual funds for the portion of overall interest earned by each fund. If done correctly, the interest allocation method will satisfy legal requirements, such as OMB Circular A-102 *(Grants and Cooperative Agreements with State and Local Governments)*, which provides guidelines for the handling of federal monies.

There are two apportionment methods currently in use:

- average daily cash balance by fund—in which the interest is based on the daily cash balance remaining in each fund; and
- average monthly cash balance in the fund—resulting in the interest being allocated monthly or annually based on the average monthly cash balance in each fund.

Most auditors are satisfied with either method so long as it is used consistently.

Exhibit 2-3 illustrates one method of allocating interest suitable for a small government, the annual allocation of interest based on monthly cash balances. This can easily be done with an electronic spreadsheet using a microcomputer, as was done for this example.

In Exhibit 2-3, the proportional total of ending monthly cash balances is used as a basis for allocating the total interest earned on an annual basis. Of course,

---

[2]See Chapter 4 for more information on concentration accounts.

Exhibit 2-3
Allocation of Interest Earned Among Funds

ENDING CASH BALANCE BY FUND

	GENERAL FUND	GAS TAX	PARKS	BOND	TOTAL
July 31	$ 8,258,186	$ 295,757	$ 474,768	$ 27,248	
August 31	8,257,933	277,055	474,768	26,635	
September 30	8208,124	617,592	481,783	26,525	
October 31	9,267,174	294,442	784,153	26,089	
November 30	9,162,595	294,442	784,153	30,947	
December 31	11,193,230	287,369	472,144	30,770	
January 31	10,921,419	466,440	477,587	28,972	
February 28	10,803,140	459,564	471,794	37,489	
March 31	10,764,352	421,726	340,452	37,683	
April 30	10,960,626	104,580	332,050	34,468	
May 31	11,054,038	90,731	332,060	39,513	
June 30	10,891,621	89,147	466,564	28,856	
Total	$ 119,742,438	$ 3,655,018	$ 5,533,181	$ 375,184	$129,305,821
Percent	92.604%	2.827%	4.279%	0.290%	
				Interest Earned Fiscal Year 19X	$ 786,620.73
				Accrued June 30, 19X9	114,019.70
Allocation	$ 834,029.06	$ 25,461.11	$ 38,538.40	$ 2,611.86	$ 900,640,43

interest could be allocated monthly, but this would lead to a concomitant increase in effort because of the constant need to accrue interest not yet received.

Reconciliation Reports: Purposes and Procedures

A good accounting system produces accurate and timely records of cash on hand and investments. Three types of reconciliations, described in the following sections, are useful for maintaining proper control over cash: bank reconciliations, proofs of cash and various treasurer's reports.

Bank Reconciliation. A bank reconciliation is a schedule indicating and explaining differences between the bank's record of a government cash account and the government's record. A bank reconciliation is one of the most important features of cash management because it helps the government account for:

- transactions recorded by the government not yet recorded by the bank—timing differences (e.g., outstanding checks, deposits in transit);
- transactions by the bank unrecorded by the government (e.g., a note collected by the bank on behalf of the government, bank service charges);
- errors by the government (e.g., incorrectly recording the amount of a check in the check register or cash disbursements journal); and
- errors by the bank (e.g., collection of interest on a certificate of deposit correctly recorded by the government, but inadvertently credited to the wrong account by the bank).

Exhibit 2-4
Reconciliation of Bank and Book Balances

Balance per bank statement, May 31, 19X9				$ 274,843.72
Add:				
Bank charge not recorded			$ 86.22	
Deposit in transit			45,846.52	45,932.74
				$ 320,776.46
Deduct:				
Outstanding checks #	7437	$ 150.47		
	7348	4,820.00		
	7350	76.19		
			$ 5,046.66	
Interest on First S&L CD collected but not recorded			2,000.00	7,046.66
Balance per books, May 31, 19X9				$ 313,729.80

Exhibit 2-5
Proof of Cash for May, 19X9

	Balance April 30	May Receipts	May Disbursements	Balance May 31
Per bank statement:	$ 199,583.24	$ 5,457,285.22	$ 5,382,024.74	$274,843.72
Deposits in transit:				
at April 30	39,485.11	(39,485.11)		
at May 31		45,846.52		45,846.52
Outstanding checks:				
at April 30	(22,696.54)		(22,696.54)	
at May 31			5,046.66	(5,046.66)
Other reconciling items:				
Bank charges at April 30	100.13		100.13	
Bank charges at May 31			(86.22)	86.22
First S&L CD interest		(2,000.00)		(2,000.00)
Per Books:	$ 216,471.94	$ 5,461,646.63	3$ 5,364,388.77	$ 313,729.80

The general form of a bank reconciliation, shown in Exhibit 2-4, is known as a bank to books reconciliation, since it starts with the balance obtained from a bank statement as of a certain date and ends with the book cash balance on that same date.

Items recognizing timing differences require no action by the government since they will eventually be recorded by the bank. However, all other reconciling items require some response by the government. If the item represents a bank transaction unrecorded by the government (such as the bank charges and the unrecorded interest) or an error by the government, an adjusting entry is required. On the other hand, if the item represents a bank error, the bank will have to be notified of the mistake and corrective action taken on its part.

Exhibit 2-6
Treasurer's Reconciliation Report

	FUND ACCOUNT				
	GENERAL FUND	GAS TAX	PARKS	BOND	TOTAL
Balance, May 31, 19X9	$ 11,054,038	$ 90,731	$ 332,050	$ 39,513	$ 11,516,332
June 1 Deposit	50,000				50,000
2 Warrant	(80,000)		(70,000)		(150,000)
3 NSF check	(50)				(50)
•	•	•	•	•	•
•	•	•	•	•	•
•	•	•	•	•	•
30 Deposit	45,865	1,584			47,449
Balance, June 30, 19X9	$ 10,891,621	$ 89,147	$ 466,564	$ 28,845	$ 11,476,177

	CASH ACCOUNT			
	GENERAL CHECKING	SAVINGS	INVESTMENTS	TOTAL
Balance, May 31, 19X9	$ 121,332	$ 95,000	$11,300,000	$ 11,516,332
June 1 Deposit	50,000			
2 Warrant	(150,000)			
3 NSF check	(50)			
•	•	•	•	•
•	•	•	•	•
•	•	•	•	•
30 Deposit	47,449			
Balance, June 30, 19X9	$ 68,731	$ 95,000	$ 11,312,446	$ 11,476,177

Proof of Cash. A second type of control schedule is a four-column reconciliation, known as a proof of cash. This statement reconciles an entire month's activity, not just the balance on a particular day. The work paper starts with the bank reconciliation as of the first of the month (the reconciliation at the end of the previous month), continues with the reconciliation of all receipts and disbursements for the month, and concludes with the same end-of-month reconciliation demonstrated in Exhibit 2-4. An example proof of cash is shown in Exhibit 2-5.

Because the proof of cash reflects all activity in a particular cash account for an entire month, it is more powerful than the standard bank reconciliation and is used by auditors when they conclude that internal control surrounding cash is weak.

Treasurer's Reconciliation Report. For many smaller governments with poor internal control over cash, a treasurer's reconciliation report serves as an excellent internal control device. This report is used by the treasurer to keep track of all daily activity in each accounting cash fund and every cash and investment

Exhibit 2-7
Sample of Statutory Requirement

§ 53646. Treasurer's reports and statements of investment policy

Text of section operative until Jan. 1, 1991.

(a) The treasurer or chief fiscal officer . . . shall annually render to the legislative body of the local agency a statement of investment policy.

(b) The treasurer or chief fiscal officer shall render a monthly report to the chief executive officer and legislative body of the local agency showing the type of investment, institution, date of maturity, amount of deposit, current market value of all securities with a maturity of more than 12 months, rate of interest, and such data as may be required by the local agency. The monthly report shall specify in detail investments made pursuant to subdivision (i) of Section 53601, Section 53601.1, and subdivision (i) of Section 53635.

(1) The monthly report shall state its relationship to the statement of investment policy.

(2) In the monthly report, a subsidiary ledger of investments may be used in accordance with accepted accounting practices.

(3) The monthly report shall also include any information which the treasurer or chief fiscal officer determines would demonstrate that the local agency's expenditure requirements can be met in the following month.

(4) A school district is not required to render a monthly report on any of its funds in the custody of the county treasurer.

(c) This section shall remain in effect only until January 1, 1991, and as of that date is repealed, unless a later enacted statute, which is enacted before January 1, 1991, deletes or extends that date. If that date is not deleted or extended, then, on or after January 1, 1991, pursuant to Section 9611 of the Government Code, Section 53646 of the Government Code, as amended by Section 8 of Chapter 105 of the Statutes of 1983, shall have the same force and effect as if this temporary provision had not been enacted.

---

account owned by the government. Thus, the activity by fund and by account and investment is constantly maintained, assuring that the total balance per books is always in agreement with the balance per bank. A simple telephone call to the bank is sufficient to obtain the bank balance, but a computer is necessary to supply information about reconciling items.

For governments without the wherewithal to maintain this schedule on a daily basis, a monthly report can be substituted. Exhibit 2-6 illustrates a sample treasurer's reconciliation report. The treasurer's report facilitates the preparation of the treasurer's monthly schedule of investments report, discussed below.

Because of the risk categorization disclosure in the comprehensive annual finance report (CAFR) required by Governmental Accounting Standards Board (GASB) Statement No. 3, *Deposits with Financial Institutions, Investments (Including Repurchase Agreements), and Reverse Repurchase Agreements,* it may be wise for the treasurer to list investments in the report by category to facilitate preparation of this information for the CAFR. This procedure will also require the treasurer to consider risk classifications of new investments as they are purchased.[3]

Treasurer's Investment Report. Many states require the treasurer to submit

[3]See Chapter 3 for more information on this subject.

Exhibit 2-8
Sample Treasurer's Investment Report

CITY OF ACME
INVESTMENT PORTFOLIO—MONTH ENDING 30-APR-88

	Cost	Percent	Average Remaining Life Days	Yield
S&L Certificates of Deposit..............$	4,958,000	33.72%	229	7.805%§
Local Agency Investment Funds ....$	4,365,000	29.68%		8.000%§
Federal/Agency Issues.....................$	2,836,562	19.29%	1,850	8.199%§
Negotiable Certificates of Deposit.......		0.00%		
Bankers Acceptances.......................$	2,297,213	15.62%	41	6.967%§
Commercial Paper..........................$	197,837	1.35%	41	6.670%§
Passbook Savings..........................$	50,010	0.34%		5.127%§
Grand Total Investment Portfolio ....$	14,704,622	100.00%†		

1986-87 Actual Interest Income ....$	807,547
1987-88 Budgeted Interest Income......$	741,000
Actual Year-to-Date Interest Income ....$	730,132
Percent of Interest Received to Date.....	98.53%
1987-88 Estimated Interest Income .....$	802,000
City Weighted Average Rate of Return .	7.784%§

§ All averages are weighted.
† May not add due to rounding.

I verify that this investment portfolio is in conformity with all State laws and the Treasurer's investment policy which is approved annually by the Acme City Council. Treasurer's cash management program provides sufficient liquidity to meet next month's estimated expenditures.

Mary Smith
City Treasurer

Copies to: City Council, City Manager, Deputy Treasurer, City Clerk, Account Technician

Date

a list of all investments monthly as well as an annual position statement on investment policy to the administration of the government and the legislative branch. Exhibit 2-7 reproduces section 53646 of the California State Code detailing this requirement in that state.

A sample investment report is shown in Exhibit 2-8. Besides detailing the investments, this report also compares budgeted interest to actual as well as the estimated actual for fiscal year 1987-88. The report includes the prior year's budget and actual interest income figures and calculates actual yield weighted by

Exhibit 2-8 (continued)
Sample Treasurer's Investment Report

CITY OF ACME
INVESTMENT PORTFOLIO—MONTH ENDING 30-APR-88

Description	Cost	Rate	Yield	Purchase Date	Maturity Date	Life To Maturity Days	Remaining Life Days	GASB 3 Category
*** S&L CDs ***								
First S&L	$ 99,000	7.500%	7.500%	18-May-87	17-May-88	365	17	1
Second S&L	99,000	7.500%	7.500%	22-Feb-88	23-May-88	91	23	1
•	•	•	•	•	•	•	•	1
•	•	•	•	•	•	•	•	1
	$4,958,000	7.691%	7.805%			652	229	
*** Local Agency Investment Fund ***								
LAIF	$4,365,000	8.000%	8.000%					N.A.
*** Federal/Agency Issues ***								
FNMA Notes◊	$ 185,560	7.600%	8.190%	25-Sep-87	01-Sep-88	342	124	1
FNMA Notes◊	279,875	6.900%	7.400%	07-Jan-88	22-Dec-88	350	236	1
•	•	•	•	•	•	•	•	1
•	•	•	•	•	•	•	•	1
	$2,836,562	8.310%	8.199%			2,103	1,850	
*** Bankers' Acceptances ***								
Bank of Somewhere	97,706	7.000%	7.160%	06-Jan-88	03-May-88	118	3	1
Something Bank, LA	99,460	6.700%	6.740%	12-Apr-88	11-May-88	29	11	1
•	•	•	•	•	•	•	•	1
•	•	•	•	•	•	•	•	1
	$2,297,213	6.781%	6.967%			101	41	
*** Commercial Paper ***								
Big Company	$ 197,837	6.600%	6.670%	12-Apr-88	10-Jun-88	59	41	1
*** Passbook Savings ***								
Bank of Acme	$ 50,100	5.000%	5.127%					1

◊ Fannie Mae Discount Notes

amount of investment and time to maturity.[4] For internal control purposes most governments should not store their own investments but rather have the securities held in safekeeping by a third-party trust department.

[4]Details about this report can be found in Andrea Daroca and Frank P. Daroca, "Computerized Portfolio Reporting," *Government Finance Review,* December 1987, pp. 22-24.

This report is an invaluable cash planning tool because it contains an updated list of all investments by maturity date, thus permitting the matching of disbursements with investment maturities.[5] For those governments lacking computers, a simple card file of investments filed by maturity date is helpful. The file must be updated as securities mature and new investments are purchased.

External Documents. All of the reports discussed in this chapter are interdependent with the bank reconciliation shown in Exhibit 2-4. There are several documents needed to reconcile bank accounts and to calculate resultant journal entries. These consist of bank statements from the jurisdiction's servicing bank; confirmations from dealers, brokers or institutions verifying the purchase, maturity or interest of investment instruments; and safekeeping receipts and trust department safekeeping reports.

Summary

Dynamic changes in municipal governments, the revolution in information technology, the ever-shifting economic environment—these and other factors point to the need for a well-developed control and reporting system so that governments may control their future. Such a system should include planning of the government's overall cash objectives and controls to assure their achievement.

---

[5]This type of report is very useful in cash forecasting. See Chapter 7 for more information on that subject.

3

ACCOUNTING AND FINANCIAL REPORTING FOR DEPOSITS AND INVESTMENTS

by David R. Bean

The release of the Governmental Accounting Standards Board's (GASB) Statement No. 3, *Deposits with Financial Institutions, Investments (Including Repurchase Agreements), and Reverse Repurchase Agreements,* significantly changed the extent of display and disclosure requirements for local governments. Although these changes were designed primarily to highlight complex investment transactions, the statement also provides guidance that applies even to simple checking accounts.

In the remainder of this chapter, GASB Statement No. 3 will be discussed in detail, with the focus on the following: its background; its basic requirements; and, the financial statement presentations that it requires. Because the complexity of transactions is not directly correlated with the size of a government, *all* display and disclosure requirements for deposits and investments will be reviewed.

Background

Before GASB Statement No. 3, display and disclosure requirements for deposits and investments were limited. Generally, disclosures presented within a government's financial statements only included a description of the valuation basis for investments (i.e., cost or amortized cost) in the Summary of Significant Accounting Policies (SSAP). Soon after the five-member GASB was established under the auspices of the Financial Accounting Foundation (FAF) in 1984, several developments occurred in the financial community that affected many governments and their investment policies. During this period, financial institutions in certain areas of the country were failing at an alarming rate. Moreover, several broker/dealers engaged in the sale of securities and the issuance of repurchase agreements failed. In addition, certain governments purchased medium- or long-term securities with the proceeds of *short-term* reverse repurchase agreements. This practice opened such governments to sharp criticism when cash flow difficulties required the liquidation of these medium- and long-term investments at a loss.

As a result of these events, questions were raised by users of financial statements regarding the adequacy of limited cash and investment display and disclosure requirements. Although the GASB had several important projects on its technical agenda, the board members believed that display and disclosure issues related to repurchase and reverse repurchase agreements warranted their immediate attention. After initial research was conducted on this project, the GASB concluded that the inherent risks associated with financial instruments justified expanding the scope of the project to encompass all deposits and investments.

Basic Requirements

The basic disclosure requirements of GASB Statement No. 3 have been incorporated into three sections of the 1987 *Codification of Governmental Accounting and Financial Reporting Standards* (referred to as 1987 *Codification* in the remainder of the text): C20, "Cash Deposits with Financial Institutions," I50, "Investments Including Repurchase Agreements," and R10, "Reverse Repurchase Agreements." Disclosure requirements for deposits and investments included in these sections can be divided further into three categories: legal and contractual provisions, balance sheet data and activity information.

Legal and Contractual Provisions

The 1987 *Codification,* Sections C20.105, I50.161-.162, and R10.106 establish disclosure requirements for legal and contractual provisions. Such provisions are established in a number of sources: constitutions, charters, ordinances, resolutions, governing body orders, and intergovernmental grant or contractual requirements. Legal or contractual provisions for deposits include deposit maturity, collateralization, and in certain cases, how collateral may be held. Similar provisions also are encountered for investment transactions.

The 1987 *Codification,* Section I50.161, requires that authorized investments be disclosed in the notes to the financial statements by type of investment. When authorized investments are not addressed in legal or contractual documents, the government's formal investment policy should serve as a basis for this disclosure. Although the GASB did not formally define "type of investments," the nonauthoritative illustration provided in GASB Statement No. 3 (1987 *Codification* Section I50.601-.602) can be used as a guideline. Typical investment types include U.S. government securities, U.S. instrumentality securities, bankers' acceptances, commercial paper and repurchase agreements. Those governments whose investment practices are governed by the "prudent man" rule should briefly explain the effects of this provision on the government's investment policy.

One of the most common compliance errors involving this standard is the misclassification of certain deposits as investments. Some governments believe that all interest-bearing instruments (e.g., certificates of deposit, time deposits) should be classified as investments. However, the 1987 *Codification,* Section I50.104 uses certificates of deposits as an example of a deposit. As a general rule, if an instrument is subject to state or federal depository insurance, it should be classified as a deposit.

Significant violations of any legal or contractual provisions associated with deposits and investments should be disclosed in the notes to the financial statements. A common noncompliance disclosure related to deposits occurs when collateral levels do not meet legal requirements. For example, when an ordinance requires that public deposits be collateralized at 105 percent of total deposits and the collateral level falls to 80 percent during the year, this fact should be disclosed. Noncompliance disclosures associated with investments include the acquisition of unauthorized types of investments and the use of unauthorized methods of holding securities during the year. For example, if a state statute requires that all investment securities be held by the government or its agent, but the government usually permits counterparties to hold securities related to repurchase agreements, this fact should be disclosed.

Balance Sheet Data

The 1987 *Codification,* Sections C20.106 and I50.164 outline the basic disclosure requirements based on deposit and investment data as of the balance sheet date. These disclosures were developed by the GASB to provide financial statement readers with information needed to assess risk associated with deposits and investments. The GASB identified two major types of risk: market risk and credit risk. The GASB defines market risk as "the risk that the market value of an investment, collateral protecting a deposit, or securities underlying a repurchase agreement will decline." The most apparent example of market risk was encountered on October 19, 1987 when the stock market experienced a significant decline.

Credit risk is defined by the GASB as "the risk that another party to a deposit or investment transaction (counterparty) will not fulfill its obligation." The GASB divides credit risk into three categories: risk associated with the issuer of a security, risk associated with a financial institution holding deposits, and risk associated with the custodian of securities or collateral. Although the GASB standards address both market and credit risks, the primary emphasis of the disclosure requirements is on credit risk.

There is a correlation between the level of balance sheet data disclosures required, the complexity of transactions, and the level of credit risk assumed by the government. For example, if the bank balances of deposits are insured or collateralized entirely with securities held by the government or by its agent "in the entity's name," the only disclosure requirement is that this fact be stated in the notes to the financial statements. When a government does not meet the requirement for this limited disclosure presentation, the disclosure requirements can become extensive.

In the pages that follow the disclosure requirements for deposits and investments will be described in greater detail, and explanations provided for some of the terminology used.

Deposits. The following disclosures should be made if deposits are *not* entirely insured or collateralized with securities held by the government or by its agent in the entity's name:

A. Carrying amount of total deposits, if not separately displayed on the balance sheet.
B. The amount of total bank balance classified in these three categories of credit risk:
   (1) Insured or collateralized with securities held by the entity or by its agent in the entity's name;
   (2) Collateralized with securities held by the pledging financial institution's trust department or agent in the entity's name;
   (3) Uncollateralized. (This category includes any bank balance that is collateralized with securities held by the pledging financial institution, or by its trust department or agent but not in the entity's name.)

These disclosures can be presented in a columnar format, however, most governments have chosen a narrative presentation.[1]

The term "bank balance," which serves as the foundation for this disclosure, was not specifically defined in GASB Statement No. 3. This has led to varying interpretations in practice. All parties have agreed that the bank balance generally is not equal to the carrying value of deposits. Further agreement, however, may be difficult to obtain. Some governments equate bank balance with the available balance per the bank's records. On the other hand, there are other governments that define bank balance as the amount that is eligible for collateralization or depository insurance. They believe that only amounts that have cleared through the banking system (i.e., have been collected) should be included in the bank balance. Although this latter view was supported by an informal Federal Deposit Insurance Corporation (FDIC) staff response to an inquiry on depository insurance coverage, governments should review this interpretation with their own FDIC regional office or state insurance officials before implementing such an approach.

Other terms (i.e., insured, agent, "in the entity's name") introduced in this disclosure requirement will be explained further in the section on terminology, since they apply to both deposit and investment transactions.

Investments. The GASB requirements for investment disclosures also are based on the categorization of credit risk. In addition to disclosing the market value of the entity's investments by type of investment, the carrying value should be classified into the following three categories:

A. Insured or registered, or securities held by the entity or its agent in the entity's name.
B. Uninsured and unregistered, with securities held by the counterparty's trust department or agent in the entity's name.
C. Uninsured and unregistered, with securities held by the counterparty, or by its trust department or agent, but not in the entity's name.

---

[1]See exhibits 3-1 and 3-2 for examples.

These disclosures normally are presented in a columnar format.

When the credit risk of the oversight unit for deposits and investments is not apparent because of significant balances of component units, or the "mix" of component units' credit risk categories differs significantly from that of the oversight unit, additional disclosure is required (e.g., 75 percent of investments classified in category 3 are held by the public employee retirement system).[2]

In addition, if unrealized losses of a fund or component unit are not apparent from the disclosure of market and carrying values by type of investment, then the unrealized loss, carrying value and market value for that component unit or fund should be disclosed separately. For example, if an unrealized loss in a pension trust fund for U.S. Treasury obligations (e.g., bonds) is offset by an unrealized gain in the investment pool's U.S. Treasury obligations (e.g., notes), additional disclosures for the pension trust fund are required.

A factor that complicates the classification of investments is the use of book-entry systems (e.g., depository trust company, federal reserve banks). Often securities (e.g., U.S. Treasury notes) are not issued in paper form; instead, these securities are recorded in data bases and transfers of ownership are accomplished through a central depository facility. Because the securities are not in a physical form a government cannot hold them. Moreover, the membership requirements of most central depositories generally preclude government participation. Therefore, governments must rely on outside parties to consummate these transactions. When determining the proper classification of these securities, governments must assess "In whose vault are the entity's securities held?" (e.g., agent, counterparty).

Terminology. In this section, several terms associated with both deposit and investment transactions will be explained, including: insurance, trust department, agent, counterparty and "in the entity's name." For example, both deposits and investments can be insured. In defining "insurance," the GASB expanded it beyond its traditional boundaries. Traditional sources of insurance coverage in the event of a default include: the Federal Deposit Insurance Corporation (FDIC), the Federal Savings and Loan Insurance Corporation (FSLIC), state insurance programs (for deposits) and the Securities Investor Protection Corporation (SIPC) (for investments).

Federal depository insurance generally is limited to $100,000 per institution; however, additional coverage may be available in certain circumstances. For example, if legal requirements provide for separate official custodians (e.g., treasurer and clerk), each custodian may be insured separately by the FDIC or FSLIC. The possession of separate federal tax identification numbers by the custodian provides evidence that the officials truly are separate legal custodians.

Another instance where additional insurance coverage may be available occurs with deposits held in trust (e.g., public employee retirement system members).

---

[2]A component unit is defined by the GASB in its 1987 *Codification* as a "separate governmental unit, agency, or nonprofit corporation that, pursuant to the criteria in Section 2100, is combined with other component units to constitute the reporting entity. An oversight unit is defined as "the component unit that has the ability to exercise the basic criterion of oversight responsibility over other component units."

For trust deposits, the FDIC and FSLIC generally have established coverage at the individual member level. However, this insurance coverage can be reduced when it is determined that the pension system's assets exceed the pension obligation. It should be noted that the FDIC and FSLIC do not generally calculate the system's funding status on the same basis as the plan. Therefore, governments are encouraged to consult the Code of Federal Regulations (see 12 CFR330) for additional clarification of these issues.

In addition to the traditional sources of insurance coverage, the GASB believes certain multiple financial institution collateral pools also qualify as "insurance." These pools are established with the legal understanding (e.g., contract, statute) that if a member fails the entire pool is available to satisfy depositors' claims. Moreover, if the value of the pool is inadequate to cover claims, additional amounts would be assessed to members of the pool on a prorata basis. The ability to assess members effectively insures the government's deposits.

The term "trust department" when used in the context of deposit and investment disclosures should be limited to trust departments of financial institutions. Although some broker-dealers may have a trust department, these are not legally separated in the same way as they would be for financial institutions. Therefore, the GASB believes that a greater credit risk (i.e., category 3) should be disclosed for investments held in the entity's name by a broker-dealer's trust department.

Governments also should not confuse a financial institution's trust and safekeeping departments when classifying deposits and investments. A safekeeping department is not considered to be legally separated from the financial institution. Therefore, securities held in a counterparty's safekeeping department would be classified in category 3.

A financial institution or broker-dealer may act as a government's agent for one transaction and as a counterparty for another transaction. An "agent" is defined in the 1987 *Codification,* Section I50.501, as a financial institution or broker-dealer that has a contractual relationship with the government to hold, at the discretion of the government, securities owned by or pledged to the government.

This contractual arrangement can take many forms. For example, both the government and financial institution in which the government places deposits may jointly enter into an agreement with a third party to act as a custodian for collateral related to the deposits. Although the third party may, in effect, be an agent for the financial institution, the presence of a third-party agreement does not prevent the third party from acting as an agent for the government on this transaction. There are certain provisions that can be included in such three-party agreements that would clearly establish the government/third-party agency relationship. For example, if the financial institution could not remove collateral from the third party without the permission of the government, an agency relationship between the government and the third party would exist.

The term "counterparty" can be confusing when certain transactions are analyzed. For example, a financial institution may act as a paying agent and still hold the security in an agent capacity. However, when the financial institution places an order for securities or uses securities from its own portfolio to fill the government's order, the financial institution should be classified as a counterparty. It should be noted that acting as a counterparty for certain transactions does not jeopardize the financial institution's agent classification for the remaining securities held for the government.

For securities to be held "in the entity's name," certain criteria must be met, but these criteria have not been defined well in the authoritative literature. However, the GASB staff through the issuance of a technical bulletin (1987 *Codification,* Section I50.603), clarifies the proper use of this term for book-entry system transactions. These basic criteria could also be applied to how the term in the entity's name should be used for all securities held by custodians. This nonauthoritative section states that for book-entry systems "conditions that indicate securities are held in the name of the entity include having the securities held in a custodial or fiduciary account and identified as owned by or pledged to the entity in the custodian's internal accounting records." Although a custodial or fiduciary account may not specifically identify that the securities are owned or pledged to the government, it does indicate that the securities are not owned by the custodian. Securities owned by a custodian generally are included in a separate trading account.

In addition, the ability to limit or prevent the transfer of securities without the government's knowledge and/or permission also can be used as a criterion for assessing the government's right to those securities. The underlying premise of all these criteria is the establishment of a government's right to the securities *in the event of a default.* As will be discussed in a later chapter, written contracts (e.g., master agreements) are an excellent method to set forth clearly the responsibilities and rights of all parties.

Once a security is determined to be held in the entity's name, the government's and/or counterparty's relationship with the custodian should be used to determine the proper classification of the securities. For example, if the securities are held by the counterparty's agent, the securities would be classified in category 2. However, when the counterparty holds the securities, the proper classification would be category 3.

Activity Information

The final category of disclosure requirements includes information on deposit and investment activity during the year. These requirements were established to disclose any "window dressing" that may have occurred at year end. When the amount of deposits or investments held in category 3 during the year significantly exceed the amount held at year end, this fact must be disclosed. For example, if the counterparty holds *all* deposit collateral during the year (e.g., category 3), but at year end the collateral is transferred to the government's agent and held in the government's name (e.g., category 1), the government should disclose this situation in the notes. A more common situation of this type faced by governments occurs during periods of significant tax collections. Collateralized deposits classified in categories 1 and 2 during these periods may fall below amounts held in these categories at year end.

Another activity disclosure is required when types of investments that were held during the year are not present at year end. For example, a government may periodically enter into repurchase agreements and/or reverse repurchase agreements during the year but may not hold these types of investments at year end.

The final activity disclosure relates to losses due to counterparty default. The amount of any losses and any amounts recovered from prior-period losses should be disclosed in the notes to the final statements if not separately displayed on the operating statement.

The requirements to disclose deposit and investment activity information highlights the need for adequate recordkeeping during the year. As discussed in Chapter 2, "Cash Controls and Reporting Systems," information should be contained in the monthly treasurer's report or maintained by the counterparty to provide an adequate audit trail for investment activities. Without this trail, the cost of gathering this information at year end increases significantly.

Financial Statement Presentations

Although GASB Statement No. 3 focuses primarily on disclosure requirements, this pronouncement also provides display guidance. These requirements are associated with the balance sheet and operating statement presentations of repurchase agreements and reverse repurchase agreements.

Repurchase Agreements

The GASB divided repurchase agreements into three categories: standard repurchase agreements, fixed-coupon repurchase agreements and yield-maintenance repurchase agreements.

The GASB provided the following definitions in the 1987 *Codification,* Section I50.500:

Standard Repurchase Agreements (often referred to as plain or plain vanilla). The government transfers cash to a broker-dealer or financial institution; the broker-dealer or financial institution transfers securities to the government and promises to repay the cash plus interest in exchange for the return of the *same* securities.

Fixed-Coupon Repurchase Agreement. As above, except the returned securities have the same stated interest rate as, and maturities similar to, the securities transferred.

Yield-Maintenance Repurchase Agreement. As above, except the securities returned provide the broker-dealer or financial institution with a yield specified in the agreement.

The 1987 *Codification,* Section I50.172, provides "Income from repurchase and fixed-coupon repurchase agreements shall be shown as interest income." Therefore, the effects on governments' financial statements generally is to reclassify "cash" to "investments" (i.e., repurchase agreements) and to recognize interest income. Before this guidance was issued a few governments considered all of these agreements to be purchases and sales of securities and reported the income as gains upon expiration of the agreements.

The GASB believes that this practice has merit with regard to yield-maintenance repurchase agreements. Because the agreement can be fulfilled with the return of securities that have no relationship with the original underlying securities (e.g., U.S. Treasury bills vs. U.S. Treasury notes), the 1987 *Codification,* Section I50.173, states that yield-maintenance repurchase agreements should be accounted for as purchases and sales of securities.

Reverse Repurchase Agreements

The GASB also divided display guidance for reverse repurchase agreements into the same basic categories: standard, fixed coupon and yield maintenance. The 1987 *Codification,* Section R10.115, states that yield-maintenance reverse repurchase agreements should be accounted for as the sales and purchases of securities. In addition, this section of the 1987 *Codification* provides that reverse repurchase agreement transactions should not be netted. Before GASB Statement No. 3 was issued, governments often would report only the securities purchased with the proceeds of the agreement or would net the interest earnings of these securities against the cost of the agreement. The 1987 *Codification,* Sections R10.113 and R10.114, strictly prohibit these practices.

Specifically, these paragraphs provide that "securities transferred under reverse repurchase and fixed-coupon reverse repurchase agreements should be reported as obligations under reverse repurchase agreements and the underlying securities should be presented as investments." Moreover, interest cost associated with these reverse repurchase agreements should be reported as expenditures/expenses and not netted against interest earnings on related investments.

Summary

The implementation of GASB Statement No. 3 causes many governments to reassess their current investment policies. The disclosure of the level of credit risk may be important to financial statement users; however, when applying the GASB standard, governments should not let the status (i.e., categorization) of their investments dictate their overall investment policy. Users may question the status of certain investments, but their assessment ultimately should be made within the context of the government's investment objectives.

Exhibit 3-1
Sample Note Disclosure of Limited Deposit and Investment Activities

Assumptions

Deposits. Deposits (including certificates of deposit) are carried at cost plus accrued interest. The carrying amounts of deposits are not separately displayed on the balance sheet.

	Carrying Amount	Bank Balance
Insured (FDIC)	$ 100,000	$ 100,000
Uninsured, collateral held by the government, agent (custodial bank) in the government's name	50,000	40,000
Total deposits	$ 150,000	$ 140,000

Investments. Investments are stated at cost plus accrued interest.

	Carrying Amount	Market Value
U.S. Treasury bills Uninsured, unregistered and held by the government's agent in the government's name	$ 25,000	$ 22,500
Investment in state treasurer's investment pool	200,000	200,000
Total investments	$ 225,000	$ 222,500

Note X. Cash and Investments

Deposits. The government's deposits at year-end (carrying value - $150,000) were entirely covered by federal depository insurance or by collateral held by the government's custodial bank in the government's name. State statutes authorize the government to participate in the state treasurer's investment pool and invest in securities that are direct obligations of the U.S. Government.

Investments. The government's investments at year-end are presented below. The U.S. Treasury bills are held by the government's agent in the government's name. Because the government does not own specific securities within the state treasurer's investment pool, details as to the type of securities the pool holds and how they are held are not available.

	Carrying Value	Market Value
U.S. Treasury bills	$ 25,000	$ 22,500
Investment in state treasurer's investment pool	200,000	200,000
Total investments	$225,000	$222,500

Note: The valuation method (e.g., cost) used for deposits and investments should be disclosed in the SSAP.

Exhibit 3-2
Sample Note Disclosure of Complex Deposit and Investment Activities

Assumptions

Deposits. Deposits (including certificates of deposit) are in a single financial institution and are carried at cost plus accrued interest.

	Carrying Amount	Bank Balance	Fund
Insured (FDIC)	$ 100,000	$ 100,000	Pool
Insured (FDIC)	2,000,000	2,000,000	Pension
Uninsured:			
Collateral held by the government's agent in the government's name	550,000	450,000	Pool
Collateral held by the counterparty bank's trust department in the government's name	200,000	225,000	Pool
Collateral held by the counterparty bank	50,000	40,000	Pension
Total deposits	$ 2,900,000	$ 2,815,000	

A government ordinance establishing the cash and investment pool requires that all collateral be held either in a third-party financial institution or by the government.

Exhibit 3-2 *(continued)*

Investments. Investments in the government's cash and investment pool are stated at cost, plus accrued interest. Pension investments are stated at cost or amortized cost, with accrued interest displayed separately on the balance sheet. Agency fund investments are stated at market value.

	Carrying Amount	Market Value	Fund
Repurchase Agreements:			
Agreement No. 1: Securities held by the broker-dealer	$ 250,000	$ 250,000	Pool
Agreement No. 2: Securities held by the counterparty bank's trust department in the government's name	100,000	100,000	Pool
Other Investments:			
Corporate stocks: Insured and held by broker-dealers (3)	1,250,000	1,500,000	Pension
Held by broker-dealers	2,500,000	2,650,000	Pension
Corporate Bonds: Registered and held by the broker-dealer	500,000	450,000	Pension
U.S. Government: U.S. Treasury Bills: Held by the government's agent in the government's name	750,000	745,000	Pool
U.S. Treasury Notes: Held by the broker-dealer's agent in the government's name	900,000	875,000	Pension
Investment in Mutual Fund	600,000	600,000	Agency
Total investments	$6,850,000	$7,170,000	

Also during the year the government entered into a number of reverse repurchase agreements. All of these agreements had expired by year-end.

Exhibit 3-2 *(continued)*

NOTE X: CASH AND INVESTMENTS

The government maintains a cash and investment pool for all funds except the pension trust fund and IRC 457 deferred compensation plan (agency) fund. Deposits and investments for these funds are held separately.

Deposits. At year-end the carrying amount of the government's deposits was $2,900,000 and the bank balance was $2,815,000. Of the bank balance, $2,550,000 was covered by federal depository insurance or by collateral held by the government's agent in the government's name, $225,000 was covered by collateral held in the counterparty bank's trust department in the government's name and $40,000 of the pension trust was covered by collateral held by the counterparty bank.

An ordinance requires that all collateral for the cash and investment pool be held by either a third-party financial institution or by the government; however, several times during the year and at year-end, collateral was held by the counterparty bank's trust department in the government's name.

Investments. State statutes authorize the government to invest in obligations of the U.S. Treasury, bankers' acceptances and repurchase agreements. The government is also authorized to enter into reverse repurchase agreements. In addition, the pension trust fund is authorized to invest in corporate stocks and bonds of investment quality and the deferred compensation (agency) fund is authorized to participate in a mutual fund.

The government's investments are categorized below to give an indication of the level of credit risk assumed by the government at year-end.

Category 1 includes investments that are insured or registered or for which the securities are held by the government or its agent in the government's name. Category 2 includes uninsured and unregistered investments for which the securities are held by the bank's trust department or the broker-dealer's agent in the government's name. Category 3 includes uninsured and unregistered investments for which the securities are held by the broker-dealer, bank, or by the bank's trust department or the broker-dealer's agent, but not in the entity's name.

	Category			Carrying	Market
	1	2	3	Amount	Value
Corporate bonds	$ 500,000	---------	---------	$ 500,000	$ 450,000
Corporate stock	1,250,000	---------	$ 2,500,000	3,750,000	4,150,000
Repurchase agreements	---------	$ 100,000	250,000	350,000	350,000
U.S. Government securities	750,000	900,000	---------	1,650,000	1,620,000
	$ 2,500,000	$ 1,000,000	$ 2,750,000	$ 6,250,000	$ 6,570,000
Investment in mutual fund				600,000	600,000
Total investments				$ 6,850,000	$ 7,170,000

The pension trust fund owns 90 percent of the investments in category 2 and approximately 91 percent of the investments in category 3.

During the year, the government entered into reverse repurchase agreements. All of these agreements had expired by year-end.

Note: The valuation method (e.g., cost) used for deposits and investments should be disclosed in the SSAP.

4

EFFECTIVE COLLECTION AND DISBURSEMENT PROCEDURES

by Paul R. Ferm

An effective cash management program will maximize the amount of investable cash available to a governmental unit. By maximizing the amount of investable cash, a government can increase its investment earnings and reduce the burden on taxpayers. Collection and disbursement procedures are an integral part of effective cash management. Effective collection methods are those that speed up the collection and deposit of revenues due the government. Effective disbursement methods, on the other hand, are those that slow the outflow of funds from a government's treasury.

New technologies, particularly in the data processing and telecommunications areas, have had a significant impact on the cash manager during this decade. The use of technologies, such as electronic wire transfers or machines that can read scannable documents, can improve the efficiency of the collections process and enable governments to disburse funds to their creditors at the appropriate time, thereby increasing the amount of cash available for investment and possibly boosting investment earnings.

While increasing investment earnings is a major goal of an effective cash management program, it should be noted that cash managers have a fiduciary responsibility with regard to the public monies that they manage. This means that the protection of principal should be of paramount concern in any cash management activity.

In addition to the basic fiduciary responsibilities, the cash manager should be fully aware of various state and local laws that affect cash management activities. Cash managers should also be aware of local precedents and procedures with regard to investments, banking relationships, etc., that might have an effect on any significant change in collection or disbursement procedures.

This chapter will examine options available to the cash manager for improving the speed and efficiency of the collections process and the timing and efficiency of disbursement procedures.

Collections

The major goal of any revenue collection system is to increase the amount of investable cash by speeding collections to a government's bank account. Funds cannot be invested until checks that are deposited in a government bank account are presented to the bank on which the checks are drawn. At this point, check deposits become investable cash. Until such time that the government's bank account has investable cash, the checks deposited are considered deposit float, not investable cash. For the purpose of investment it is better that checks and other receivables be deposited in a single account, such as a concentration account.[1] The slow processing of such items can result in foregone revenue opportunities.

Improved collection efficiency can be accomplished in a number of ways. This section discusses the different types of collections, how governments can make effective use of staff, and improving the efficiency of the collections process. The reader should keep in mind that this section focuses on the traditional collection system in which the government collects payments from taxpayers and others, and then makes deposits into the banking system (see Exhibit 4-1). The following section examines ways that governments can improve the speed of the fund deposit process and focus on changes in the traditional system of government revenue collection and fund deposit.

Identifying Types of Collections

The first step in developing effective collections procedures is to identify the various types of collections. This is important because different types of collections place different demands on staff time, and have differing administrative costs. Identifying the types of revenue collections can help a government to better manage those demands. There are generally four types of collections:

- collections driven by services provided;
- collections dictated by state or local law;
- immediate and unpredictable collections; and
- federal or state grant receipts.

These are not mutually exclusive categories. Nor do they represent the only way that government collections can be classified.

Collections driven by services provided by the governmental unit involve the generation of a bill to be returned with payment. Some examples are bills for water service, garbage collection or, in some cases, for ambulance service. There are three ways to bill for these types of recurring services:

- pre-billing before the service is delivered;
- billing upon service delivery; and
- billing after service has been provided.

[1]Concentration accounts are single accounts established at a commercial bank in conjunction with one or more zero-balance disbursement accounts.

Exhibit 4-1
Traditional Collection System

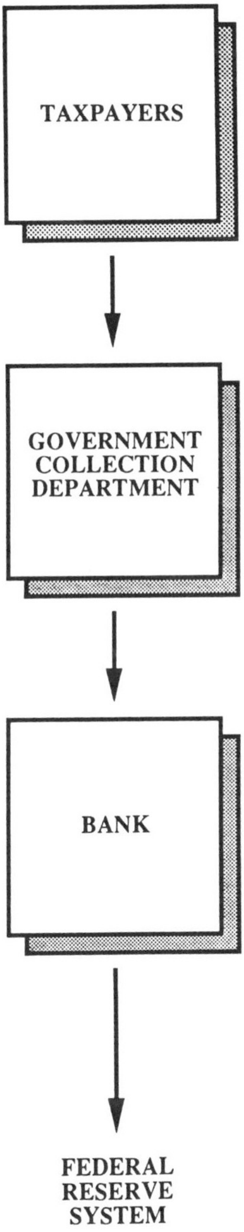

These collections typically account for a large proportion of a government's collection activity. Accordingly, they can require large amounts of staff time.

Collections which are the product of various state or local laws and are collected on an annual or more frequent basis represent the second type. These could be quarterly or semi-annual receivables generated by sales or excise taxes, or in certain instances, property taxes. These receivables tend to involve larger dollar amounts per transaction than other types of collections. Some revenues are collected on an annual basis, such as property taxes, licenses and permits. The timing of their collection is usually determined by state law. Their collection often requires large amounts of processing time by staff.

Governments also receive monies from immediate and unpredictable collections. These will be for such items as traffic and parking fines, court fines, registration for building permits, etc. Most of these involve smaller dollar amounts and represent a smaller percentage of total city collections. Often the deposit of the money collected is delayed due to the legal process involved.

The last major type of collections are those from the federal or state governments in the form of grants-in-aid, or other assistance. In such cases, the revenue stream is of a limited duration. With regard to grants, the revenue can be predicted by time of year or month. With regard to other specific receipts, collection is often based on expenditure by the city with a request for reimbursement.

Improving Collections Procedures

An important step in the development of efficient and effective collections procedures is the determination of staffing requirements. This can be accomplished through an examination of collection patterns that identifies peak receipt times, and peak demands on collections staff. Once this is done, staffing requirements can be minimized and the effectiveness of the collections process improved through a leveling of those peak receipt times. Improvement in collections operations can speed up the collection of funds, and increase the amount of investable cash available to the government. This can be accomplished through changes in a government's billing procedures.

Cycle Billing. One of the ways governments can utilize staff more efficiently and effectively would be to implement a cycle billing program. Cycle billing involves certain areas of a community receiving bills released on the first week of the month and other areas of the community on the third week of the month. This gives collections personnel better control over the process by creating a regular pattern of generating and processing bills. With the cycle approach, the peaks and valleys of collections can be minimized, and staff used more efficiently. A similar method involves the staggering of due dates for various types of receivables. Both methods can increase the amount of investable cash.

Other Methods. Cash managers may also want to consider the use of other methods to speed up the collections process. One such method involves the early mailing of bills to taxpayers and government service users. It is quite likely that a number of those billed will make payments prior to the due date. Cash managers should also consider increasing the frequency of collections. For example, if cigarette taxes are collected on a quarterly basis, more revenues will be available earlier if collections are made on a more frequent basis, such as monthly. Processing costs may increase, however; therefore the benefits and costs of utilizing this option should be looked at closely.

Other methods can be utilized to improve a jurisdiction's collection rate, and increase the amount of a government's investable cash. Penalties and interest charged on late payments by taxpayers could be increased. This may act as an incentive for delinquent taxpayers to pay up on time. Cash managers may also want to institute a program of aggressive follow-up of delinquent taxpayers. This would involve increased auditing of delinquent accounts, and legal action where necessary. The use of this type of method may be beyond the wherewithal of many small governments, however, because it will place greater demands on available staff and resources.[2]

Instituting these methods may require changes in local or state law, or in local policies. With an effective review of collection practices, however, the recommendation of changes can be made and defended.

Deposit of Funds

Cash managers not only must increase the speed of the collection of government receivables, but also increase the speed of funds deposit, as interest does not begin to be earned until funds have been deposited in an interest-bearing bank account or used to purchase an investment security.

The traditional system of collecting and depositing government revenues involved governments collecting the revenues and then depositing them in a bank account. That method of depositing government monies has been altered in the last decade, with the collecting and depositing of funds occurring almost simultaneously. No longer does it have to take days for government revenues to be deposited in the bank. Today banks often collect much of the revenue due a government and credit government accounts almost immediately (see Exhibit 4-2). In this section we will examine the forms government revenue receipts take, current fund deposit practices and discuss ways small governments can make use of them.

Revenue Receipt Forms

The sooner a government can deposit receipts the sooner it will have investable cash that can generate interest earnings. The form that government receipts take is a determining factor in the amount of time necessary to convert them into investable cash. Governments receive their revenues in one of three forms:

- cash that is presented on site for payment of service delivery, fines, registration, etc.;
- checks received on site or through the mail; and

---

[2]Some small governments may be able to pursue an aggressive follow-up strategy if they possess a computer system that can help them to identify delinquent taxpayers.

Exhibit 4-2
Modified Collection System

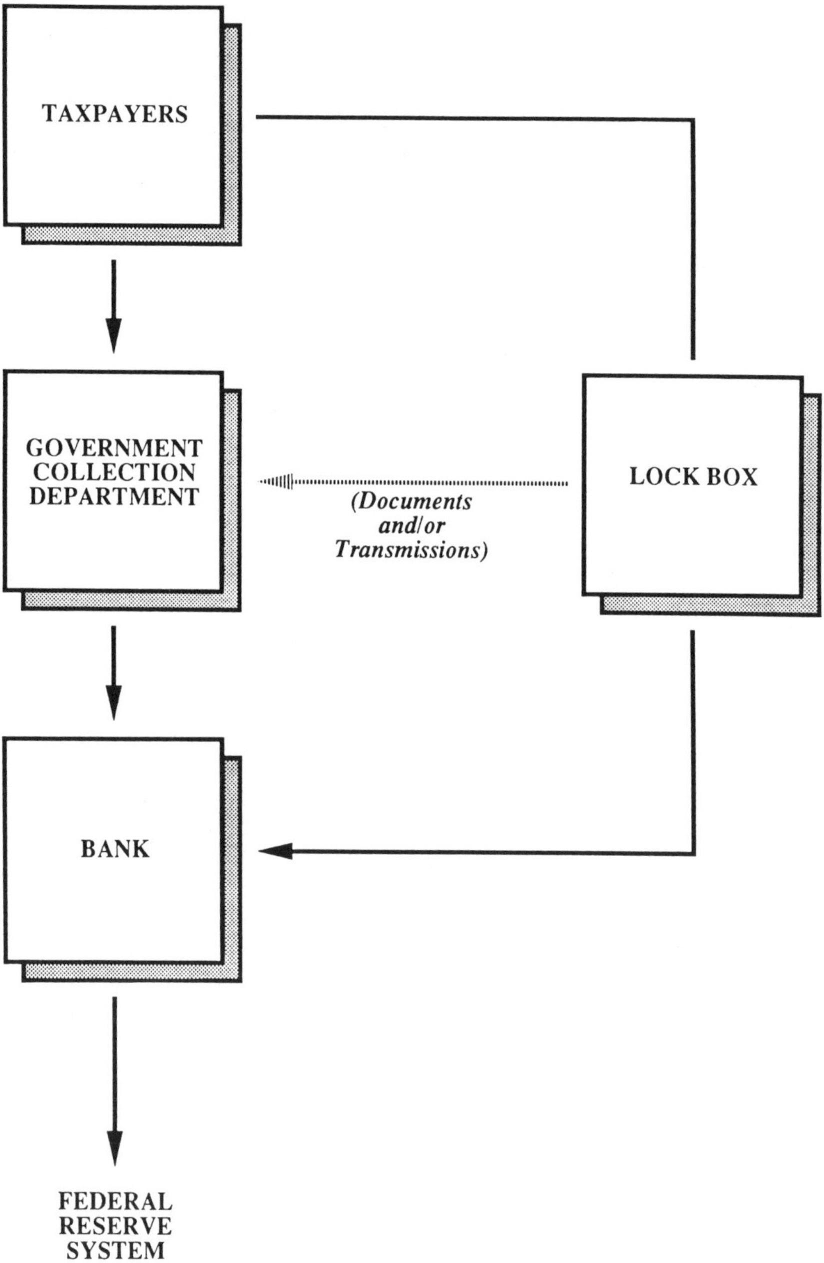

- wire transfer or other electronic methods of funds receipts (e.g., Automated Clearing House Association—ACH).

Each of these types of receipts is treated differently by the nation's banking system. Two forms of payment, cash and wire fund transfers, are considered absolute payment. Both enable the government to immediately invest dollars received. Checks, which represent the bulk of government receipts, are credited to bank accounts before they clear the banking system, but are not available for investment purposes until payment has been made by the payee's bank. This is called float, and is the time interval between when a check is received by a government and when it is subsequently paid by the bank on which it is drawn. Credits through an Automated Clearing House (ACH) are funds available for immediate investment.

Improving Deposit Procedures

By increasing the speed of the collection and deposit process cash managers can increase the amount of investable cash available to them and possibly improve investment earnings. There are four things cash managers can do to achieve this objective:

- reduce float in receivables;
- collect accurate accounting information;
- take advantage of lock box processing; and
- utilize Automated Clearing House (ACH) and other electronic funds transfer technology where appropriate.

Reducing Float. The receipt of government revenues can be accelerated by reducing the float that occurs in checks received. There are three types of deposit float:

- mail float;
- administrative float; and
- collection float.

Mail float is the amount of time a payment remains in the mail system from the time sent to the government until the government has physical possession of the check. Mail float can be reduced by assigning P.O. box numbers for government receipts. Different P.O. box numbers could be used for different revenue streams. Mail float can further be reduced by multiple pick-ups throughout the day that bring items into the processing stream faster.

Administrative float is the amount of time necessary to process the check, and is totally under the government's control. Through the use of technology, such as machines which can read scannable documents, and trained personnel, administrative float can be minimized.

Collection float is the amount of time necessary to credit a government's bank account after a check has been received. In other words, the time necessary for a government to receive good funds on a check. Collection float is a function of banking procedure and the bank selected by the government for its deposits. Governments should request a bank's availability schedule which states how long checks must be deposited with the deposit bank until the government has investable funds. Availability schedules are not the same for all banks. Availability can either be assigned or actual. It is the responsibility of the government's treasurer to assure that the government has the best possible availability from the bank selected.[3]

Collecting Accounting Information. The timely collection and recording of accounting information is an important component of any plan to improve deposit procedures. It is often said that money is of no value to a government until the accounting stream the funds belong to is determined. The government must determine which fund the receipts belong to and determine if additional accounting information is necessary to fulfill state or federal accounting requirements. Accurate identification of the taxpayer or the utility payer is also critical. As funds are received, it is imperative that the government's accounts are updated to reflect receipts. Whether the government accounting system is a paper-based general ledger system or a computerized system, there is often a time delay before checks are deposited into the government's bank account. From a management point of view, it is imperative to determine what information must be collected before a check can be deposited. If staff can work from a photostatic copy of the check long after the check has been deposited in the bank, the process of collecting and depositing checks can be accelerated while, at the same time, the necessary updates to the government's accounting records are provided on a timely basis.

Lock Box Processing. One primary method of accelerating funds collections, and easing a government's administrative burden, is through lock box processing performed by a bank or commercial vendor. Lock box processing involves the interception of the designated receivables of a government by one or more of those third parties. There are three major steps in this process: the government assigns a unique post office box number to bills generated; the government then authorizes a designated third party, usually a bank, to pick up receivables addressed to that specific post office box number; and, the bank in turn processes these receivables under the government's direction.

The lock box processor can generate a data file that a government can use to update receivables files in the format used by that government. Lock box processing can be as simple as the bank depositing the check and forwarding a copy of the check and accompanying data to the government to update receivables files in-house. On the other end of the spectrum, government can generate a scannable billing document that includes all the accounting data necessary to update the receivables file. The bank upon receiving the scannable document can read the document and generate an accounting file that includes dollar amounts

[3]The Expedited Funds Availability Act of 1987 (also known as "Reg. CC") changed federal law governing the processing of checks and the availability of funds, resulting in a reduction in collection float.

received. This accounting file can be transmitted to the government or physically delivered as a computer tape or a printed listing for those governments on paper-based systems.

Some of the advantages of lock box processing by a bank or commercial vendor include the fact that processing occurs around the clock seven days a week. It is not unusual for a lock box bank to have more than fifteen pick-ups from the post office each day and multiple deposits in the government's bank account throughout the day. Lock box processing enables governments to smooth out their workloads by assigning significant collection responsibilities to a lock box processor. By utilizing an external processing source, the government is able to avail itself of the latest in collections technology without purchasing such equipment or employing the necessary technicians to operate it.[4]

ACH Technology. Electronic payments made through the Automated Clearing House Association (ACH) are evolving into new forms, including two that should be of interest to government cash managers: corporate trade payments, and the U.S. Treasury Department's "Vendor Express" program.[5]

Corporate Trade Payments (CTP) utilize ACH technology with addendum records that enables bills to be paid electronically while including necessary accounting or invoice information. ACH movement is significantly less expensive than wire transfer movement because the originator is creating the data file. In wire transfer technology, the originating bank is creating the data file while the receiving bank is deciphering the data file into meaningful information for its customer. The use of corporate trade payments for receipts and disbursements will be of increasing value to local governments over the next five years.

In 1987 the U.S. Treasury Department created an electronic payments program through the ACH system called "Vendor Express" and expects this to be the primary mechanism for disbursing federal funds in the future. The Treasury estimates that 77 million payments will move from paper checks to Vendor Express by 1990. Vendor Express is a collection mechanism that will impact governments throughout the country as the federal government makes payments using this mechanism. As a result, your local bank will need to provide this service in the not-to-distant future. Either your bank will do it directly or through a regional bank providing such service. Vendor Express uses the Cash Concentration and Disbursement (CCD) format. Local governments should also consider using this same format as an electronic disbursement mechanism.

Disbursements

The major goal of a government's disbursement system is to slow the payment of funds so that the maximum amount of monies are available for investment for the longest possible time period, while at the same time ensuring that timely

[4]See Chapter 5 for a more detailed discussion of lock box systems.

[5]Automated Clearing Houses have been established in large population centers to process debits and credits among various banks for the purpose of clearing checks.

payments are made. By taking advantage of disbursement float, which is the period between the time when a check is prepared and the time when it is presented for payment, and utilizing effective disbursement procedures, cash managers can accomplish this objective.

In this section we will examine ways cash managers can improve the efficiency and effectiveness of their government's disbursement procedures. Developing an efficient disbursement system generally involves two things:

- an analysis of disbursement patterns; and
- efficient management of disbursements.

Analyzing Disbursement Patterns

An analysis of disbursement patterns can help governments identify disbursement float and opportunities for greater investment.

Disbursement Patterns. Determination of payment due dates is a key component of effective disbursement management. The intent of government should be to pay all bills on time. On time means on the due date, not before or after. A study of payments can assist a government in determining disbursement patterns. Some of the larger payment patterns revolve around the salary disbursement account, utility payments and large vendor or service providers to government. By reviewing the types of payments, the cash manager can create a record of due dates. This will be of assistance for several reasons. First, it will determine the in-house lead time to prepare a disbursement document. Second, it will enable the cash manager to match large disbursements with investment maturities. Third, it will maximize the time to payment except when prepayment discounts are cost-effective.

Disbursement Float. By taking advantage of the disbursement float that is a byproduct of the banking system, cash managers can potentially boost investment earnings. Disbursement float has three components:

- Delivery float: the time it takes to deliver a check after it has been prepared for disbursement.
- Processing float: the time it takes for an organization to process receipts for deposit or an invoice for payment.
- Transit float: the time that it takes a check to clear the banking system, from its deposit to its deduction from a government's account balance.

Disbursement float, as indicated above, can be identified and exploited through an analysis of disbursement patterns.

Managing the Disbursement of Funds

The efficient and effective disbursement of funds requires the use of effective disbursement procedures and the effective management of a government's banking arrangements.

Disbursing Funds. Once a data base of due dates has been established and estimates of disbursement float developed, it is necessary to determine the most cost-effective way to manage disbursements. The two main ways governments disburse funds are through:

- commercial bank checks; and
- wire transfers.

A commercial bank check is still the most widely used disbursement mechanism employed by governments today. A check is simply an order to pay money on demand to the payee from the payor's bank account. It is not cash, but rather a credit instrument that is presented for cash. Modifications of the commercial bank checking account are being utilized effectively to assist in funds management. One such method is the zero-balance account discussed in the next section.

Wire transfers move funds between banks electronically over telephone lines. Because funds can be moved almost immediately, payments can be made to vendors at the last possible moment, allowing cash balances to remain for a longer time in a government's central bank account.[6] This can result in improved investment earnings. Wire transfers are costly, however, and probably should not be used for small transactions.[7]

There are several other ways that governments can disburse funds, including warrants (also called payable-through-drafts), and depository transfer checks. Since they are not widely used in government we will not attempt to cover them in detail here. Warrants are instruments very similar to checks. The major difference is that funds are not automatically released when a warrant is presented for payment. Rather, the payor is allowed a second chance to review the transaction before payment is made. Depository transfer checks are also similar to checks except they are used exclusively for transfers between government accounts in different banks.

Disbursement Accounts. The effective management of a government's disbursement accounts is crucial to the success of its cash management program.

One of the keys to increasing investment earnings is to centralize all government funds in a single, centralized bank account. In most cases governments will want to utilize a concentration/zero-balance account system.[8] Under this system a concentration account is established to hold the government's available funds, while a number of other accounts, containing zero balances, are set up to handle disbursements. As checks are presented for payment, these disbursement accounts are drawn upon. At the end of each business day, funds are transferred electronically from the central account to the disbursement accounts to cover checks presented throughout the day. Excess funds remain in the master account of the government and can be used to pay banks for services provided. (This is known as a compensating balance.)[9]

---

[6]Direct deposit of payroll is an example of this type of transfer.

[7]Chapter 5 contains information on cost/benefit analysis for wire transfers.

[8]See Chapter 5 for more information on this type of arrangement.

[9]Demand deposits held by a bank have three components. The first is the ledger balance which

Direct deposit of payroll is one of the original electronic technologies used by many governmental units. In direct deposit of payroll a data file is generated by a government and given to a commercial bank before the disbursement date. The commercial bank then transmits the data to the local automated clearinghouse association and moves funds from the government account to the recipient's account on the designated business day.

New enhancements of this proven technology are developing today with regard to other types of payment. The most promising is known as Corporate Trade Payments (CTP). There are different formats available, including CTP, and CTX (Corporate Trade Exchange). The method uses the traditional ACH exchange (discussed earlier) to make corporate payments. The CTP allows the remitter to add one or more addendum records in order to provide more accounting detail to the money movement. Use of this type of technology enables the cash manager to coordinate payments on the due date rather than send checks several days before a due date. Because this technology is still developing, many commercial banks do not currently provide this service.

Another method cash managers should consider is controlled disbursement. In such a situation, government disbursements are made from a remote bank location either in the same area or another portion of the country. This account has one presentment of checks on a daily basis and is funded by the government's primary account. Controlled disbursement can extend the time required for checks to clear a government's account.

Summary

The development of efficient and effective collection and disbursement procedures can have a positive impact on a government's cash management program. By maximizing the amount of cash available for investment, cash managers can boost investment earnings and reduce the burden on the taxpayer. For governments in difficult financial positions, this could mean the difference between budget surplus and deficit.

---

is normally referred to as the bank balance. The second component is float, which in this case is the dollar value of deposits in the process of collection. Float may exceed the average ledger balance in certain situations. The third component of demand deposits is collected balances. This is the amount of funds available to the government for investment purposes. This collected balance (less bank reserves) can be used to pay for services by the bank in lieu of cash payments by a government. [Editor's note: The use of compensating balances to pay for banking services is just one way governments can pay for bank services. The direct payment of fees is another. See Chapter 6 for further information on bank payment methods.]

5

BANKING RELATIONS: PART I

by Rhett D. Harrell

This chapter will discuss the establishment of banking relations in a local government. The success in establishing banking relations will be determined to a large extent by the political considerations and capabilities of the banking community as well as the ability of the local government to develop the best banking arrangement. Various alternatives for obtaining banking services will be explored, as will the roles of the key officials within a local government.

To obtain the best banking arrangement, the local government should be aware of the types of banking services available in the local area. For some services such as custodial, however, local governments may need to look beyond local banks to satisfy their needs. Once the desired services are determined, the local government needs to understand the negotiation process that must follow. Finally, the evaluation of the banking proposals will allow the local government to select the best service arrangements.

Establishment of Policy for Dealing with Banks

Political Considerations

It is difficult to discuss banking services for governments without addressing political considerations. Political involvement in a government's banking relations can range from minimal to extensive. In many local governments, banking relations are determined solely by politics. The main problem posed by politics is that it hinders free and open competition in the procurement of banking services at the best price for the services rendered. A growing number of governments, however, have been able to set aside politics and approach their banking relations on a business-like basis.

Political involvement often takes one of the following forms:

- a requirement that the government treasurer maintain bank accounts at each of the financial institutions within the community; or

- a requirement that the government treasurer rotate the banking business to each bank within the community on an annual or other periodic basis.

Use of All Local Banks

Sharing the government's deposits with all or most of the banks in a community is the most common arrangement for handling banking relations. Unfortunately, it is also the least desirable method. Once established, this method is difficult to reverse, since all of the banks are benefiting from the government's business.

The sharing method evolved many decades ago as a means by which elected officials compensated banking officials for assistance provided in previous elections. Furthermore, it had the advantage of maintaining political tranquility among the banks and between the banks and the government. In some communities, these reasons continue to be as compelling today as they were many years ago.

While the advantages of this arrangement are political, the disadvantages are economic, producing very ineffective cash and investment management programs and inefficient operations. Some of the disadvantages associated with the sharing arrangement are:

- multiple bank accounts reduce the ability to pool cash for improved investment earnings;
- minimum account balances are maintained for each account, thus reducing potential investment earnings;
- processing costs associated with handling multiple accounts are significant;
- multiple accounts prevent pooling of cash to handle unforeseen cash emergencies; and the treasurer is hampered in using cash forecasting techniques due to the large number of accounts to be considered in the forecast.

Multiple accounts hinder an effective investment program since they require a significant effort on the part of the treasurer's staff to prepare the checks and deposit tickets required whenever an investment transaction is performed. Besides the handling of checks and deposit tickets, there is a need to constantly monitor the investments so that at maturity they are either rolled over or sold, with the proceeds returned to the appropriate accounts. This effort may reach the point that the treasurer feels it is not warranted, resulting in idle funds remaining in the various accounts for significant periods of time.

In summary, multiple accounts can result in lost interest, reduced yields due to smaller amounts invested, and additional personnel costs associated with maintaining records. Although the sharing method may occasionally be politically advantageous and economically acceptable when investable funds legally must be segregated, it generally is discouraged since no one gains. None of the banks acquire sufficient deposits to make the endeavor profitable, and the government does not earn sufficient interest to offset the cost and inefficiencies encountered.

Rotation of Banks

Rotating banking business, although not as common, is preferable to the sharing arrangement. Under this arrangement, the accounts are maintained in one bank in the community and then periodically rotated to other banks. Usually this rotation occurs without the benefit of bidding. Once again, competition is limited, and the local banks are not motivated to offer additional or improved banking services to the government.

In comparison with the sharing method, the rotation method has several advantages:

- Certain efficiencies are achieved by having all accounts with one bank, even though the accounts are not necessarily pooled under this method.
- Processing costs associated with multiple banks are reduced.
- Investment earnings have the potential to be increased, since all accounts are with one bank and can be pooled.

There are also several disadvantages to the rotating method:

- Rotation is generally based on informal policies that are subject to change.
- The rotation policy may not include a process for handling new banks or mergers within the local community.
- In larger communities, the rotation period is usually one year long since there are so many banks to rotate among. Constant changing of banks can be expensive in terms of new checks, revised procedures, etc.
- There may be disagreement over the length of the rotation period for each participating bank. Due to their size, larger banks believe that they should have a longer rotation period than that of other, smaller banks.

Although preferable to the sharing method, the rotation method is not the best approach for a government to use in obtaining banking services. The rotation method is in reality just another means to achieve political peace with the local banking community and has only marginal financial benefits to the government. However, rotation might serve as a way to increase competition and eventually lead to a bidding process.

As will be demonstrated in the next chapter, a formal bidding process involving all the banks in the community or local area is strongly recommended.

Process for Developing Banking Policies

Banking arrangements should be the result of formal, written policies. In developing these policies, the finance director or treasurer should play a major role in setting the agenda and seeing the project through to completion. In that regard, the finance director serves as the catalyst for change, particularly if there are no polices in existence. In developing these policies, the finance director should set the agenda using the following broad points:

1. Determine the current banking arrangement (or policy) and the reasons why the arrangement exists. The reasons may or may not still be valid. If they are not, then a plan to revise the reasons must be developed.
2. Determine the type of banking arrangement that should be developed, using the existing resources of the bank(s). In this step, the use of a formal

bidding process is strongly recommended. In some cases, however, the political atmosphere may not allow a full bidding process, where the best bank wins all or a substantial portion of the local government's banking business. As a possible scenario, an allocation process can be developed, wherein the banking business is divided into two or more major segments, and each segment is then bid. A word of caution, however, is necessary. If the major activity accounts are divided between two banks, very little, if any, of the planned efficiencies will be gained. For example, the major disbursement accounts should be kept in one bank.

3. Develop a plan for revising the current banking arrangement into the planned banking arrangement. Remember that this must be a workable plan (e.g., one that can be implemented by all parties).
4. Obtain consensus of all key players in the decision-making process. Generally this includes the chief executive officer, such as the city or county manager, and key legislative members, such as the mayor or chairperson for the finance committee.
5. Prepare banking services request(s) for proposals (RFPs) according to the plan developed in step 3 above. Services needed by the local government should be incorporated into the RFP.
6. Evaluate the proposals and award the banking services to the bank(s) that demonstrate they can handle the business in the most cost-effective manner.
7. Continually monitor the banks that have been awarded the banking services for compliance with the specifications contained in the RFP, and for any new services that may become available in the banking industry.

Range of Banking Services Available

The first step in selecting the best mix of financial services is to define the available services. These services can be conveniently categorized as:

- collection services;
- disbursement services;
- investment services;
- and credit services.

Each service category relates to a specific function within the cash transaction cycle. The collection and disbursement services actually provide support roles to the entire cash management function. Exhibit 5-1 provides a framework outlining each service category and typical services provided.

Collection services have a primary objective of accelerating cash receipts. Acceleration of cash receipts is achieved by a reduction of the collection float, which refers to the normal processing of cash receipts through the mail and the government's internal procedures. By effectively utilizing various collection services offered by banks, a government can realize an increase in funds available for investment purposes.

Various collection services offered by most banks are discussed in detail later

Exhibit 5-1
Bank Services

Collection Services

- Wire Transfers
- ACH Collections
- Pre-Authorized Checks
- Lock Box Systems
- Depository Transfer Checks
- Over-the-Counter Payment Systems
- Armored Car Services
- Night Depository Services
- Coin Counting Services

Investment Services

- Money Market Instruments
- Custodial Arrangements for Repurchase Agreements
- Investment Advice
- Retirement Plan Services

Disbursement Services

- Wire Transfers Services
- Payable-Through-Drafts (PTDs)
- ACH Payments
- Concentration/Zero Balance Accounts
- Controlled Disbursements
- Account Reconcilement Services
- Check Truncation
- Disbursement Float Summary
- Serial Check Float
- Microfilm Checks
- Computer Services
- Balance Reporting

Credit Services

- Lines of Credit
- Municipal Commercial Paper
- Short-Term Notes
- Bond Purchaser
- Bond Underwriter
- Bond Transfer and Registration Services
- Lending Activities Related to Community and Economic Development Projects
- Leasing

in the chapter. Electronic wire transfers and lock box systems are the two most popular services used by local governments. Although these two services provide the most dramatic results, a government should continually monitor additional services available from its banking community.

Disbursement services have the primary objectives of decelerating cash disbursements by lengthening the disbursement float and minimizing idle cash held in a bank account through special techniques and communications. Later in the chapter, several of these techniques and communication methods are explored, ranging from a simple daily phone call to the more complicated concentration/zero balance account structure. Governments that can effectively use a combination of these techniques can anticipate a more rapid notification of larger cash balances available for investment purposes.

Investment services and specific investment techniques are available to governments to assist them in their investment programs. Most governments are accustomed to dealing with their banking communities for investment services. A key issue within the investment services area is whether these services are used by governments more for political than for economic considerations.

Credit services are available to governments that borrow money for short- or long-term purposes. Later in this chapter the variety of bank credit services available to governments will be discussed. Generally, these services can range from direct loans to support functions relating to the administration of a government's bond issue. A new service receiving increased emphasis is bank participation in local community or economic development projects initiated by federal, state and local governments.

These brief descriptions of the service categories provide an overview and introduction to some of the material that follow. Specific service areas offered by a particular bank may include some or all of the services covered. Determination of the specific services available to a local government from local banks is an important step in managing banking relations.[1]

Collection Services

Banks provide a number of services designed to improve the processing of funds into a government unit. The primary objective of these services is to accelerate the availability of funds by decreasing the collection float. Collection float refers to the time lag caused by the normal processing of cash receipts through the mail and the government's internal procedures. Government units that aggressively pursue a reduction in processing time can anticipate an increase in funds available for investment purposes.

Collection float occurs at the following three critical points in processing:

- the time between the mailing and receipt of a check;
- internal recording and processing time needed to prepare the receipts for deposit; and
- check-clearing time between the deposit and subsequent notification by the bank of the availability of the funds. Banks accept all checks subject to funds being received from the remitter's bank. Most banks, however, provide credit before the funds are actually received. This important feature should be required of banks competing for the government's business.

---

[1]It should be noted that not all of the bank services listed in Exhibit 5-1 will be discussed in this chapter. For those desiring a more comprehensive discussion of these services, see the GFOA book *Banking Relations: A Guide for Government.*

Collection float can be improved through the use of one or more of the banking services described in the following paragraphs.

Wire Transfers. Wire transfers, a form of electronic funds transfer (EFT), provide an excellent means of accelerating receipt and deposit of large incoming payments. Used in lieu of checks, transfers involve the electronic transmission of payments from one bank to another through the Federal Reserve Communications System (the Fed Wire). The Fed Wire is used for several important reasons: transaction costs are generally less; there is daily settlement between banks; all banks may participate; and security of the transfer is guaranteed by the Federal Reserve, rather than by the participating banks.

Because wire transfers can be expensive, it is recommended that government treasurers perform a break-even analysis to determine the minimum amount for which wire transfers will be cost-effective. To calculate such a break-even point, three information items are needed.

1. Unit cost of the transfer = cost
2. Days saved in transit time = days
3. Annual interest rate on idle balances = rate

$$\text{Break even point} = \frac{\text{Cost}}{\text{Days} \times \dfrac{\text{Rate}}{365}}$$

The following example illustrates a situation in which wire transfers are cost-effective for any receipts in excess of $9,126.

1. Cost = $5.00
2. Days = 2
3. Rate = 10%

$$\text{Break even point} = \frac{\$5.00}{2 \times \dfrac{.10}{365}} = \frac{\$5.00}{.0005479} = \$9{,}126$$

Transactions for which wire transfers may be cost-effective include intergovernmental grants, proceeds from investment sales, proceeds from debt issuances, and tax or utility payments from out-of-town organizations. Although a wire transfer can be cost-effective for a remitting organization in light of the cost of preparing and mailing a check, the remitting organization often perceives wire transfers as inconvenient even when they are in fact cost-effective.

Lock Box Systems. Lock box systems, which are used extensively in the private sector, can be used effectively in the public sector as well. These systems are designed to reduce the mail and internal processing time delays before receipts can be converted into usable funds. A lock box system works as follows:

- a local post office box is rented by the bank in the government's name;

- remittances are mailed to this specific post office box rather than to the post office box for the government's regular mail;
- the bank agrees to collect the remittances periodically during the day, depending on volume, perhaps as often as once every two hours or as infrequently as once a day;
- a bank staff person opens the remittances and sorts the payments and accompanying data;
- checks that agree with the particular bill, invoice, or other data are processed for deposit that day;
- exceptions may or may not be processed according to the special customized computer program. Those that are not processed are turned over to the government for action; and
- copies of all normal or accepted remittances and accompanying data (invoice, utility bill, etc.) are forwarded daily to the government for its internal processing.

An alternative to the above is for the bank to process all payments, including exceptions. A determination on which method to use will depend on several factors, such as past experience with exceptions, procedures for follow-up action, and the preferences of the local government and the bank.

The lock box system can be used for any type of remittance that meets both of the following conditions: (a) the remittance is in response to a formal billing/collection effort of the government, e.g., tax and utility payments, special assessments, license renewals, fees and registrations, and traffic fines; and (b) the remittance is accompanied by some form of remittance advice, known as a turnaround document, e.g., a tax or utility bill, special assessment notice, license or fee registration notice, or traffic ticket. The key to the above criteria is to have some form of identifiable control over incoming receipts.

A lock box system has several benefits:

- Mailing time is reduced through frequent and more timely collections of the mail from the box.
- Internal office processing delays occurring before deposit of receipts are eliminated since the checks are credited to the government's bank account prior to being processed and posted to the general ledger.
- Clerical workloads in the government treasury operations are significantly reduced, as mail-opening and deposit preparation functions are eliminated.
- Cyclical work overloads are reduced. Incoming payments often cluster around certain key dates, necessitating overtime and causing clerical frustration accompanied by occasional errors. Shifting increased responsibility to the bank reduces these problems.
- Usable cash balances are accelerated by several days as a result of a reduction in the mail/processing delays. This results in a one-time permanent injection of cash into the treasury. Consequently, short-term borrowing can be reduced or possibly eliminated at the same time that investment interest earnings are increased.

- Accounts receivable files are updated faster.

Retail lock boxes are used for high volume, low dollar payments, such as tax and utility payments, business licenses, special assessments, traffic fines, and other similar types of payments.

Most governments will use only the retail lock box; however, a wholesale lock box can be useful in specific types of situations. A medium-size hospital on the west coast of Florida that had a retail lock box established a wholesale lock box to receive the three to four Medicare payments that were mailed monthly by Blue Cross/Blue Shield to hospitals in the state. The reduced mail and processing times were sufficient to justify the cost of this service.

In selecting a wholesale lock box the key consideration is reduced mail and processing time, whereas in a retail lock box the key consideration will be per item costs.

Wholesale lock boxes come in three different classifications:

- manual processing accompanied by photocopies of turnaround documents (if requested) and a manual update of accounts receivable (a wholesale lock box may not have a turnaround document; therefore, it must be processed manually);
- data entry of turnaround documents with an automated update of accounts receivable; and
- machine readable turnaround documents with an automated update of accounts receivable.

Most wholesale lock boxes will be of the first two types due primarily to the low volumes.

Retail lock boxes are generally fully automated, encompassing machine readable documents, with little manual intervention. Machine readable documents enable the system to read the MICR (magnetic ink character recognition) encoded line on the check and the MICR type code on the turnaround documents. These codes will contain at least the customer's account number, the amount due and the minimum amount due, if applicable. Turnaround documents (invoices, remittance advises, bills, etc.) are important to the proper functioning of a retail lock box system. These documents must be properly prepared using complex specifications or the system will reject them.

Rejected items cause lost processing time and higher banking fees. In one recently negotiated lock box system, there were eight pages of extremely complex detailed requirements for the paper, ink and characters. Terms such as reflectance, opacity, porosity, gloss, drop-out inks, and print contrast signals are best understood by a professional printer. It is highly recommended that a copy of the media specification requirements be obtained prior to printing turnaround documents for either existing or prospective lock box systems. When bidding for services, copies of these requirements should be obtained along with the bids. Generally, if turnaround documents meet one bank's standards, they will meet other's; however, it is best not to assume anything. A little planning and research will save a great deal of time and money.

From discussions with several bank officials, it seems that even the type of printer used can be very important in developing successful turnaround documents. Laser printers, for example, print consistent quality documents in accordance with the specifications with only about a 1 percent reject rate. Impact printers, on the other hand, initially print documents in accordance with the specifications but slipping does occur after thousands of impacts, resulting in a rejection rate of between 3 and 5 percent. Thus, in a large printing, the quality is acceptable at first, then slips to unacceptable toward the end of the printing job. This may explain why some governments experience higher rejection rates as they process the turnaround documents.

As indicated earlier, improperly formatted turnaround documents will cause rejections in the processing. Most banks will allow a small percentage of rejects as part of their fee structure. Rejects in excess of these minimums will be charged on an increasing scale back to the user.

State of the art lock box systems now use image processing instead of scan lines. Image processing captures video images of checks and turnaround documents by digitizing them for storage on computer disk or tape. Once the process occurs, the physical documents no longer need to be handled by the operators, resulting in greater accuracy and more efficiency.

In developing a lock box system, the entire billing and payment process will need to be revised to gain optimal benefits. One aspect of the payment process is the design of the return envelope. A return envelope should use the "Zip + 4" zip code to speed the envelope processing within the mail system. Another popular technique is the use of bar codes, similar to the Uniform Product Code (UPC) found on many grocery items.

Many organizations use distinctive colors or markings to distinguish their envelopes from other envelopes. These markings can be put on the top, side or some combination. Some even place the markings at a diagonal across the envelope.

Calculation of the Benefits and Costs of Lock Box Systems. Lock box systems can dramatically increase cash availability. However, this represents only one portion of the time versus cost dimension of cash transactions. In order to evaluate whether lock box services are of significant net value, it is necessary to analyze the tradeoff of benefits versus costs. The benefits from speeding cash availability can be measured in terms of the added interest earnings potential and the reduction of internal processing costs in the government treasurer's office. Exhibit 5-2 provides some basic calculations designed to highlight the cost-benefit relationship. Under benefits, the incremental investment returns from a lock box system are shown to depend on the increase in usable balances and the interest earned by investing these incremental balances. Usable or available cash balances are calculated as the product of:

- the number of receipt items processed per day;
- the average dollar value per receipt; and
- the average number of days in reduced transit/processing time.

Adding the savings from reductions of clerical staff in the treasurer's office

Exhibit 5-2
Calculating Benefits and Costs of Lock Box Systems

Benefits

Increase in usable balances	=	Total number of receipt items	X	Average dollar value of items	X	Number of days in reduced transit/ processing time per item
Incremental investment return		=		Increase in usable balances	X	Average daily interest rate on investments
Total benefits		=		Incremental investment returns	+	Savings in costs to government for clerical tasks

Costs

Bank charge	=	Cost per item	+	Number of items	+	Fixed Charge
Total costs		=		Bank charges	+	Other costs of implementation

Example

The following example demonstrates the calculation of total net benefit when the following values pertain:

Number of Items per Year = 12,000	Average Rate on Investments = 11%
Average Dollar Value per Item = $1,200	Clerical Savings, Other Costs = $0
Bank Charges = $0.20 per Item	Reduced Transit Time = 3 days
Bank Fixed Charge = $0	

Incremental Investment Returns:

$$12{,}000 \times \$1{,}200 \times 3 \times \frac{.11}{365} = \$13{,}019 + 0 = \text{Total Benefits}$$

Bank Charges:

$$.20 \times 12{,}000 + 0 = \$2{,}400 + 0 = \text{Total Costs}$$

New Benefit:

$13,019 $2,400 = $10,619

to the incremental investment returns provides a measure of total benefits from a lock box system.

Commercial banks incur significant costs in providing lock box systems, for which they expect to be compensated. In large part, the costs to banks represent clerical functions that would otherwise be required by the treasury office. However, the fact that banks can service many different customers with the same staff and support systems allows banks to pass on some economies from specialization. The prices charged by banks for lock box services often include a fixed fee, per item processing charge, or an assortment of other charges, such as post office box rental charges, transportation costs for turnaround documents, and data transmission charges. If the lock box bank is different from the bank in which a government's funds are deposited, then there will be a cost for transferring the funds. Total bank charges, therefore, are determined by the number of items processed, rather than by the average dollar value of receipt items.

Other costs incurred by the government unit may include start-up costs for redesigning turnaround documents and modifying the internal treasury processing system.

Disbursement Services

As with collection services, banks also provide a number of services designed to improve the processing of funds out of a government. With disbursement services, the objective is to retain the available funds for a longer period of time. This can be accomplished by lengthening or maximizing the disbursement float. The disbursement float is really the mirror image of the collection float.

Disbursement float refers to the normal processing of checks through the mail, the vendor's (employee or other recipient) internal procedures and the banking system before the government's bank account is charged with the check. The float is commonly measured, quite simply, by the difference between the cash balances on the government's books and the account balance on the bank's books.

Disbursement float is composed of the following three types of time lags:

- Delivery float refers to the time elapsed between the recording of a disbursement in the government's accounting system and the receipt of the check by the recipient (vendor, employee, or other party).
- Processing float is the time required by the recipient to process the check through its internal accounting procedures and deposit the check in its bank.
- Check-clearing float (transit float or bank float) refers to the time elapsed between the deposit of the check by the recipient and the date that the check is deducted by the bank from the government's account balance.

Disbursement float can be enhanced through the use of one or more of the following techniques.

Wire Transfers. Wire transfers can be utilized for delaying disbursements in much the same manner as they are used for accelerating collections. Wire transfers, as compared with checks, will reduce the disbursement float rather than lengthen it, since wire transfers provide an additional time period in which the funds can remain invested before the transfer is made. Thus, the tradeoff would appear equal, except for the wire transfer fee charged by the bank. The one true advantage of wire transfers over checks is that a definite period is established during which funds can remain invested, as opposed to an estimate of how long it will take a check to clear the bank. This is particularly advantageous for a large payment due on a specific date. Not only does a wire transfer guarantee its prompt arrival, it also prevents any embarrassment caused by overestimating the disbursement float and having insufficient funds in the bank.

Another very important usage of wire transfers is the initiation of investment transactions outside the local area. When a local government wants to purchase certificates of deposit from banks in distant large urban areas, it will need to wire transfer the appropriate funds. Purchase of money market instruments in New York (or some other city) through a broker will also necessitate a wire transfer through the local bank to the broker's bank in New York.

In a general discussion of wire transfers as a collection service it was noted that banks often pass on their costs to the remitter. Thus, it is necessary to calculate a break-even point to determine when a wire transfer should be used for disbursements. To calculate such a break-even point, three information items are needed:

1. Unit cost of the transfer = cost
2. Days saved in transit time = days
3. Annual interest rate on idle balances = rate

$$\text{Break-even point} = \frac{\text{Cost}}{\text{Days} \times \frac{\text{Rate}}{365}}$$

The following example illustrates a situation in which wire transfers are cost-effective for any disbursements exceeding $16,592.

1. Cost = $10.00
2. Days = 2
3. Rate = 11%

$$\text{Break-even point} = \frac{\$10.00}{2 \times \frac{.11}{365}} = \frac{\$10.00}{.0006027} = \$16{,}592$$

Note that the cost for originating a wire transfer is generally higher than to receive a wire transfer.

ACH Payments. Automated Clearing House (ACH) systems can be used to process electronic payments. To date, ACH has been used primarily in the direct deposit of payroll, and to some extent in pension payments. Direct deposit of payroll is convenient and a benefit to the employees; however, it is a costly endeavor for governments. Many government units have established direct deposit payroll systems in response to employee requests with little or no consideration to costs.

On completion of an evaluation, a net savings should indicate the service is cost-effective to implement. A net cost should not deter the government because there may be off-setting reasons to implement direct deposit. The pain of a less-than-expected pay increase could be soothed somewhat by implementation of a direct deposit program. In labor negotiations, a positive response to the union's request for direct deposit could offset other requested benefits, such as pay increases, shorter hours, etc.

In calculating the costs, special consideration should be given to lost float. With direct deposit, the entire payroll must be ACH transferred from the government's bank account either one or two days before payroll day. However, only a majority of the payroll checks are cashed on payroll day. Remaining payroll checks are cashed within the next few days.

How important is the lost float? In a study by the Federal Reserve on direct deposit vs. check payment, they found the cost advantage of direct deposit was eliminated when lost float was considered.

There are, however, several advantages to direct deposit that need to be quantified in the evaluation process, such as:

- reduced per item check processing charges by the bank;
- reduced processing charges internally;
- reduced account reconciliation effort and costs;
- reduced number of lost/stolen paychecks;
- reduced special arrangements for absent employees;
- reduced employee lost time for cashing checks; and
- reduced storage requirements for cancelled checks.

Concentration/Zero-Balance Account. A concentration/zero-balance account (ZBA) structure is an excellent tool for managing disbursement float. As the name implies, all balances are maintained in the concentration account. Checks are presented against the various ZBAs which have zero balances, thus causing the ZBAs to be overdrawn by the amount of checks presented. At the end of each business day, or early the next day, funds are automatically transferred from the concentration account to each ZBA so that their balances become zero. Exhibit 5-3 depicts a typical concentration/zero balance account structure.

Ideally, the transfers from the concentration account to the ZBAs should be done automatically during the evening of the day the checks are presented. Smaller banks that lack the sophisticated equipment of larger banks may need to perform the actual transfer manually at the beginning of the next business day. This should not present any problems, as long as the daily balance reporting system shows the transfer as having occurred and the ZBAs with zero balances. ZBAs can be established for any type of payment, the same as regular checking accounts. Typically, ZBAs are established for accounts payable and payroll. More accounts can be added, or if desired, all accounts combined into one ZBA.

Daily deposits, regardless of the collection method, are generally deposited into the concentration account. Those deposits that are not immediately available (collected funds) will remain in the concentration account unusable until they become available. A concentration account containing both available and unavailable funds can be difficult to manage.

Funds within the concentration account can be used for either disbursement or investment, provided they are available. Any funds not needed for disbursing

Exhibit 5-3
A Concentration/Zero-Balance Account Structure

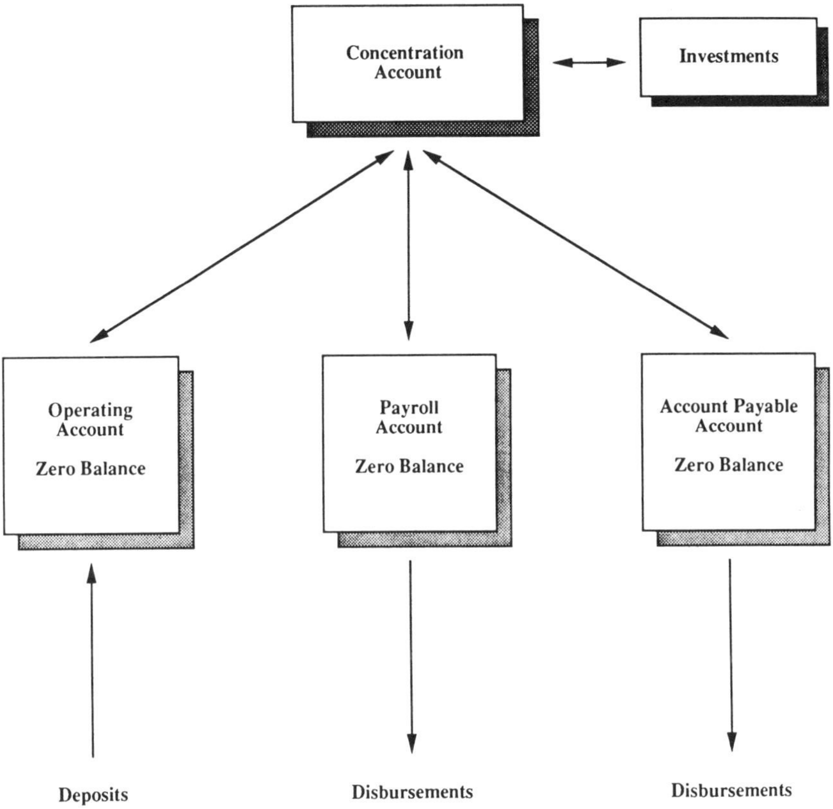

can be invested, either overnight or over a range of maturities. Many governments invest a certain percentage, or a certain amount of the available investment funds in an overnight or open repurchase agreement for liquidity purposes.

An overnight repurchase agreement (repo), although extremely liquid, does require that all funds be invested overnight and returned the following morning. This can be ineffective if the overnight repo is for $5 million and only $500,000 is needed to fund the ZBAs that day. The other $4.5 million simply goes out on a ride that evening and returns home the next morning. Undoubtedly, going out again the same evening; a busy repo.

An alternative is to use an "open" repurchase agreement, that stays open until cancelled by either party. Using an open repo allows only the money needed to fund the ZBA to be returned that evening. The other funds continue to be invested.

In bidding banking services it is advisable to include an automatic open repurchase agreement feature in the RFP. The RFP should require that all available funds be withdrawn each evening from the concentration account and placed into the open repo. Because some banks have limits on available collateral, a maximum amount should be stated in the RFP that will be invested according to the specified interest rate provision. Amounts over that limit would be invested on a "best efforts basis."

In establishing the interest rate calculation to be used in the RFP for repos, it is recommended that it be based on the Federal Funds Market (Fed Funds) and be easily verifiable. The Fed Funds market is an electronic exchange between financial institutions (and brokers) where institutions that have excess reserve balances can sell those balances to institutions needing reserves to meet their reserve requirement. Thus, Fed Funds are balances at the Federal Reserve that are lent unsecured to other institutions generally on an overnight basis.

A common calculation is to use the daily Fed Funds rate minus a certain number of basis points to cover the bank's profits. In many cases, a deduction of 50 basis points (½ of 1 percent) is acceptable. Aggressive banking markets may allow as little as a 20 basis point deduction. Others may require a deduction of 100 basis points.

Governments should note that they are unable to directly participate in the Fed Funds market because it is limited to financial institutions and brokers. Accordingly, governments should not expect to receive the same rate, thus the necessity for the deduction. Governments receiving the Fed Funds rate without a deduction can be assured they are paying for the deduction elsewhere in their banking services.

Verifying the Fed Funds rate may not be easy unless the government uses one of the money market services, such as Telerate. Virtually all banks use some type of service and should be able to perform the appropriate calculations. Some governments, however, desire to verify or monitor the Fed Funds rate used by the bank and thus, desire more independent verification.

The difficulty in verifying the Fed Funds rate is further compounded by the need to determine which Fed Funds rate will be used. There are several variations such as the opening, closing, high, low, average, or the rate at a particular time in the day, say noon. One recommended rate is the effective Fed Funds rate. The effective rate is the average of all rates during the day, weighted for the volume of trades occurring at each rate. Generally, the effective rate will be higher than the average of the high and low rate during the day.[2]

A concentration/zero-balance account structure can be the best cash management tool in banking services, particularly when combined with an effective investment program that can provide liquidity to the account structure through a repurchase agreement.

Account Reconcilement Service. Account reconcilement services are a

---

[2]Verification of this rate can be performed easily by subscribing to the weekly statistical release by the Federal Reserve Board titled, *Selected Interest Rates* H.15 (519) available as follows: Publications Services, Federal Reserve Board, Washington, D.C. 20551. The Fed charges a small fee to cover postage.

tremendous time saver for governments. Most bank services provide a computer magnetic tape and/or computer listing of all checks paid, listing the check number, amount and date paid. Some banks provide a comprehensive program by first obtaining a magnetic tape from the government containing all checks paid during a month, or some other time period. From this tape, the bank will extract the information and produce not only the above information, but also a list of outstanding checks. Voided checks will have to be handled manually to preserve check number sequence. This is an excellent cost-effective service that can be used by virtually all government units.

Serial Check Sorts. Generally, this service is provided along with the account reconciliation service, although it can be done separately. This service, sometimes referred to as a "fine sort," simply means the checks will be returned in check numerical order. This service is particularly cost-effective for large, volume accounts such as payroll.

Microfilm Checks. This is a growing service and should be considered by government units as they face the costly problem of check storage. Most governments would want the use of their checks for a short term following the receipt of the bank statement. Physical possession would allow for faster retrieval, should any questions occur. After some time, say 60-90 days, checks are not referred to as frequently and could be microfilmed.

An alternative would be to have the bank microfilm the checks as they are paid. The only drawback is the microfilmed checks may not be in numerical order. However, since microfilmed checks are generally indexed, it may be as fast as another system where sequential order was maintained.

Governments wishing to explore the feasibility of this service would be advised to request the banks bid on this service as an option. This would not force the government unit to accept the service and the bid. It is important to have banks bid on this service because prices vary greatly.

Computer Services. Computer services, available through many banks, can be used in lieu of acquiring a computer system or as a supplement to an existing computer system. Typical services offered include payroll, utility billing, and general ledger accounting. The type and quality of such services will vary among banks. Some banks may try to use private-sector-oriented computer programs for public-sector applications. Such an application for payroll is generally successful, since the objectives are the same for either sector. Utility billing and general ledger applications, however, require programs specifically designed for the public sector. These applications are usually offered only if there is a sufficient market. Before using these services, other government units having experience with them should be surveyed to determine whether the services are satisfactory.

Although small governments extensively utilize computer services offered by outside organizations, large governments may also find such services advantageous. Outside organizations should be considered whenever the computer services offered are superior to the government's own system; the government unit is undergoing a revision in its system and needs a dependable processing source; the government does not have an integrated system and it is cost-effective to utilize an outside source for a specific application; or the government no longer has sufficient capacity.

Balance Reporting. The final service in our list of disbursement services is the computerized daily balance reporting service provided by a number of banks. Many banks are becoming increasingly involved in providing not only balance reporting services, but many more cash management options. While these options may be useful to certain government units, it is not necessary to subscribe to a package of information just to manage the daily cash position.

Small government units not desiring or unable to justify a sophisticated computerized balance reporting service should not despair. In this era of communications, the same information is readily available through telephone calls from the bank. Exhibit 5-4 illustrates a sample report, filled out by the Treasury Division of the Manatee County, Florida Finance Department from information provided over the telephone by the bank. Notification is done initially by telephone and a written report similar to Exhibit 5-4 is sent later.

Investment Services

Good cash management programs can accelerate receipts, delay disbursements, and minimize idle balances; however, the investment practices provide the real measure of overall effectiveness. Government units should pursue a good investment program with the same zeal that goes into developing a good cash management program.

Investment services offered by banks vary in degree and quality. Government officials trying to evaluate services offered by banks should be aware of several factors which can complicate this evaluation. Among other complications, these include:

- the argument from the banks that investments should be made locally in order to bolster the local economy; and
- aggressive marketing programs that may make offers difficult to distinguish.

Although banks offer various types of investment services to government units, it is widely recommended that governments retain the investment responsibility for themselves. Contracts for banking services should expressly state that the government reserves the right to make investment decisions with any bank or brokerage firm it chooses. Shopping for investment services should be kept separate from shopping for other bank services.

Government officials should never lose sight of the fact that the investment services offered by banks can be accepted or rejected. Government officials should not hesitate to consider all alternatives when they are shopping for investment services.

In evaluating these services, government units are encouraged to consider national money market yields and other opportunities that are available outside the local banking community.

Exhibit 5-4
Sample Balance Reporting Form

1.	Repurchase Agreement Balance	$______
2.	Concentration Account Balance	$______
3.	Available Funds (transfer from Operating)	$______
4.	Repurchase Agreement Interest	$______
	Adjustment (+)	$______
	Adjustment (-)	$______
5.	SBA Balance (provided by County)	$______
6.	Zero Balance Accounts:	
	Payroll	$______
	Accounts Payable	$______
7.	Over the Counter Check Presentation (Est.):	
	Payroll	$______
	Accounts Payable	$______
	Subtotal	$______
8.	Incoming Wires (list):	
	a. ______	$______
	b. ______	$______
	c. ______	$______
	d. ______	$______
	Total Incoming	$______
9.	Outgoing Wires (list):	
	a. ______	$______
	b. ______	$______
	c. ______	$______
	d. ______	$______
	Total Outgoing	$______
10.	Projected Account Balance	$______
11.	Repurchase Agreement Transaction	$______
12.	Proposed Ending Balance	$______
	New Overnight Repo Balance	$______
	New Overnight Repo Rate	______ %

Prepared by ______

Reviewed by ______

Investment services offered by a bank will depend on the bank's location and size. These services might include:

- the offering of several money market instruments, including the bank's own certificates of deposit;

Exhibit 5-5
Money Market Instruments

Short-term U.S. Treasury Securities

Short-term U.S. Government Agency And Instrumentality Securities

Repurchase Agreements

Reverse Repurchase Agreements

Bankers' Acceptances

Commercial Paper

Bank Certificates Of Deposit

Money Market Mutual Funds

- investment advice, with or without a corresponding offer of money market instruments;
- the traditional offering of time deposits (savings accounts); and/or
- investment services oriented solely toward a government's retirement plan.

Governments are generally most likely to use money market instruments for their investments because of the liquidity and marketability provided.

Money Market Instruments. The money market is not a formal organized market like the stock market; rather, it is an informal telephone market operating, for the most part, without any regulation. The money market comprises 36 or so primary government securities dealers and very large banks. Anyone else desiring to participate in the money market must do so through one of the primary government securities dealers.

Instruments that are traded in the money market come in a variety of sizes and shapes; however, they all have the common denominator of being high quality, short-term debt instruments. Exhibit 5-5 identifies specific money market instruments; however, it is important to note that not all of these instruments are legal investments in all states.

Although banks serve a valuable function by providing a mechanism for government treasurers to acquire money market instruments, government officials also have the option of using major brokerage houses. Regardless of whether investments are made through a bank or through a brokerage house, that organization probably will encourage investment in its own certificates of deposit or other instruments in which it holds an advantageous position rather than in other investment vehicles. Treasurers should concentrate on market fundamentals and, to the greatest degree possible, ignore aggressive sales pitches.

Government units that regularly trade in a variety of money market instruments frequently use a major brokerage house rather than a bank for this purpose.

Since the government's bank will have to use a correspondent bank to execute the transactions unless it is one of the primary government securities dealers, it is generally more convenient and cost-effective to deal directly with a brokerage house that is a primary dealer.

Credit Services

Banks offer a variety of credit services related to debt management that historically have been overlooked by government officials when they solicit banking contracts. These credit services may be identified either as short term or as long term. Services classified as short term may appropriately be included in the regular banking services contract. However, services related to longer-term credit are probably best handled through separate contracts not associated with the recurring, regular banking services contract.

Short-term services are essentially those services which can be easily initiated and terminated within a one- or two-year period. These short-term credit services include:

- establishment of a standard line of credit;
- establishment of a line of credit for municipal commercial paper; and
- purchase of short-term notes.

These services place a premium on flexibility and dependable access to credit. A line of credit enables a government unit to borrow money from a bank at any time up to a predetermined limit. To receive a line of credit, the government will have to submit its financial statements to the bank for a detailed analysis. Once approved, the bank will request periodic updated financial statements in order to maintain the line of credit.

Government units which frequently borrow may find that having an established line of credit is very beneficial when temporary financing is needed. Once a line of credit is established, it is relatively easy to obtain a loan against the line. This can be particularly important for governments facing temporary cash flow shortages, such as a payroll date with insufficient funds in the checking account. However, it must be remembered that governments relying on these credit lines generally pay a fee to the financial institution that extends the credit. For instance, the fee for revolving credit lines will normally range from three-eighths of a percent to 1 percent. Letters of credit, which are the most secure of the lines of credit, also cost more than a normal credit line. It is generally not cost-effective to pay for the privilege of having a line of credit which is infrequently or never used. It is recommended that loans be priced at the time they are needed. If a line of credit is included in the banking service contract, the bank should provide a separate price for this service.

Generally, the interest rate charged once the line of credit is activated will be a percent of the New York prime rate, typically 70 to 90 percent. Government units that are frequent users of lines of credit may wish to include this service in their request for proposal. When doing so, it is recommended that a particular rate, such as the New York prime rate, be used so that each bank's percentage can be compared to the same base rate.

Government units have not always considered bank credit services when soliciting banking contracts. These services were often handled separately at the time the need arose. Recently, more communities have attempted to integrate certain credit services into their banking contracts, while maintaining separate contracts for those services which do not lend themselves to routine and relatively short-term banking services contracts. In deciding which services to include, it is recommended that those credit-related arrangements which will not extend beyond the contract term be considered. Longer-term credit needs should be handled through separate contracts.[3]

Summary

This first chapter on banking relations discusses the political considerations that must be evaluated whenever a change in banking relations is being contemplated. The process of combining all bank accounts into one account in one bank is often overshadowed by political movements to keep the status quo, or spread the banking business around to all banks. Governments wishing to improve their banking arrangements should never underestimate these political forces. However, as a matter of ethics often the treasurer or finance director needs to wear the "black hat" and recommend the most beneficial economic alternative even if it is not popular.

In the second part of this chapter, typical banking services were discussed. Banks are capable of providing a wide range of services that should be explored by the government unit. Governments desiring to improve their banking arrangements should carefully define their own needs before initiating negotiations with the banking community.

---

[3]For more information on bank credit services, see the GFOA book *Banking Relations: A Guide for Government.*

6

BANKING RELATIONS: PART II

by Rhett D. Harrell

The previous chapter examined the development of a policy for dealing with banks and described the range of banking services available to small governments. This chapter discusses negotiating for banking services, including the development of a request for proposal (RFP), and the evaluation of proposals and bank services.

Negotiating For Banking Services

Providing services to government units is a very profitable business for banks, and maintaining this relationship has been important to them. It was not unusual a few years ago to find bank and government relationships lasting several decades. As more and more new banks opened, there was increasing pressure to divide the business among all the banks in an area. Recently, there has been an increasing trend by local governments to use competitive bidding in selecting banks.

Almost without exception, competitive bidding will prove beneficial to government units. Some of the benefits that can be obtained through competition are:

- additional interest earnings resulting from improved yields if investments are divorced from routine banking services;
- additional interest earnings resulting from an overall increase in amounts available for investments through better use of a bank's collection services;
- additional bank services available for the same amount of bank service charges or compensating balance currently remaining at the bank;
- reduced bank service charges or compensating balances as a direct result of the competition; and/or
- an overall increase in efficiency of cash management operations.

There will also be certain costs associated with competitive bidding. These may include:

- costs related to the bidding process (e.g., staff time, legal fees, advertising, and possible use of consultants); and

- costs incurred when changing established procedures (e.g., forms, computer software, training, and errors arising from misunderstandings and unfamiliarity with the new procedures).

Generally, the competitive bidding process will include the following steps:

- review of the present system and determination of what bank services are desired and available;
- preparation of a request for proposal (RFP) and distribution to all banks in the designated area (city, county, region, or state);
- holding of a pre-bid conference for all potential bidders to answer questions and to clarify the RFP;
- preparation and submission of proposals by banks;
- evaluation of proposals by the government;
- recommendation of the best proposal to the legislative body;
- award of a contract to the recommended bank;
- execution of a banking services contract; and
- implementation of the contract.

Other steps that could be added to the above process include appointment of a bank advisory panel and preparation of a preliminary request for proposal that would be discussed with potential bidders. These additional steps are highly recommended for governments approaching competitive bidding for bank services for the first time. Involvement of the bankers early in the process can help head off later problems and misunderstandings.

Reviewing in greater detail each of the steps involved in competitive bidding should provide additional insights that will prove very useful.

Determination of Bank Services Desired

It is necessary for the treasurer (or responsible committee) to thoroughly understand the existing banking system. A study of the existing system will provide an excellent foundation for identifying desirable services. The government unit should also review pertinent cash management literature and talk with other local governments that have been involved in competitive bidding situations.

Many of the services available from banks were covered in the previous chapter. The government unit must determine which services will meet its needs. Once a tentative list of services is developed, banks should be contacted to determine whether the services are currently available. Services frequently requested by governments include:

- wire transfers, including a specified method of notification;
- lock box services, including specification of frequency and length of time prior to credit to the local government's account;
- coin counting services;
- provision of the concentration/zero balance type of account;
- a specified type of daily account notification;

- account reconciliation services;
- check sorting services;
- special computer services; and
- special account reports (e.g., earnings allowance and float analysis).

Governments should be careful to request only services which are truly needed. Demanding services which are only marginally needed or which cannot be provided on a cost-effective basis by banks should be avoided. Also, the government should be prepared to pay for all services requested. Checks, deposit tickets, and even daily balance telephone calls require an effort on the part of the bank for which it expects to be compensated.

Preparation of a Request for Proposal

Requests for proposals vary significantly from one jurisdiction to another. Some are as short as three pages, while others are 30 pages or more in length. A key consideration is the degree of detail and clarity required.

In developing an RFP, some governments are tempted to use another jurisdiction's RFP by changing only the name. While this practice occurs, it is never recommended. A government unit should always perform the necessary analysis of the services it desires and incorporate these services into its own RFP.

Before developing the actual RFP, one must establish the approach to take. An increasing number of governments have adopted the approach of setting strict specifications for banking services. Banks which are unable or unwilling to respond take exception, and these exceptions are costed and added to the basic bid package. More importantly, however, is that this approach eliminates the variables in bank bidding and the focus becomes the actual per item charges as illustrated in Exhibit 6-1.

Some of the more common variables that should be defined in the RFP are as follows:

- terms of the contract, with specified provisions for renewal and for selected cost increases;
- availability schedules (should be requested and compared);
- formula for setting the daily repurchase agreement (or sweep) for idle funds;
- provisions to handle interest reimbursement on failed wire transfers;
- defining the reserve requirement to be used in the compensating balance formula; and
- defining the earnings allowance to be used in the compensating balance formula.

Governments that define these variables in the RFP have gone a long way toward improving their proposal process. Albeit the work is much harder in developing the RFP, but the rewards come later in the ease of evaluating the proposals.

Exhibit 6-1
Banking Services Consolidated Bid Form

Bank Submitting Bid ______________________________

Bank Depository Services	Estimated Annual Volume	Charge Per Item	Annual Service Charges
Account Maintenance	48		
Checks Paid:			
Accounts Payable	25,000		
Payroll	26,000		
Items Deposited:			
Other	4,000		
Returned Checks	120		
Stop Payments	132		
Wire Transfers:			
Incoming	75		
Outgoing	75		
Bank Transfers Between Accounts	756		
Daily Balance Reporting	252		
Daily Report on Concentration Account	252		
Monthly Service Charge Report	12		
Account Reconciliation:			
Computer Tape	51,000		
Checks Sorted	51,000		
Other Banking Services			
Daily Repurchase Agreements	252		
Safekeeping Fees	252		
Coin Sorting -estimated volume to be 10,000 coins annually			

Total Proposed Bid	$__________
Average Monthly Amount (Total Proposed Bid ÷ 12)	$__________
Balance required monthly to support $1.00 of services	$__________
Required monthly compensating balance	$__________
Minimum amounts required for open repurchase agreement:	
Initial Amount	$__________
Increment	$__________

In all fairness to the banks, the RFPs must be impartial and reasonable. RFPs requesting impossible services and/or responses do not serve the government well. Banking services are like any other service; both parties must be objective in their needs.

Generally, an RFP will contain several standard sections, identified as follows:

- Section 1, Introduction;
- Section 2, Scope of Banking Services;
- Section 3, Bidding Instructions;
- Section 4, Bank Credit Evaluation; and
- Section 5, Bidding Forms.

Section 1: Introduction. This section will usually contain the following classes of information:

- background;
- objectives of the competitive bidding process;
- bidding instructions;
- bid evaluation/selection criteria;
- length of contract period; and
- standard terms and conditions relating to the government unit's bidding procedures.

Section 2: Scope of Banking Services. This section should include a list of desired services such as those described in Chapter 5. If alternatives are permissible, these should also be discussed. It is important for the RFP to describe how the proposals should address the desired services, as well as the alternatives.

In listing the services desired, the RFP should briefly describe how the service should operate and what the government expects from the bank. Any deadlines or time constraints for receiving specified services should be indicated. This section is the heart of the banking RFP and should be carefully thought out and not be just a listing of services.

Section 3: Bidding Instructions. One of the most important responsibilities of a government unit is to provide clear and concise bidding instructions. Where appropriate, the government unit should provide bid forms to standardize the responses and make subsequent evaluations easier. The amount of information included on the bid form may vary between government units, but the instructions should be specific as to what the banks need to provide.

One aspect of the compensating balance formula that causes problems is the earnings allowance. It has been my recommendation for several years that the average of the previous month's three-month Treasury bill auction results be used. However, the coupon or bond equivalent yield should be used instead of the widely reported discount rate.

The reasons for using coupon equivalent yield (CEY) are very simple:

- CEY is used in making investment decisions;
- CEY is a more accurate reflection of the yield; and
- CEY will result in a higher earnings allowance and a lower compensating balance.

Section 4: Bank Credit Evaluation. Selection of a bank should not be based solely on an evaluation of its creditworthiness, except in the case of a tie bid when the traditional coin toss is not appropriate. Instead, evaluating a bank should focus on qualifying a number of institutions as being acceptable, without necessarily ranking them in any order. Nevertheless, some government units prefer to make the evaluation a portion of the overall selection decision-making process by assigning a percentage weight.

This section should include a summary of the qualifying ratios that will be used in determining basic eligibility. Since it will be difficult to ascertain a bank's peer group average prior to the actual bidding process, averages should not be reported in the RFP. It is sufficient to say that in order to qualify, a bank must be at least equal to or better than the peer group averages.

Governments desiring to use the Uniform Bank Performance Report (UBPR) may request the bank provide its latest annual and/or its latest quarterly UBPR with its proposal. Other governments may prefer to receive the UBPR from the Federal Financial Institutions Examination Council (FFIEC). In either case, a listing of the ratios to be used in the evaluation process at least puts the banks on notice as to how they will be evaluated.

Some governments may choose to use an outside bank credit rating organization to determine eligibility. Although most of these organizations use the UBPR as their data base, they will apply different ratios in arriving at their recommendation. Banks should be informed of this outside process and the minimum eligibility requirements.

Banks should also be requested to submit their annual financial reports for the past two years. As mentioned below, the objective of this process is to review the auditor's opinion, notes to the financial statements, and management's discussion of the past year and prospects for the future. This review will provide insights unavailable by restricting oneself to only financial data.[1]

Section 5: Bidding Forms. Government units should develop the standard bid forms to be used by the responding banks. Bid forms can range from a simple format to a more complex format. Whenever additional services are requested or an alternate method of payment is desired, a separate bid sheet is recommended.

Copies of the monthly service charge reports to be filed should also be included in the package of bidding forms to prevent any later misunderstanding about their content.

Master repurchase agreements should also be included in the bid package if a government unit has developed one. Otherwise, the banks should be requested to submit a copy of their master agreement. The Master Repurchase Agreement should be the latest model developed by the Public Securities Association (PSA), with the annex provisions recommended by the Government Finance Officers Association (GFOA).[2]

---

[1]For more information on evaluating bank credit, see the GFOA book *Banking Relations: A Guide for Government.*

[2]The sample annex to the PSA agreement is presented to stress the additional items of concern

Exceptions to bid specifications are a normal part of any bidding process. It is recommended that an "exception list" be provided so that the banks can group all their exceptions in one place for proper evaluation and costing by the government unit.

Finally, it is recommended that a lead sheet be included in the bid package that will list all the forms and information required to be submitted. This lead sheet should identify the bank, its address, bank officer to contact, and the bank's telephone number.

Pre-Bid Conference

Government units using a competitive bid approach for the first time, or who have significantly revised their requested services, should hold a pre-bid conference. Many governments mandate attendance at such a conference as a prerequisite to submitting a bid. This makes certain that all of the bidding banks have the same information and that none are at a disadvantage. In order to minimize politicization, many government officials choose to refuse any other communication (in excess of normal operating discussions) with the banking community during the bidding process. If such communications are allowed, they should be in written form and responses should be sent to all qualified bidders.

Preparation of Proposals

Banks that have never submitted a competitive proposal often have difficulty in preparing a response. Thirty days is generally considered sufficient time for a bank to receive and respond to an RFP. Government units should protect themselves by personally delivering, or sending by registered mail, the RFP to the president or a key officer in each bank that is a potential bidder.

Banks may add items to their proposals that were not requested. This additional information can be confusing during the evaluation of the proposals and may, in some circumstances, lead to the selection of a bank which did not submit the best proposal.

To alleviate this potential problem, a local government should require banks to respond only on the standard forms provided. While supporting material may be attached, it will not necessarily be considered in the review and evaluation process. If alternatives are permitted, then the proposal should specify the format of their presentation.

Evaluation of Proposals

It is important that all the banks know what criteria will be used in evaluating the banking services proposals. Government units should develop their evalua-

---

which cash managers may want to use to ensure or enhance the security of their investment (the repo transaction). Cash managers seeking futher guidance in this area should contact the Chicago office of the GFOA for a copy of *Considerations for Governments in Developing a Master Repurchase Agreement.*

tion and selection procedures and include them in the introductory section of the RFP. Incomplete proposals or proposals that do not follow the bidding instructions should be disqualified.

Generally, the bank which submits the lowest overall cost or compensating balance requirement and which meets the other criteria will be awarded the contract. Abnormally low bids should be carefully evaluated to assure that the bank can deliver the services promised. Other government units or corporate customers of the bank can be contacted as part of the evaluation process. The government should always reserve the right to refuse all bids and start the process over again, if necessary.

Recommendation of the Best Proposal

The government unit should list the acceptable bids starting with the lowest cost, since cost is the primary criterion. Additional explanatory material should accompany the recommendation. This may be appropriate in the case of a very low bidder that is selected or where the difference between banks ranked number one and two is so close that a change from one to the other may not be cost-effective. Obviously, the latter situation should be well documented. Selection of the lowest cost, of course, assumes that the proposal satisfactorily meets or exceeds the other evaluation criteria. A bank not meeting all of the other criteria should be disqualified.

Award of Contract

No award should be considered final until the award has been made by the legislative body. Occasionally, the government staff or the legislative body may decide to change the final selection.

Execution of a Banking Services Contract

Generally, the contract is signed immediately after the legislative body has voted. The government unit should include appropriate provisions from the RFP in the contract. Reference to the proposal should also be included in the contract to assure that all provisions are fulfilled.

Implementation of the Contract

A 30- to 60-day transition period between the old and new banking contracts should be sufficient time for all parties. Additional time may be granted if necessary.

Evaluating Banking Services

This section discusses the evaluation of proposals from banks for their services, the evaluation of payment methods, and the evaluation of bank financial conditions.

Evaluating Proposals

The job (or process) of evaluating the proposals received from banks may be simple or complex, depending on the philosophy in preparing the initial RFP.

RFPs that are developed using an aggressive approach will take longer to prepare and include more specifications. However, it will be much easier to evaluate the proposal and observe deviations from those specifications.

On the other hand, RFPs that are prepared using a less aggressive philosophy will generally take much longer to evaluate. They will have few or no specifications, and thus each of the responding banks will prepare its proposal from its own viewpoint and not from the local government's perspective. This methodology usually results in the local government receiving what the banks want to give them, not necessarily what the local government wants.

The local government should always price out any exceptions taken by a bank, so that all proposals are evaluated on the same basis. Assuming the local government adopted the approach described earlier in this chapter, the evaluation should then center on the adherence to the specifications, the number and type of exceptions, and finally the cost. In this arrangement, other things being equal, the bank with the lowest cost will generally win the banking proposal, since it will have met most, if not all, of the specifications.

Evaluating Payment Method

Most local governments continue to use the compensating balance method of paying for banking services, although recently many governments have begun to pay direct fees for such services. It is unlikely, however, that paying direct fees will overcome the compensating balance approach.

In using the compensating balance method, the local government maintains deposits at the bank sufficient to pay for any banking services provided. This method avoids any direct invoicing, or debit to the bank account, thus it does not appear that the banking services cost the local government. In reality, the banking services cost the government indirectly in the form of lost interest due to the compensating balance.

Compensating balance is the most popular form of paying for banking services, primarily due to several reasons:

- Banks prefer to have deposits on hand, rather than fees.
- Compensating balances are non-budget items, thus avoiding any scrutiny from the elected officials.
- It is easy to administer.

Compensating balances, however, can be very costly to local governments if the compensating balance is not carefully defined in the banking services RFP. For instance, the earnings credit needs to be defined using Treasury bills (or some other verifiable money market rate) rather than the internal bank rate of return, which is often substantially less. In the absence of an RFP specification regarding the reserve requirement, the banks will use 12 percent, which is the reserve requirement for demand deposit accounts. By specifying that the compensating balance should be retained in a time deposit, the reserve requirement will drop to 3 percent. Compensating balances maintained in a repurchase agreement are not subject to reserve requirements.

Paying for banking services using a direct fee approach avoids both the reserve requirement and the earnings allowance issues. The only charge will be the direct cost of receiving banking services.

The only difference between the two methods is the reserve requirement and the earnings allowance. With the direct payment approach the reserve requirement is not a factor since there are no deposits retained by the bank to pay for the banking services. The earnings allowance also is not a factor since the local government is making all investment decisions.

For those governments that have an aggressive investment policy, the direct payment approach is usually the best and least expensive method.[3]

Evaluating Bank Credit Conditions

There are two basic reasons for evaluating bank credit. The first reason, quite simply, is to avoid any embarrassment that may come from keeping money in a bank that subsequently is closed by the FDIC. The reason usually is important enough to perform some preliminary credit analysis, even if there is no actual risk to the local government in terms of deposits.

The second reason is to protect the assets of the local government in those states where there are no collateral laws concerning local government deposits. In these states, the local government is at risk for all deposits at the bank, whether they be demand or time deposits. Obviously, the potential loss can be quite staggering.

Credit analysis of banks can be performed using one of two methods. The first method is the "do-it-yourself" analysis that has the advantage of being the least expensive, but also the most complicated. The second method of using outside help is more expensive, but is much easier to implement.

There are many complexities in using the do-it-yourself method, such as obtaining the necessary financial information, performing the analysis, and evaluating the results. In the final analysis, it is often recommended that this method not be used, except in those cases where the local government staff is adequately trained in the various elements of bank credit analysis.

For those governments desiring to use outside assistance in evaluating banks, a list of vendors is provided in Exhibit 6-2. Most of the outside vendors can provide a sophisticated analysis at a reasonable cost. Some, however, can be very expensive.[4]

In summary, bank credit evaluation is too important to be left to inexperienced staff. If the evaluation needs to be done, then it should be done by someone on the staff that is experienced, or outside assistance should be obtained.

---

[3]For more detailed information regarding bank payment methods, see the GFOA book *Banking Relations: A Guide for Government,* pp. 80–81.

[4]For those governments desiring to learn more about this type of analysis, they are encouraged to read Chapter 9, "Evaluating Bank Credit," in the GFOA book *Banking Relations: A Guide for Government.*

Exhibit 6-2
Bank Advisory Firms

1. Bank Safety, Inc.
P.O.Box 94
Lake Bluff, IL 60044
(312) 295-6346

2. Cates Consulting Analysis
74 Trinity Place
New York, NY 10066
(212) 964-7002

3. Duff and Phelps
55 East Monroe Street
Chicago, IL 60603
(312) 263-2610

4. Dun & Bradstreet
190 South Orange Avenue
Livingston, NJ 07039
(800) 526-4915

5. Keefe, Bruyette & Woods
One Liberty Plaza
New York, NY 10006
(212) 349-4321

6. McCarthy, Christiani & Maffei, Inc.
71 Broadway
New York, NY 10006
(212) 509-5800

7. Prudent Man Analysis
P.O.Box 1020
Lisle, IL 60532
(312) 963-0733

8. Sheshunoff and Company, Inc.
P.O.Box 13203, Capital Station
Austin, TX 78711

9. Veribanc, Inc.
P.O.Box 2963
Woburn, MA 01888
(617) 245-8370

Summary

Governments can obtain the best banking services at the most competitive prices when they choose to bid for banking services. In preparing to bid for those services, government units should prepare a request for proposal that contains a description of the services requested. This chapter presented several recommendations for preparing an RFP and suggestions for evaluating proposals. Governments preparing aggressively defined RFPs will often find they will obtain better results and the evaluation process will be much easier.

The second part of this chapter addressed the evaluation of banking services. Cash managers should commit an adequate amount of time and resources to a proper evaluation of proposals received from the banking community, including an analysis of proposed payment methods. It is also becoming increasingly important, given the large number of bank failures, to thoroughly evaluate a bank's financial condition.

7

CASH FORECASTING

by Ian J. Allan

Cash forecasting is an important, but often overlooked, component of an effective cash management program. Cash forecasts are projections of anticipated receipts, disbursements and cash balances over a certain period of time, typically a year. An accurate cash forecast is an important cash management tool for the following reasons:

- it can improve investment earnings by forecasting the amount of cash that will be available for investment, and for what time period;
- it can identify temporary cash deficits that require short-term debt financing, and ensure compliance with federal arbitrage regulations;
- it can ensure liquidity by providing estimates of the amount of cash on hand for timely disbursements;
- it can enhance creditworthiness, through improved cash management practices, thereby reducing the costs of borrowing to debt issuers; and
- it can warn of impending problems with the annual fiscal budget through the identification of potential revenue shortfalls or unexpectedly large disbursements that could result in budget deficits.

Those interested in improving cash management practices should develop a cash forecasting capacity.[1]

There are several types of cash forecasts. While the main object of each is to forecast cash position at some future point in time, each has different purposes, benefits and costs. There are also different approaches to cash forecasting that range from the informal to the sophisticated. In developing a cash forecasting capacity, cash managers must take these things into account and select the method which best suits their situation.

---

[1]It should be emphasized that cash forecasting is not an optional technique since all cash managers must make some projections of receipts and disbursements, even if it is just to meet payroll and pay bills.

The balance of this chapter is devoted to discussing the development of a cash forecasting capacity. Several aspects of cash forecasting will be examined, including: choosing an appropriate forecast format; constructing a cash forecast; using the cash forecast; and, updating the cash forecast.

Choosing an Appropriate Forecast Format

While all cash forecasts estimate a government's cash position over the course of time, they differ in the period for which cash position is measured. The three most common are:

- annual forecast;
- monthly forecast; and
- weekly forecast.[2]

Annual cash forecasts provide monthly estimates of cash position, including the level of positive and negative cash balances. They are useful in determining the amount of cash available for investment in instruments with maturities of 30 days or more.

Monthly cash forecasts provide weekly estimates of cash position. They can be used to monitor the accuracy of the annual forecast and are useful in making decisions involving investment instruments in the 0–90 day range.

Weekly forecasts provide daily estimates of cash position. They can be used to monitor the accuracy of the monthly forecast, and can be used for investment decision making involving instruments with maturities of fewer than seven days. The daily monitoring of cash position can improve investment opportunities and lead to greater investment earnings.

At the least, cash forecasts should be prepared on an annual basis with cash position estimated monthly. Whether cash managers forecast on a more frequent basis will depend on a number of factors, including:

- the time and resources available for the exercise, and the user's sophistication;
- the amount of funds under management, and other characteristics of a government's cash flows;
- the desire to improve the cash management program; and
- the need for accurate information regarding cash position.

There are different costs associated with each type of forecast. Cash managers need to evaluate cash forecasts in terms of their potential costs and benefits, and then make a determination as to whether the increased income attributable to the forecasting effort matches the cost of producing it. Generally speaking, the less detailed the forecast, the easier it is to develop, and the more inexpensive it is. On the other hand, more sophisticated forecasts are usually cost-effective only for governments with substantial cash balances.

---

[2]These cash forecast formats are not mutually exclusive. All could be employed simultaneously and, indeed, sophisticated cash managers would use all three.

Choice of a particular cash forecast format is left to the discretion of the individual cash manager.

Constructing a Cash Forecast

This section describes the methodology cash managers might use to develop an annual cash forecast. While there are other possibilities, this forecast is particularly appropriate for small governments.

It should be emphasized from the outset that cash forecasting, like most other forms of forecasting, is more an art than a science. The expert judgment and experience of the cash manager can be just as important as the methodology used in constructing the forecast. It should also be noted that cash forecasts are useful to the cash manager only so long as they are accurate and help to guide investment and borrowing decisions. Cash forecasts that are not accurate should not be utilized.

Receipt and disbursement flows are different for each government. The property tax, for example, which most local governments rely on for the largest proportion of their total revenues, can vary considerably in the frequency of its collection. Some governments collect property taxes on an annual basis, while others collect it semiannually or quarterly. This creates differing sets of cash flow and cash forecasting circumstances. For example, cash position over time will be different, as will opportunities for investing, and borrowing needs.

Cash managers can estimate a government's future cash position through an examination of historical patterns of receipts and disbursements and an analysis of budgeted revenues and expenditures. Such forecasts involve the development of an analysis that depicts a government's cash position over time. The key to developing an accurate cash forecast is to determine the timing of cash receipts and disbursements.

The receipts and disbursements that flow to and from a government can be characterized as either:

- recurring; or
- nonrecurring.

Recurring flows are regular and predictable. The timing and amount are usually known well in advance of their occurrence. Examples of recurring flows are receipts from property taxes (personal and real) and disbursements for salaries and wages.

Nonrecurring flows are irregular and unpredictable. The timing and amount are usually not known very far in advance of their occurrence. Examples of nonrecurring flows are receipts from the sale of a government's assets and disbursements for capital projects. Accurately forecasting the timing of disbursements for these projects will be the biggest challenge facing cash managers in the development of the cash forecast.

In constructing a cash forecast, information must be gathered on these flows. Information can be obtained from a number of sources, including the following:

- monthly financial reports for the previous three years (or five years depending on the preference of the cash manager) that include revenues by type and amount and expenditures made by type and amount;[3]
- the current year fiscal budget for both revenues and expenditures;
- capital project spending projections; and
- a summary of maturity dates for the current investment portfolio.

Due to the nature of governmental accounting, receipts and disbursements flow to and from a number of governmental funds, including the general operating fund.[4] While cash forecasts can be developed for each of the different funds, there are advantages to consolidating the cash flow forecast and cash for investment purposes:

- the consolidated cash flow stream is often smoother than that for individual funds; and
- the pooling of cash can lead to greater investment earnings due to the fact that, in many instances, investment yield is higher for larger investments.

This approach assumes some flexibility in interfund borrowing to cover shortfalls in individual funds. Cash managers may also want to consider the development of a consolidated cash forecast and a separate forecast for the general fund. This can make it easier to identify general fund shortfalls and track budget performance.

The development of a cash forecasting capacity requires interdepartmental cooperation. The accounting department will provide much of the information on prior receipts and disbursements that cash managers need for historical analysis. The budget office will provide information on revenues and expenditures for the fiscal year. Other departments will provide information on their expected monthly expenditures over the course of the year. In order for an accurate cash forecast to be produced, the cash manager will have to secure the cooperation of all of these entities.

The remainder of this section will discuss how cash managers can accurately forecast receipts and disbursements over the course of a year.

Forecasting Receipts

The object of forecasting receipts is to determine the level of tax and non-tax revenues a government can expect to receive by month (or some other period, e.g., week) over the course of the fiscal year.[5] There are generally three steps in the forecasting process:

---

[3]Some governments require their operating departments to prepare an annual spending plan for the fiscal year, perhaps as part of an allotment process. This information may be helpful in projecting expenditures.

[4]It should be noted that cash forecasting can be more difficult if the basis of accounting is different for these funds. To ensure accuracy, the use of accrual- or cash-based accounting methods must be taken into consideration when developing the cash forecast.

[5]Some forecasts are for a mix of time periods. For example, cash position could be forecast weekly or biweekly for two to three months, with monthly or quarterly projections following.

- reviewing the annual fiscal budget;
- developing an historical analysis of receipts; and
- creating a forecast of monthly receipts.

In order to accurately forecast receipts, cash managers need to gather information from two sources:

- the current fiscal budget; and
- monthly financial reports from prior years.

An estimate of the revenues anticipated to be collected can be obtained from the revenues section of the annual fiscal budget. Estimates contained in this budget are based partly upon historical experience, partly upon knowledge of the jurisdiction's tax bases and rates, and partly upon knowledge of certain other events that affect revenues, such as changes in the economy.

There are a number of revenue sources that cash managers should evaluate, including:

- property taxes;
- sales and use taxes;
- excise taxes (such as cigarette or gasoline taxes);
- federal and state assistance;
- user fees; and
- other revenues.

Because cash forecasts attempt to determine a government's cash position at different points over time, just knowing the amount of revenues a government expects to receive in any given year will not be of much help. Cash managers need to know when to expect those revenues.

In order to determine when it is most likely that revenues will be collected, an analysis of recent revenue collection history is necessary. By examining historical records of revenue collections by month, cash managers can develop an estimate of anticipated revenues by month for the coming fiscal year.[6] This estimate is the percentage of revenues collected in a given month from a particular revenue source. Information for the previous three years (or five years) should be available in a government's monthly financial reports.

Exhibit 7-1 shows monthly property tax revenue information for a three-year period for a hypothetical small government. In determining the distribution of receipts by month, a simple average of the monthly percentages for prior years can be used. Exhibit 7-2 depicts the monthly distribution of property tax revenues estimated for the new fiscal year using this method. Trends and predicted changes in the timing or amount of receipts should be accounted for, with the cash manager using expert judgment to adjust the monthly averages. Since the sum of the percentage of receipts expected monthly must equal 100, any increases in monthly percentages must be accompanied by corresponding decreases elsewhere.

---

[6]Cash managers should also review state and local laws governing payment schedules for taxes and other forms of revenue.

Exhibit 7-1
Historical Analysis of Monthly Receipts: By Category
($000s)

Tax on Real Property

Year	January	% of Total	February	% of Total	March	% of Total	April	% of Total	May	% of Total	June	% of Total
FY 86	$2,250	18.8%	$ 750	6.3%	$ 0	0.0%	$2,300	19.2%	$ 700	5.8%	$ 0	0.0%
FY 87	2,500	18.9	800	6.1	0	0.0	2,550	19.3	750	5.7	0	0.0
FY 88	2,500	17.9	1,000	7.1	0	0.0	2,700	19.3	800	5.7	0	0.0
3-Year Average		18.5%		6.5%		0.0%		19.3%		5.7%		0.0%

Year	July	% of Total	August	% of Total	September	% of Total	October	% of Total	November	% of Total	December	% of Total
FY 86	$2,350	19.6%	$ 650	5.4%	$ 0	0.0%	$2,200	18.3%	$ 800	6.7%	$ 0	0.0%
FY 87	2,600	19.7	700	5.3	0	0.0	2,500	18.9	800	6.1	0	0.0
FY 88	2,600	18.6	900	6.4	0	0.0	2,700	19.3	800	5.7	0	0.0
3-Year Average		19.3%		5.7%		0.0%		18.8%		6.2%		0.0%

Exhibit 7-2
Projected Property Tax Receipts by Month—FY 19X9

Month	Budgeted Annual Property Taxes ($000s)		Percent Distribution By Month*		Projected Monthly Property Tax Receipts ($000s)
January	$15,000	X	18.5%	=	$2,775
February	$15,000	X	6.5%	=	$975
March	$15,000	X	0.0%	=	$0
April	$15,000	X	19.3%	=	$2,895
May	$15,000	X	5.7%	=	$855
June	$15,000	X	0.0%	=	$0
July	$15,000	X	19.3%	=	$2,895
August	$15,000	X	5.7%	=	$855
September	$15,000	X	0.0%	=	$0
October	$15,000	X	18.8%	=	$2,820
November	$15,000	X	6.2%	=	$930
December	$15,000	X	0.0%	=	$0

* Based on 3-Year Averages

Once this analysis has been completed, the results should be summed by month to arrive at the revenue forecast. Exhibit 7-3 is an example of a revenue forecast for a small government.

A rule that cash forecasters often use is to evaluate only those sources that account for 15 percent or more of a government's total revenues; the rationale being that the other revenue sources will not have a significant impact on the cash forecast. This usually means that only four or five revenue sources will be studied. This may have some validity; however, cash managers should remember that they are attempting to accurately forecast their future cash position, and to do so requires accurate estimates of both receipts and disbursements. Accurate estimation may require cash managers to account for all receipts and disbursements. At the least, cash managers should aggregate the smaller items and forecast them as a group.

Forecasting Disbursements

The object of forecasting disbursements is to determine the level of disburse-

Exhibit 7-3
Projected Monthly Receipts—FY 19X9

Receipts	Jan.	Feb.	Mar.	Apr.	May	Jun.	Jul.	Aug.	Sep.	Oct.	Nov.	Dec.
Property Tax	$ 2,775	$ 975	$ 0	$ 2,895	$ 855	$ 0	$ 2,895	$ 855	$ 0	$ 2,820	$ 930	$ 0
Sales Tax	223	239	286	218	199	186	204	210	215	228	233	220
Water & Sewer	209	209	209	209	209	209	209	209	209	209	209	209
Other Local Receipts	85	85	85	85	85	85	85	85	85	85	85	85
State Aid	2,017	0	0	2,017	0	0	2,017	0	0	2,017	0	0
Miscellaneous	5	5	5	5	5	5	5	5	5	5	5	5
Total	$ 5,314	$ 1,513	$ 585	$ 5,429	$ 1,353	$ 485	$ 5,415	$ 1,364	$ 514	$ 5,364	$ 1,462	$ 519

ments a government can expect to make by month over the course of a year. There are generally four steps in the disbursement forecasting process:

- evaluating the annual fiscal budget;
- collaborating with the various operating departments on a report of projected expenditures by month;
- developing an historical analysis of disbursements; and
- creating a disbursement forecast from the information obtained.

In order to accurately forecast disbursements, cash managers need to collect information from three sources:

- the annual fiscal budget;
- a report of projected monthly expenditures for the fiscal year, including capital project spending projections; and
- monthly financial reports from the previous three years (or five years).

While the annual fiscal budget sets limits on the amount of expenditures a government can make, it does not tell the cash manager when disbursements will be made during the course of the year. To determine the timing of disbursements, cash managers will need to develop monthly projections. While all disbursements should be considered in the development of the cash forecast, there are several of prime importance, including:

- salaries and wages;
- payroll taxes;
- debt service;
- capital expenditures;
- materials and supplies;
- pension and employee benefit plan payments;
- utility payments; and
- other expenditures.

Cash managers must work with staff of the various government departments, including purchasing, on the development of a report that estimates disbursements by month for both recurring (such as for payroll) and nonrecurring (such as for capital projects) items. As many actual disbursements as possible should be accounted for given time and resource constraints. Exhibit 7-4 is an example of such a report.

It is relatively easy to account for recurring items, such as payroll expenditures. On the other hand, it can be quite difficult to predict the timing of disbursements for nonrecurring items, particularly those for capital expenditures. It is very important, however, that cash managers make a strong effort to account for these items.

Some significant government expenditures are not departmental in nature, such as debt service, or payments to other governments. These must also be included in the report on monthly disbursements and in the cash forecast.

The report on projected monthly disbursements by department (shown in

Exhibit 7-4
Projected Monthly Disbursements—FY 19X9
Department of Sanitation
($000s)

Category	Jan.	Feb.	Mar.	Apr.	May	Jun.	Jul.	Aug.	Sep.	Oct.	Nov.	Dec.
Payroll	$ 183	$ 183	$ 183	$ 183	$ 183	$ 195	$ 195	$ 195	$ 183	$ 183	$ 183	$ 183
Equipment	10	10	10	10	10	10	10	10	10	10	10	10
Material & Supplies	28	28	28	28	28	30	30	30	28	28	28	28
Contractual Services	25	25	25	25	25	25	25	25	25	25	25	25
Total	$ 246	$ 246	$ 246	$ 246	$ 246	$ 260	$ 260	$ 260	$ 246	$ 246	$ 246	$ 246

Exhibit 7-4) can then be compared with an historical analysis of monthly expenditures developed from information contained in monthly financial reports from prior years. As with receipts, cash managers may want to develop percentages of average monthly disbursements from the three year (or five-year) history. Exhibit 7-5 depicts an historical analysis of disbursement projections for a category of expenditures. While this type of analysis can usually provide accurate estimates of the timing of disbursements for recurring flows, the effect of major nonrecurring items, which tend to distort the accuracy of the percentages determined through this method, must be taken into account.

The cash manager should evaluate the report on projected monthly expenditures in light of the government's past expenditure experience, and determine whether those projected expenditures are reasonable, given that experience. Then, using expert judgment and the information at hand, a forecast of disbursements by month should be created. Exhibit 7-6 shows what such a forecast would look like.

Creating the Cash Forecast

The cash forecast is the sum of the monthly revenue and expenditure streams and the beginning cash position. Beginning cash position, which includes both cash and investments, is important because it represents the starting point for the cash forecast.[7]

To get a sense of liquidity and cash availability, the existing investment maturities should be added to the forecast. This provides a basis for estimating the amount of cash available to cover disbursements and for investment.[8]

Cash forecasts are usually shown in either tabular or graphic form. Exhibits 7-7 and 7-8 provide examples of each format.

Using the Cash Forecast

While there are many similarities among small governments, such as reliance on the property tax to fund operations, there are also many differences. One of the interesting characteristics of governments is that cash flows and cash position are unique for each.

Some governments are always in a strong cash position, with substantial positive cash balances throughout the year. Governments in this position have been less inclined to formalize the cash forecasting process. The likelihood of their experiencing a cash deficit will be low and they may not be as concerned about the success of their short-term investment program.

---

[7]It should be noted that beginning cash position does not equal the amount of cash available for investment. To compute this amount cash managers would have to subtract the level of funds required as compensating balances to pay for banking services (assuming this method of payment is being used).

[8]To ensure liquidity, investments should be timed to mature when cash is needed to cover disbursements.

Exhibit 7-5
Historical Analysis of Monthly Disbursements: By Category
($000s)

Payroll

Year	January	% of Total	February	% of Total	March	% of Total	April	% of Total	May	% of Total	June	% of Total
FY 86	$1,025	8.4%	$1,000	8.2%	$ 975	8.0%	$ 988	8.1%	$1,038	8.5%	$1,050	8.6%
FY 87	1,050	8.3	1,000	7.9	1,025	8.1	1,000	7.9	1,075	8.5	1,050	8.3
FY 88	1,125	8.2	1,100	8.1	1,138	8.3	1,150	8.4	1,125	8.2	1,150	8.4
3-Year Average		8.3%		8.1%		8.1%		8.1%		8.4%		8.4%

Year	July	% of Total	August	% of Total	September	% of Total	October	% of Total	November	% of Total	December	% of Total
FY 86	$1,075	8.8%	$1,038	8.5%	$1,050	8.6%	$1,013	8.3%	$1,000	8.2%	$ 988	8.1%
FY 87	1,125	8.9	1,075	8.5	1,088	8.6	1,050	8.3	1,050	8.3	1,025	8.1
FY 88	1,125	8.2	1,138	8.3	1,175	8.6	1,138	8.3	1,150	8.4	1,150	8.4
3-Year Average		8.6%		8.4%		8.6%		8.3%		8.3%		8.2%

Exhibit 7-6
Projected Monthly Disbursements—FY 19X9
($000s)

Category	Jan.	Feb.	Mar.	Apr.	May	Jun.	Jul.	Aug.	Sep.	Oct.	Nov.	Dec.
Payroll	$ 1,204	$ 1,175	$ 1,175	$ 1,175	$ 1,218	$ 1,218	$ 1,242	$ 1,218	$ 1,242	$ 1,204	$ 1,204	$1,189
Contractual Services	50	50	38	38	38	50	50	50	38	38	43	50
Material & Supplies	70	70	70	70	70	78	78	78	70	70	70	70
Equipment	28	30	28	30	28	30	28	30	28	30	28	30
Utilities	55	55	43	40	40	48	55	55	48	40	43	50
Debt Service	55	55	55	55	55	55	55	55	55	55	55	55
Capital Expenditures	---	---	150	275	325	325	325	288	250	225	125	---
Retirement Contribution	2,600	---	---	---	---	---	---	---	---	---	---	---
Benefit Plan Payments	402	391	391	391	406	406	416	406	416	402	402	396
Insurance	193	193	193	193	193	193	193	193	193	193	193	193
Other Expenditures	10	10	10	10	10	13	13	13	10	10	10	10
Total	$ 4,667	$ 2,029	$ 2,153	$ 2,277	$ 2,383	$ 2,416	$ 2,455	$ 2,386	$ 2,350	$ 2,267	$ 2,173	$2,043

Exhibit 7-7
Annual Cash Forecast—FY 19X9
($000s)

	Jan.	Feb.	Mar.	Apr.	May.	Jun.	Jul.	Aug.	Sep.	Oct.	Nov.	Dec.
Beginning Fund Balance	$ 3,200											
Projected Receipts	5,314	1,513	585	5,429	1,353	485	5,415	1,364	514	5,364	1,462	519
Projected Disbursements	4,667	2,029	2,153	2,277	2,383	2,416	2,455	2,386	2,350	2,267	2,173	2,043
Net (Receipts - Disbursements)	647	(516)	(1,568)	3,152	(1,030)	(1,931)	2,960	(1,022)	(1,836)	3,097	(711)	(1,524)
Cumulative Balance	3,847	3,331	1,763	4,915	3,885	1,954	4,914	3,892	2,056	5,153	4,442	2,918

Exhibit 7-8
Annual Cash Forecast—FY 19X9

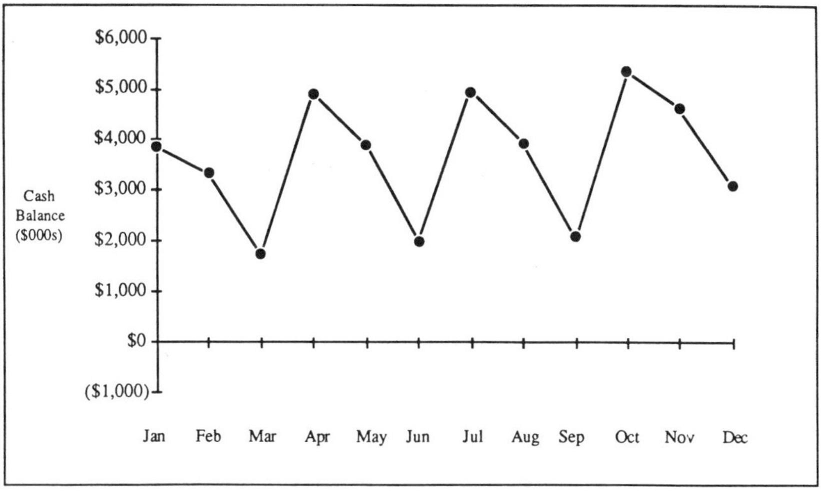

Other governments are in weak cash positions, experiencing minimal or negative cash balances throughout the year. Governments in this position have been more inclined to formalize the cash forecasting process because they require accurate information on cash position on a frequent basis to ensure liquidity and perhaps because they wish to realize the benefits forecasting can bring to their short-term investment program.

Many governments fall between these extremes. The point is that, regardless of cash position, all governments can benefit from cash forecasting, as this is the only sure way to estimate how much cash will be available for investment, and for what time period. This information can allow the cash manager to invest the greatest amount of money for the longest time period, which can result in improved investment earnings (given a positive sloping yield curve), and this is important to all governments, regardless of their cash position. Cash forecasting can also identify short-term borrowing needs, enable governments to comply with federal arbitrage regulations, and ensure liquidity.

Short-term Investing. The key to developing a successful investment strategy is knowledge of how much cash is available for investment and for what length of time. This information is provided by the cash forecast, which should set the parameters for the investment program.

Exhibit 7-9 depicts the cash position for a hypothetical community, called Sometown, USA, for fiscal year 19X9. Sometown's cash position over the course of the fiscal year is characterized by two peaks and troughs which serve as effective constraints on its ability to invest cash balances in the short-term. Aware of this, however, the cash manager can make plans to invest available cash in a manner that will maximize investment earnings, while protecting principal and ensuring liquidity.

Exhibit 7-9
Annual Cash Forecast—FY 19X9
Sometown, USA

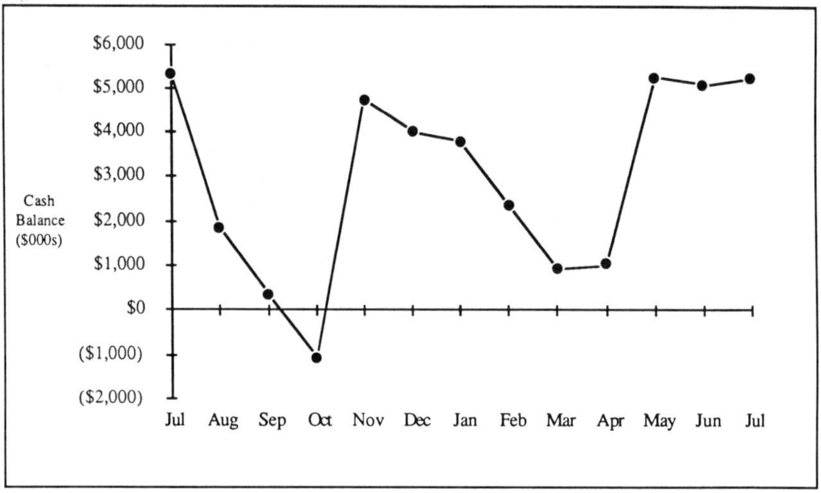

Sometown starts the year with a steeply declining cash position that results in a temporary cash deficit in October. In this instance, Sometown needs cash in a hurry to meet its short-term cash needs and will have scheduled its investments to mature in order to meet expenditure demands. In November, Sometown recovers strongly from its negative cash position and has a substantial cash balance ($5 million) to invest. However, the amount of Sometown's investable cash is forecast to decline steadily until it reaches the low point of a trough in March. Once again, Sometown must keep its maturities short in order to meet its expenditure needs. Following the low point in March, cash balances return to peak levels in May until they begin their descent into the next trough in the new fiscal year.

Sometown's cash forecast indicates to the cash manager that investments will have to be limited to those with shorter maturities. Without such a forecast, Sometown would have difficulty determining its future cash position, and no guidance for the investment of its monies. While cash forecasts will not tell the cash manager how to invest available funds, they should serve as the parameters for investing funds. With knowledge of cash availability and expenditure demands, the cash manager can structure the investment portfolio in such a way that investment earnings can be maximized.[9]

Short-term Borrowing. Cash forecasts not only identify the amount of cash available for investment, they can also provide cash managers with advance

[9]For more information on short-term investing, see Chapter 9.

warning of cash deficits. Such advance notice is important to the efficient operation of government and the development of a short-term borrowing strategy to finance the deficit. The preparation of a cash forecast, which represents a cash management improvement, can also lead to enhanced creditworthiness and reduced borrowing costs.

The key to a successful short-term borrowing strategy is knowledge of the amount of the cash deficit and the length of time that it will exist. This information should be provided by the cash forecast. Once this information is known, the cash manager should borrow money as it is needed, but in a manner that minimizes the amount borrowed and the costs of borrowing.

Returning to Exhibit 7-9, it can be seen that Sometown anticipates experiencing a temporary cash deficit in the month of October. By anticipating the deficit and having an estimate of its amount and duration, the cash manager can make plans to finance it well in advance of its occurrence.

In Sometown's case, the deficit is forecast to be $1 million and to last for approximately one month. Prior to its occurrence the cash manager can arrange for short-term financing, such as tax or revenue anticipation notes, to cover cash requirements and ensure continued liquidity. Through the development and use of a cash forecast the cash manager is able to do this, and also ensure compliance with the federal government's arbitrage regulations.

Until passage of the Tax Reform Act of 1986, some cash managers engaged in the practice of maximizing short-term borrowing to take advantage of interest arbitrage. Since passage of the tax act, borrowing in the short term for the purpose of investing in higher-yielding instruments to obtain arbitrage interest earnings has been severely restricted.[10]

Updating the Cash Forecast

Once the cash forecast has been completed, the cash manager should be prepared to update it on a regular basis. Adjustments made to the forecast should reflect actual results. By updating the forecast on a regular basis, cash managers can improve the accuracy of their current forecast, and establish a database for future cash flow projections. Many governments forecast on a continuing basis, adding a new month or quarter as each one is finished. This is known as a "rolling" forecast.

Updating the forecast to reflect actual cash flow experience is crucial to the success of the cash management program, and the efficient and effective operation of government. Significant differences between projected and actual experience can indicate the need for changes in short-term investment and borrowing strategies, as well as inappropriate forecasting methodologies, and serve as a warning of unanticipated fiscal problems.

Differences between projected and actual receipts and disbursements may be

---

[10]For more information on short-term borrowing and arbitrage, see Chapter 11.

the result of unanticipated events. Such events can affect the timing and amount of receipts and disbursements. In either case, the cash forecast must be altered to reflect their impact. Unanticipated changes that affect cash flow and the cash forecast include:

- changes in the tax rate or base;
- changes in the economy;
- changes in administrative procedures;
- one-time changes, such as the sale of an asset; and
- unforeseen demand for government services.

At the end of the fiscal year, cash managers should conduct an audit of the cash forecast to compare projected results vs. actual results, identify the reasons behind the variances, and improve the next forecast.

Summary

Cash managers interested in improving cash management practices should consider the development and use of a cash forecast. Cash forecasts are essential components of effective short-term investing and borrowing strategies. Use of a cash forecast can result in improved investment earnings and provide cash managers with sufficient time to develop plans for financing temporary cash deficits.

8

DEVELOPING INVESTMENT POLICIES

by Bonnie R. Kraft

No matter how small a governmental entity might be, if it has any investable cash, it should have a written investment policy. A formal policy protects not only the assets of the organization (which belong to the public), but also the elected officials and the finance and management staff. Although the actual investment activity and reporting for a small jurisdiction are vastly different from that of a larger entity, the basic components of a formal investment policy are essentially the same. The three objectives which should direct any investment policy are safety, liquidity, and return.

It is no accident that safety is listed first. Because public investment officials have a fiduciary responsibility with regard to the monies that they manage, safety, or the preservation of capital, must be their primary concern.

Liquidity, the ability to sell or dispose of an investment, is also important. Invested funds must be available when the government needs to make expenditures. This can be accomplished by timing the maturity of investments to ensure that funds are available when a major expenditure must be made (such as for payroll or a capital project). It can also be accomplished by ensuring that the instruments in the portfolio are liquid and have a ready market.

Rate of return, or the income which is derived from investments, is the third objective. While additional income from investments is important, particularly to governments faced with declining or stagnant revenues, it must never become the prime consideration in the investment of public funds.

The remainder of this chapter discusses the development of a formal investment policy with the focus on the following: legal and political considerations; steps in developing an investment policy; components of the investment policy; and, implementation of the investment policy.

Legal and Political Considerations

Once the decision has been made to develop an investment policy, an examination of the organizational environment should be conducted. The key question to ask is: What factors determine how the organization operates its investment program?

One important factor is the existence of legal constraints. Before undertaking the development of the policy, the writer must understand the laws which govern investment activities. Most states and provinces have specific laws which govern the investment of public funds. A local government's investment policy must conform to these laws. In addition, there may be local ordinances or charters which affect the policy. Finally, the provisions of federal law, such as the Tax Reform Act of 1986, can have a substantial impact on the investment of funds.

It is important to remember that while state and local laws might restrain certain activities, they often allow a great deal of latitude. For a small jurisdiction, the law often is more lenient than the organization should be. Policies must be developed around the capabilities of the staff, not just encompass whatever the law allows. For example, just because state law allows investment in commercial paper doesn't mean that a small, relatively unsophisticated investor should purchase that instrument.

The political environment must also be considered when developing an investment policy. Do the elected officials prefer active or passive portfolio management? In other words, should the public investment officer monitor the market and engage in swaps and other portfolio adjustments, or are the elected officials more comfortable with a buy and hold strategy? Other issues may revolve around the extent to which government funds are invested in local or regional banks.

A decision will have to be made regarding the choice of investment strategies. Here, the professionalism and availability of staff responsible for the investment program should drive the investment policy process and be the final determinant of whether investment strategies are active or passive.[1]

The issue of social investing may need to be addressed. A key question is: Should investment decisions be based on social or moral issues? Determination of whether social investing is an important issue for your government depends largely upon the views of the elected officials.

Steps in Developing an Investment Policy

There are several steps in the process of developing a formal investment policy. The first step is to meet with top management. Included in the decision-making process should be the chief finance official (such as the finance director or treasurer) and the chief administrative officer (for example, the city manager, mayor, or county administrator). It is critical that high-level staff support the concepts and goals of the investment policy.

A second critical step is the involvement of elected officials. The development of a policy should be an educational process for the council or board. In addi-

[1]See Chapter 9 for a discussion of passive and active investment strategies.

tion, it is important that the policy reflect the views of elected officials regarding appropriate investment strategies and their political or social concerns. Another method of receiving input in the development of a policy is to form a committee of financial experts from the community. These people can provide a perspective of the financial environment within which the policy must operate. However, information obtained from this source might not always be without bias.

The final step before beginning the actual writing of the policy is to study what other governments have done in this area. The Government Finance Officers Association (GFOA), through its various publications on cash management and training programs, can provide valuable assistance in this area.[2] Another strategy is to review policies from other agencies and borrow material from them. The wise finance officer will be careful with this approach, however. While it is a good idea to see what else has been done, it is important to think through the process and develop policies that are designed for the specific needs of the organization. Development of one's own policies helps in ensuring a more thorough understanding of the process and the outcome. Every component of the policy should be analyzed in the context of how it applies to the specific governmental entity.

With all of the background work completed, the writer should have enough information to begin work on the policy. The easiest way to organize the policy is to write it based on an outline consisting of several components.

Components of the Investment Policy

When developing an investment policy, several important topics should be addressed. A checklist approach works well to ensure that items of importance are at least understood and considered, and that nothing of consequence is left out. The following topics represent a checklist for consideration when developing the policy (see Exhibit 8-1).

Scope

An investment policy should contain a broad statement describing its scope. If the policy applies to the financial assets of all funds or fund types in the jurisdiction, it should be clearly stated. If the organization acts as custodian or trustee of assets of other entities, the writer must determine whether those assets also come under the guidelines of the policy.

A distinction should be made between shorter-term cash management, which is the thrust of this book, and the management of longer-term investments, such as pension funds.

This section of the investment policy should also include the legal reference under which funds can be invested. Usually, this will be the state or provincial statutes which apply, as well as reference to any applicable federal laws. In addi-

---

[2]One particular resource is the GFOA book *Investing Public Funds* by Girard Miller. The GFOA also offers technical assistance to cash managers and training programs through its Educational Services Center.

Exhibit 8-1
Components of the Investment Policy

- Scope
- Objectives
- Delegation of Authority
- Prudence
- Monitoring and Adjusting the Portfolio
- Internal Controls
- Investment Diversification
- Competitive Selection of Investment Instruments
- Qualified Institutions
- Safekeeping and Collateralization
- Accounting Method
- Reporting Requirements
- Performance Evaluation

tion, the adopted policy and other written administrative procedures should be described.

Objectives

Every investment policy should contain a concise statement of the objectives; in other words, why is the policy being written? The tone of the investment program will be set in part by the professionalism and expertise of the staff that will be involved in the investment process. The capabilities of staff should determine the parameters for investment activity.

The objectives also will be dependent on what guidance has been provided by the elected officials. As discussed earlier in this chapter, the governing board, in consultation with staff, should establish objectives based on preferences regarding active versus passive portfolio management. In addition, the elected officials must be made to understand staffing limitations, and should commit resources to ongoing staff training.

The tone and direction of the policy should be set by the governing body. The best approach is to identify the government's chief concerns. Some objectives which should be given consideration in the development of the policy are:

- preservation of capital and the protection of investment principal (safety);

- maintenance of sufficient liquidity to meet operating requirements;
- conformance with federal, state and other legal requirements;
- diversification to avoid incurring unreasonable risks regarding specific security types or individual financial institutions; and
- attainment of a market rate of return.

Should the governing body so direct, investment objectives might also address the issue of social investing.

Delegation of Authority

The policy should clearly specify who is responsible for conducting the day-to-day investment activities of the organization, and who is responsible for the overall management of the program. No persons other than those specifically mentioned in the policy should be authorized to engage in investment transactions. Included in this section should be a statement regarding the importance of allocating resources to the cash management program. This is critical if investment staff are to maintain any kind of expertise in a rapidly changing field.

Also included in this section could be a statement regarding indemnification. This should include a discussion regarding the extent to which public investors are liable for their investment decisions.

Prudence

An investment program for public funds seeks to minimize risk. How prudent the organization is regarding the investment of funds depends upon the level of credit (default) risk or market risk that it is willing to assume.

The investment policy should include specific reference to the prudent investor rule, which states, "Investments shall be made with judgment and care under circumstances then prevailing which persons of prudence, discretion, and intelligence exercise in the management of their own affairs, not for speculation, but for investment, considering the probable safety of their capital as well as the probable income to be derived."

Some policies include language regarding ethics and conflicts of interest. Such language might specifically limit the investment officer from engaging in personal or business activities which would profit from or be affected by the carrying out of their responsibilities as investors of public funds.

Monitoring and Adjusting the Portfolio

The investment objectives determine whether the organization will take an active or passive investment posture. In other words, will the investment staff engage in trading activity on a regular basis, or will the staff buy an investment instrument with the intention to hold until maturity? Again, this decision depends upon the preferences of the governing body, the expertise of the staff, and the size of the portfolio.

The issue of active versus passive management, and the degree to which a portfolio should be monitored and adjusted, can be easily quantified. Common sense and a few simple calculations can help in determining whether portfolio management should be a high priority, with expert staff engaged to handle daily operations. Is the total portfolio large enough to generate sufficient additional income through aggressive management to pay for the cost of the resources used? For example, if a more active stance would earn $30,000 in additional interest income over the year, but the increase in staff and other resources would amount to $40,000, there is no payoff from taking a more aggressive approach.

Internal Controls

The investment policy should require a system of written internal controls.[3] The procedures themselves should not be a part of the policy, but their development should be directed by the policy.

Internal controls should consider management issues such as control of collusion, separation of functions, custodial safekeeping, clear delegation of authority, written confirmation of telephone transactions, and documentation of all transactions and strategies. In addition, internal controls can ensure compliance with legal requirements. In smaller jurisdictions, developing internal controls can be difficult due to staffing limitations which restrict the ability to separate administrative functions.

Once established, written internal controls should be reviewed for effectiveness on a routine basis by an independent financial auditor.

Investment Diversification

There are three different areas of diversification which an investment policy should address: diversification by investment instrument, by financial institution, and by maturity scheduling.

Diversification by instrument is important so that the entity does not put its assets at risk by over investing in one type of instrument. This section should lay out very specifically which instruments are allowable investments for the entity. Legal investments are often dictated very specifically by state statute; however, legality is only one issue when determining which instruments to include. The choice of investment instruments should also take into account the level of staff expertise.

The policy could note the percentage of portfolio allowed to be invested in a particular instrument. While this method can be somewhat restrictive, it also protects the relatively unsophisticated investor from over investing in a particular type of security.

Diversification by financial institution reduces asset risk by preventing over investing in one institution. Limitations on investments in specific institutions can be defined by percent of portfolio, by percent of assets of the institution, or by capital adequacy guidelines.

Careful maturity scheduling ensures that the governmental unit can meet its projected cash flow needs. In a cash management context, the investment policy

---

[3]See Chapter 2 for more information on internal controls in small governments.

by definition is intended to provide guidelines for relatively short-term investments. Specific percentage minimums can be included in the policy to help define maturities; for example, 10 percent of the portfolio could have a maturity of less than 30 days; 25 percent could have a maturity of less than 90 days; and so on. As with diversification by instrument, such percentage limitations can restrict portfolio management.

The policy may need to reference guidelines for longer-term investments, such as bond sale proceeds being held for capital projects. Considerations for longer-term investments include cash flow projections and federal legislation relating to allowable arbitrage earnings.

Competitive Selection of Investment Instruments

The investment policy should require that staff select instruments for investment on a competitive basis. This not only ensures that the government gets the best rates available on its portfolio, but also helps to avoid excessive mark-up (built-in profits) for the dealer.

A list of qualified banks and brokers can be maintained for use when the entity has excess funds to invest. Competitive quotes for various instruments should be obtained from among the institutions on the qualified list. The governmental unit then chooses what best fits its portfolio based on the maturity required, liquidity requirements, the current makeup of the portfolio, and the offered rate. For informational purposes and future reference, a record should be kept of the bids offered, the bids that were accepted, and the rationale for making the decision.

Qualified Institutions

Evaluating the creditworthiness of a financial institution is probably one of the most difficult policy areas to define, particularly for a smaller jurisdiction. However, it is critical that the entity make a bona fide, good faith effort to ensure that it not deal with a bank or broker/dealer in financial trouble.[4]

Once an institution has been evaluated and determined to be sound, it can be placed on the "qualified institution" list for use in the routine competitive selection of instruments. Evaluation of banks and institutions on the list should be done on a regular basis from audited and unaudited information provided by the financial institutions.

Safekeeping and Collateralization

The investment policy should clearly identify the governmental unit's safekeeping and collateralization requirements and procedures.

Third-party safekeeping helps to guarantee delivery of securities before payment is released. The entity's money does not leave the safekeeper until the actual security has been delivered. This ensures that no funds are at risk because

---

[4]A valuable resource in evaluating financial institutions by using some fairly simple, straightforward ratios can be found in Chapter 9 of the GFOA book, *Banking Relations: A Guide for Government*, authored by Rhett Harrell.

a security was not delivered on time or never delivered. Provisions in the safekeeping agreement will also guarantee that the security is being held in the government's name. Third-party safekeeping is not inexpensive; but the costs should be considered in relation to the risk of losing principal when a dealer disappears with the organization's money. Many times, the safekeeping function can be folded into a banking services contract, thus decreasing the cost of the service.

With a deposit-type instrument, collateralization is critical. It is important that staff understand the state laws under which they operate. Some states have collateral pools; in other states, ensuring adequate collateral coverage is the responsibility of the governmental entity. The investment policy should guarantee that adequate collateral and insurance (FDIC, FSLIC) is obtained to protect the assets of the organization. The investment officer should be concerned with not only the amount of collateral that has been pledged to back a security, but also the type of securities that are being used as collateral.[5]

Accounting Method

A statement on accounting method is particularly important if the governmental entity reports according to generally accepted accounting principles (GAAP). In that case, care must be taken to ensure compliance with the Governmental Accounting Standards Board Statement 3, *Deposits with Financial Institutions, Investments (Including Repurchase Agreements), and Reverse Repurchase Agreements.*[6]

Reporting Requirements

Depending on the size of the jurisdiction, the investment policy should require a variety of daily, monthly, quarterly, and annual reports. Reports can be used to track investment activity and to determine how actual activity comports with adopted guidelines and policies. In addition, less technical reports should be generated on a regular basis with the purpose of keeping management and elected officials informed of the status of the investment portfolio, changing market conditions, and other pertinent facts. This information can be particularly helpful if your investment policy requires annual approval of financial institutions that the government is doing business with.

Performance Evaluation

At the option of the governmental entity, the policy can identify a yardstick against which investment return is measured. This measurement can be used to determine whether enough time is being spent trying to enhance investment return. A variety of yardsticks can be used to measure return, ranging from the 91-day Treasury bill rate to state pool returns.[7]

---

[5]For more information on investment safekeeping and collateralization, see the GFOA publications *Considerations for Governments in Developing a Master Repurchase Agreement* and *Considerations for Governments in Collateralizing Public Deposits.*

[6]See Chapter 3 for more information on accounting for deposits and investments.

[7]See Chapter 10 for more information on performance evaluation and reporting.

It is important that the staff and elected officials not place undue emphasis on the yield portion of the guidelines. In public investing, particularly for smaller governments, rate of return should never be placed ahead of the safety or liquidity of public funds.

Implementation

Once the policy is developed, it should be taken to the governing board and formally adopted by ordinance or resolution. This ensures that the elected officials understand the concepts that are behind the policy and agree with those concepts and the way in which they are stated.

After governing board adoption, the policy should not be placed on a shelf. It should be implemented immediately, and procedures developed using the policy as a framework. The policy can also be used to monitor actual investment activity.

The investment policy is not a static document. It should be reviewed at least annually, and changes made as new investment legislation becomes law, as staffing capabilities change, or as other external or internal issues arise. The policies should be re-adopted by the governing body each time there is a change.

9

INVESTMENT TOOLS AND TECHNIQUES

by Girard Miller

This chapter identifies and describes commonly used investment instruments purchased by public cash managers, examines the impact of the yield curve on the investing of public funds, discusses the importance of safekeeping to the preservation of public capital, and evaluates active and passive investment strategies. An appendix to the chapter discusses federal arbitrage rebate requirements and various strategies for investing bond proceeds.

The ongoing investment process involves systematic selection of securities and investment instruments that meet a local government's objectives and constraints. The tools and techniques in this chapter are therefore analyzed in the context of four criteria: legality, safety, liquidity and yield. Each instrument and technique must meet a government's legality criteria, and should contribute to an overall portfolio management program that assures safety and liquidity while obtaining at least market-average rates of return.

The Tools: Investment Instruments

U.S. Treasury Bills (T-bills). These short-term obligations are issued at a *discount* from their par maturity value. For example, a one-year T-bill issued at a 6 percent discount with a $100,000 maturity would be sold initially at 100−6=94 for a price of $94,000 and a total return to maturity of 6.38 percent (.06/.94).

Treasury bills are auctioned weekly, with cash settlement required on Thursdays. Every Treasury bill matures on a Thursday, unless a holiday falls on that date. Each weekly auction of Treasury bills includes 91-day (13-week) and 182-day (26-week) maturities. Every four weeks, a new "year" bill is auctioned, with a 364-day (52-week) maturity. Investors may purchase Treasury bills at the auction by submitting bids through dealers or banks, or directly through the Federal Reserve. To submit a bid, a tender form is submitted. The investor can submit a noncompetitive tender at the average auction interest rate, or may submit a competitive tender at a fixed price and interest rate. If the latter procedure is used,

Exhibit 9-1
Characteristics of Investment Instruments

Instrument	General Legality	Safety Factors	Liquidity	Relative Yield
U.S. Treasury bills	Most states permit.	Default risk free; custody sometimes difficult to arrange independently.	Immediately marketable (can be sold to obtain cash).	Typically the lowest yield.
U.S. Treasury notes	A few states restrict to short maturities.	Default risk free; same custody problems as T-bills. Price risks increase with maturity.	Generally marketable; price spreads widen on longer maturities.	Usually higher than T-bills.
U.S Treasury bonds	A few states restrict to short maturities.	Default risk free; many public sector losses experienced in long maturity bonds.	Marketable, but wider spreads exist in longer maturities.	Incrementally higher than notes, but often not in direct proportion.
Zero-coupon securities: a) STRIPS	Most state treat as outright ownership.	Considerable price risk for maturities over 5 years.	Less marketable than treasurys. Wireable through the Fed.	Often higher than coupon securities.
b) TIGRS, CATS, LIONS, other depository receipts	Many states do not treat them as legal equivalent of the underlying treasurys.	The theoretical risk of depository failure; long maturity and price risk are major problems.	Sometimes poor; wide price spreads.	Usually higher than STRIPS because of limited market.

Exhibit 9-1 (continued)
Characteristics of Investment Instruments

Instrument	General Legality	Safety Factors	Liquidity	Relative Yield
Federal agency discount notes	Some state require full faith and credit of U.S. government; these generally lack such guarantees.	No express federal guarantee; generally viewed as safer than longer-term agency notes and bonds. Federal "moral obligation."	Generally good; verify secondary market when you purchase.	Usually better than T-bills.
Bankers' acceptances	A few states permit.	Good credit quality on top-name domestic BAs.	In large blocks, a secondary market may exist.	Often higher than government securities.
State investment pools	25 states now operate.	Good diversification; some states do not mark-to-market, however, and maintain long maturities.	Generally good; problems can arise if interest rates rise and the pool disintermediates.	Generally higher than short-term treasury securities.
Money market mutual funds	Some states permit.	Varies with the fund. Some are AAA-rated and hold only government securities. Constant $1.00 share price.	Institutional funds permit same-day withdrawals and wire transfers; retail funds often do not.	Generally better than short-term government securities.
Municipal securities	Generally only in-state obligations permitted. Some states are amending laws to broaden authority.	Credit risk varies with issuer.	Poor. Only purpose is to invest bond proceeds.	Low. However, some high-quality bond issuers can buy tax-exempts, earn arbitrage profit, and keep it.
Government bond mutual funds and tax-exempt mutual funds	Very few states now permit.	Quality varies. Market price risk is primary risk. Should be no-load.	Can be liquidated, but losses will occur if interest rates rise.	Government bond funds often yield more than money market funds. Tax-exempt funds reflect lower rates in that sector.

Exhibit 9-1 (continued)
Characteristics of Investment Instruments

Instrument	General Legality	Safety Factors	Liquidity	Relative Yield
Guaranteed investment contracts	Very few states now permit; generally for bond proceeds only.	Depends on insurance company. No federal insurance applies.	May be poor. Difficult to withdraw without losing earnings.	Sometimes higher than money market securities.
Federal agency bonds and notes	Some are full faith and credit, others are not. Certain states permit all, many permit only a few.	Default risk is greater than treasurys. Market price risk increases with maturities.	Often less liquid than other government securities.	Should be higher than treasury bonds of same maturity.
Certificates of deposit of banks and S&Ls	Many states permit in-state bank CDs. A few permit out-of-state CDs if insured or collateralized.	43 states require collateralization. $100,000 federal deposit insurance per institution. 200 banks and S&Ls failed in 1987.	Most institutions penalize early withdrawal.	Erratic. Generally should exceed T-bills but some markets are uncompetitive.
Repurchase agreements (repos)	Some states permit explicitly; others by implication. Some impose rigid delivery requirements.	Safety improves with written agreements, delivery vs. payment, daily mark-to-market of collateral, and "haircuts."	Overnight/open repos are liquid; term repos are not.	Usually close to Fed fund rate. Typically yields rise when securities dealer inventories are large.
Commercial paper	Some states permit, usually with credit rating restrictions.	Unsecured corporate obligation under 270 days. Typically the greatest credit risk of money market securities.	Unless dealer agrees to redeem, liquidity can be poor. Usually held to maturity.	Higher than most other comparable maturity instruments.

the bid is accepted only if it falls within the bid range accepted by the Treasury. Very few small governments employ the competitive tender. Most smaller jurisdictions purchase T-bills through noncompetitive tenders at the average rate in the auction, or they purchase the bills in the secondary market.

The secondary market for Treasury bills is the market between dealers, banks and investors. This over-the-counter, telephonic market has no centralized marketplace like a stock exchange. Instead, buyers and sellers conduct their business over the telephone or other electronic media. Commissions are not paid; instead, the dealer collects a profit by matching buyers and sellers and collecting a small spread between the two. The advantage of the secondary market for public investors is that they can purchase the Treasury bills on any day of the week, and likewise can sell a Treasury bill on any day instead of waiting for maturity.

Most small government investors purchase Treasury bills and hold them to maturity. Very few small jurisdictions trade their accounts.

Ordinarily, T-bills are used only when no alternative form of investment yields a higher rate. This is because T-bills are considered risk free and very liquid instruments with a high degree of marketability. Therefore, their yields tend to be the lowest of all money market instruments. Thus, many investors elect alternative investment securities to obtain higher yields. Treasury bills do offer excellent collateral for bank deposits and repurchase agreements, however. Sometimes, when the interest rate spread between T-bills and other instruments such as bank deposits is unusually narrow, investors purchase the T-bills despite their slightly lower yields, expecting that on a future date, they can sell the bills and reinvest the cash proceeds in a higher-yielding instrument at a wider spread. Such "swap" opportunities do occasionally arise, making it worthwhile for small government investors to monitor the T-bill market.

A final advantage of the Treasury bill market is that newspapers carry the T-bill discount rates and bond equivalent yields on a daily basis for all the maturities. This enables the investor to compare other money market instruments against the T-bill yield curve (interest rate structure).

Treasury Notes and Bonds. In addition to the Treasury bill series, the U.S. government also issues coupon securities called notes and bonds. These instruments pay interest every six months just like municipal bonds. Investors must be careful, however, because Treasury bonds and notes may mature on weekends or holidays. For longer-term investments, this may not be a disadvantage; but for short-term investments, a few days of lost interest can be meaningful.

Unlike Treasury bills, which are quoted on a discount basis, Treasury bonds and notes are traded in the bond market with prices based on par equaling 100, and minimum price fluctuations measured in 32nds of one point (sometimes in 64ths). Sometimes, a period is used to separate the points from the 32nds, and investors must be careful not to confuse this with a decimal. For example, a price quote of 98.16 means 98-16/32, not 98-16/100.

Notes and bonds are virtually identical in their investment features, except that notes are issued originally with maturities of 10 years or less, whereas bond maturities are longer than 10 years, by congressional definition. Following their periodic auctions, they also can be purchased in the open secondary market. As older bonds and notes eventually approach maturity, these coupon securities can be purchased with relatively short maturities. It may be possible, for example, to locate a Treasury bond or note that matures in six months or 18 months, thereby fitting exactly an investor's specific maturity requirements.

Because each bond or note carries a different maturity and often different coupon interest rates, a mechanism is needed to permit investors to compare their relative yields and prices. This convention is called the *yield to maturity,* and represents a shortcut method of determining the effective yield on a bond or note regardless of its price. To calculate the yield to maturity, a complex mathematical formula is used, but it can be simplified by thinking of the yield to maturity as the interest rate that you would earn on your money if invested in a compound-interest bank account at the yield to maturity rate.[1]

Zero-coupon Securities. In the 1980s, securities dealers cleverly discovered that by separating the coupons from the principal payment on Treasury bonds and notes, it was possible to create a new instrument that was valuable to certain investors. A zero-coupon security is one that does not pay interest until its final maturity. By stripping the coupons from a bond, it became possible to offer investors Treasury obligations that pay principal or interest on future dates with the original investment priced at a substantial discount from the maturity value. These instruments proved popular because they avoided the need to reinvest coupon interest, which often is difficult for small investors to achieve efficiently. Zero-coupon securities also permit investors to "lock in" a specific return, without having to worry about what interest rate they will receive on the reinvestment of their future interest payments.

Originally, zero-coupon securities were created by physically stripping coupons from bonds. Sometimes these physical instruments were delivered directly to the investor, creating additional custody problems. To overcome this, several dealers created depository receipts which usually are held at a money center bank's custody division. Investors receive a depository receipt evidencing ownership of specific future coupons or principal payments. Some states do not recognize these intermediary receipts as the functional equivalent of owning the Treasury obligation; accordingly, they are not eligible instruments in certain states.

Eventually, the U.S. Treasury decided that these zero-coupon securities programs created additional and therefore desirable demand for conventional Treasury bonds. As a result, the Treasury has worked with the Federal Reserve System to create Separate Trading in Registered Interest and Principal Securities (STRIPS), which permit investors to hold direct ownership of the component parts of a Treasury obligation in book-entry form through the Federal Reserve System. Most states recognize these instruments as outright or direct ownership of Treasury obligations.

As noted above, zero-coupon securities have certain attractive features which may make them desirable for some public investment programs. However, special

[1]For those who like formal mathematics, the yield to maturity is also the rate at which interest coupons must be reinvested to produce the same compounded rate of return on the principal invested.

caution is needed when investing in longer-term zero-coupon securities. Because the entire investment income is realized through changes in price over long periods of time, changes in interest rates can dramatically affect the market price of a zero-coupon instrument. This volatility is so extreme that a two percent (200 basis point) change in interest rates can cause a 20-year zero-coupon security to fluctuate by more than 40 percent—more than the stock market crashed in 1929 or in 1987. A second problem accompanying these instruments is the tendency of some government securities dealers to charge excessive prices for the zero-coupon securities, collecting profits considerably out of line with competitive levels. Accordingly, investors should always obtain competitive prices, and compare the yield to maturity of their zero-coupon investments with other, more conventional instruments. Some local governments require special approval of the governing body before permitting investments in long-term securities because of the excessive market risk that they entail.

Federal Agency Securities. In addition to the U.S. Treasury, Congress has also authorized numerous federal agencies and government-sponsored corporations (instrumentalities) to issue debt. Some of these obligations are guaranteed by the full faith and credit of the U.S. government, but most of them carry only a "moral obligation" of the Congress to protect investors.

The securities themselves are not as widely traded as Treasury obligations, and their lack of guarantees also compels investors to seek higher yields in compensation. Because of the federal government's involvement, however, most states have authorized at least some of these instruments as eligible investments for their local governments.

Short-term investments in federal agencies can be accomplished through discount note programs, in which short-term notes are issued at a discount from par, just like Treasury bills. The advantage of these instruments, besides their generally higher yields, is that the investor can choose a specific maturity to match known cash flow requirements. This aspect of the discount note makes it well suited for buy-and-hold investing. Unfortunately, the interest rates on discount notes are not quoted regularly in the financial press, so the investor must work through a dealer or bank to monitor the market. For this reason, multiple quotes are advisable.

Longer-term agency obligations also are available, with notes and debentures available from several federal agencies. Of these, the most popular among governmental investors have been the Federal National Mortgage Association (FNMA or Fannie Mae), the Federal Home Loan Bank, and the Federal Farm Credit Bank (FFCB).

In addition, some long-term public investors have purchased Government National Mortgage Association (GNMA) pass-through mortgage securities, although these instruments are not appropriate for most small government cash management programs. GNMAs are complex long-term investments whose pricing and record-keeping complexities exceed the capabilities of many small governments. They also entail considerable market risk of rising interest rates and declining prices.

A Caution about Government Securities. Unlike many other financial institutions, dealers in U.S. government securities are largely exempt from the federal regulatory structure that governs sales practices of brokers and dealers. Numerous instances of abusive sales practices have been reported in the government securities industry, and unfortunately small governments often have been the victims of these practices. Before investing in government securities, most prudent governmental officials obtain competitive prices and thoroughly investigate the broker or dealer offering the securities.

Depository Instruments. Banks and savings and loan associations offer several instruments that can strengthen the cash management program. In fact, for years bank certificates of deposit (CDs) were the backbone of most governments' investment programs. As the financial marketplace becomes more complex, many governments are exploring additional alternatives, but very few are abandoning altogether their local depositories. Two instruments are noteworthy: the interest-bearing deposit account (NOW or MMDA) and the certificate of deposit. Eventually, banks are expected to receive securities underwriting powers under the eventual repeal of federal Glass-Steagall legislation, which also will enable them to underwrite the commercial paper of industrial corporations and money market mutual funds. Presently, however, most small governments will concentrate their cash management activities through conventional bank accounts.

Forty-three states presently require banks to collateralize public deposits, particularly for amounts in excess of the $100,000 federal deposit insurance permitted for each institution. Collateral typically is held by an independent third party, and may consist of government securities, or other marketable instruments depending upon state statutes or local practices.[2]

Certificates of deposit presently must mature in seven or more days. Most small governments purchase non-negotiable local bank CDs, and elect maturities that coincide with payroll, accounts payable distributions or debt service payment dates. The interest rate on CDs is negotiable, although most banks post a specified rate and allow the investing local government to "shop the market." Most institutions pay interest using a 360-day year, but many are still known to calculate interest using a 365-day year. When comparing investment yields, it becomes important to know the basis of the interest calculation.

Repurchase Agreements. A repurchase agreement, despite its legal complexity, is essentially a simple, two-way transaction. An investing government exchanges cash to receive government securities for a specified period of time. This can be done overnight, for a specific term (maturity), or on an indefinite (open) basis. The interest rate paid for the use of the government's cash is determined by negotiation or bidding, and typically is related closely to the Fed funds rate on overnight borrowings in the banking network. Upon maturity, the investing government returns the securities and receives cash plus accumulated interest. The

[2]A useful GFOA publication on the subject of deposit collateralization is entitled *Considerations for Governments in Collateralizing Public Deposits* and is available through the association's Chicago office.

market value of the securities transferred to the local government should exceed the amount invested. As a protection against fraud, the bank or dealer should not be permitted to hold the collateral securities in its own safekeeping department but should instead deliver them to an independent third-party institution.

Throughout the 1970s and 1980s repos revolutionized the world of local government finance. Even small jurisdictions found it possible to obtain high overnight rates of return using instruments that were secured by government securities. For ten years, the repo instrument was used without incident, and helped banks to avoid reserve requirements which detracted from their earnings and yields. Likewise, government securities dealers found repos an attractive way to finance their growing inventories of government securities. Meanwhile, local governments earned attractive interest rates and maintained considerable liquidity. Unfortunately, the collapse of several government securities dealers in the early and mid-1980s stunned the public markets and left numerous municipalities holding worthless paper. Numerous reforms have been implemented to help small governments avoid similar losses in the future, including: (a) thorough investigation of the counterparty bank or dealer's creditworthiness, (b) use of an independent custodian to hold collateral securities, (c) widespread adoption of the delivery vs. payment (DVP) procedure for settling repo transactions, (d) marking collateral to market daily, so that price fluctuations in the bond market do not undermine the value of the protective collateral and (e) overcollateralization or "haircut" factors to provide a safe margin for error and possible price fluctuations.

Governmental investors are advised to arrange all repurchase agreement transactions through the use of a written agreement—a master repo agreement. This document specifies the intentions, rights and obligations of both parties to the transaction, and provides remedies in the event of default. Industry experts consider a master repo agreement to be a vital protection against possible losses that could occur in the event of default.[3]

Commercial Paper. Over 1,000 American corporations issue unsecured promissory notes maturing in less than 270 days. These instruments are known as commercial paper, and represent an alternative to government securities and depository instruments. Obviously, because these debt instruments carry no government guarantees or insurance, they entail considerably higher credit risks. To control these risks, broad portfolio diversification is needed. Most small governments are unable to properly construct a portfolio of high-quality commercial paper, with each issue representing only one or two percent of the total holdings. Accordingly, many jurisdictions use their state investment pool or money market funds, if they are legally permitted, as the vehicle through which to invest in commercial paper.

Several rating agencies now rate commercial paper, and most governments restrict their investments to the highest quality (A-1 or P-1) ratings. Like agency discount notes, commercial paper usually can be purchased with the maturity

[3]The Government Finance Officers Association has published *Considerations for Governments in Developing a Master Repurchase Agreement,* available through the association's Chicago office.

elected by the investor. Some paper is issued in discount form, and other issuers permit interest-bearing paper. A few large issuers sell their paper directly; most employ a dealer to accomplish the distribution function. Some dealers are prepared to repurchase commercial paper from an investor whose unexpected cash flow requires them to liquidate. In these instances, however, the market price of the instrument may have changed since the time of purchase.

Bankers' Acceptances. To finance foreign trade transactions, several large banks issue acceptances of trade bills. These instruments are usually high-quality money market securities, and usually trade in denominations of $1 million or $10 million. In the states where legalized, bankers' acceptances are popular, and generally are perceived as high-quality money market securities. Recently, Japanese bankers' acceptances have become popular with west coast governmental investors because of their higher yields. Of course, any crisis in the international financial community could affect these instruments more than domestic bankers' acceptances. Most BAs trade in the secondary market on a discount basis with maturities under 60 days. Because of their large denominations, it is difficult for small governments to construct a properly diversified portfolio including bankers' acceptances.

State Investment Pools. Over 25 states have created investment pools that operate like commercial money market funds. These pools offer the advantage of daily liquidity, economies of scale through combined purchasing, and diversification and professional management. In two states, a private firm operates the state pool under a management contract. In several states, a public joint powers trust operates much like a state investment pool, although without the formal authorization and backing of the state government. As repurchase agreements became more complex and the costs of achieving delivery vs. payment and independent custody rose in recent years, state investment pools have become more popular with smaller jurisdictions seeking safety and liquidity.

Money Market Mutual Funds. Presently, 17 states permit local governments to invest in money market mutual funds. Like their retail counterparts, several investment companies offer institutional money market funds to governmental investors. These Securities and Exchange Commission (SEC) regulated instruments employ an independent custodian, and operate under a trust agreement. Most funds require delivery vs. payment for their portfolio, and conduct transactions through wire transfers so that the portfolio managers and officers never have access to the client's cash. Several investment companies permit subaccounting which allows small governments to avoid the problem of apportioning interest among various funds. In some cases, an investment income reporting service can be offered for the investment of bond proceeds.

Money market funds seek to maintain a constant $1 net asset value. Under SEC regulations, the funds must maintain an average maturity of less than 120 days, although in practice most maintain portfolio maturities averaging 30–60 days. No single instrument can be purchased with a maturity of more than one year. Historically, there has never been a loss of governmental funds through a money market fund.

Some states permit investments in money market funds that invest strictly in government securities; others permit more broadly diversified portfolios. The latter instruments offer a useful way to participate in the commercial paper and bankers' acceptance market. The disadvantage of money market funds is that they are completely liquid. Higher yields sometimes can be obtained through direct investments in money market securities with a distant future maturity.

Other Mutual Funds. A few states permit local governments to invest funds in short-term government bond mutual funds and tax-exempt mutual funds. The government bond mutual funds offer a mechanism for small governments to participate in longer maturities, without actively managing their portfolios themselves. The primary disadvantage of a bond mutual fund is that if interest rates rise, the investor may not be able to sell the mutual fund shares at the price paid at the time of purchase. Accordingly, special care is needed to ensure that funds invested in a bond mutual fund are not needed for payment in the near future.

Tax-exempt mutual funds generally are advisable for purchase only in special cases involving the proceeds of bond issuances subject to federal arbitrage rebate requirements. In these instances, the tax-exempt fund can provide a vehicle for avoiding a rebate and rebate calculation.

Municipal Securities. Small governments occasionally issue tax-exempt bonds in amounts exceeding $5 million per calendar year. If the proceeds of these tax-exempt issuances are not spent within six months, it is likely that federal arbitrage rebate requirements will apply to the investments of those proceeds. One of the few "safe harbors" to escape federal arbitrage regulations is the investment of bond proceeds in tax-exempt securities. Accordingly, some states have expanded their investment laws to permit local governments to invest bond proceeds in obligations of their state and local governments, and perhaps also the obligations of other states and local governments. Ordinarily, these instruments would not be suitable for public sector cash management, because of their inherently lower interest rates. However, in special situations such as the investment of bond proceeds, they may fulfill a portfolio need.

A special consideration to observe when investing in tax-exempt securities is the credit quality and diversification needed to protect against defaults. Some local governments have been investing in tax-exempt securities of issuers whose future creditworthiness might be dubious. Obviously, diversification and special care in selecting creditworthiness are two considerations warranting the investor's attention.

Guaranteed Investment Contracts. A few states permit local governments to invest cash or bond proceeds in guaranteed investment contracts (GICs). These uninsured, non-guaranteed obligations of insurance companies typically pay higher interest than comparable maturity bank deposits.

Because of their unsecured character, it is necessary to conduct special studies of the creditworthiness of the insurance company before investing in GICs. These instruments have been used primarily for public pension fund investments, and must be properly diversified to protect against default risk. Some GICs are sufficiently short in maturity to qualify as cash management instruments; however,

Exhibit 9-2
Normal Yield Curve

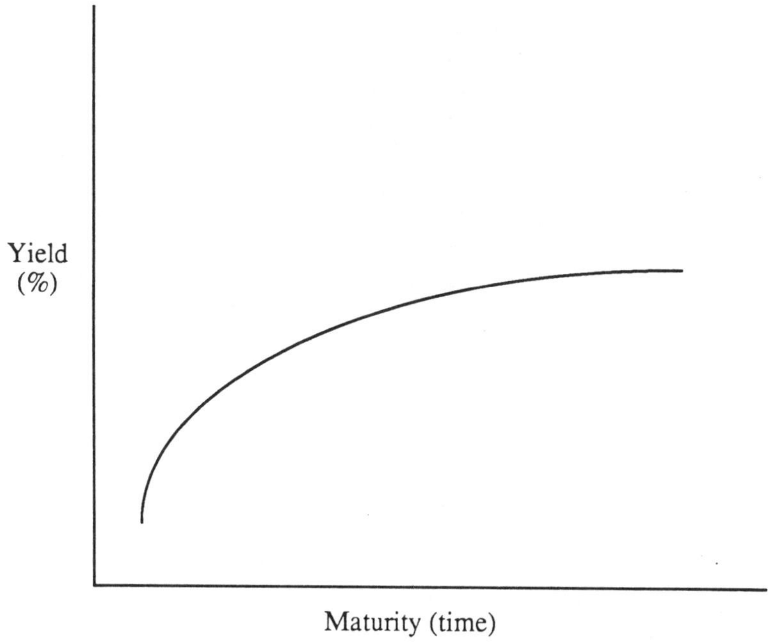

many are longer-term securities comparable to Treasury bonds or zero-coupon securities. The industry is notorious for imposing difficult penalties in the event funds are withdrawn from a GIC prior to its stated maturity. Investors should carefully review the GIC contract documents before making investments in order to ascertain the penalties and possible costs of subsequent changes in portfolio composition. Credit ratings of the issuing insurance company should also be consulted before investing.

The Yield Curve

A major concept for investment officers to understand is the yield curve—the relationship between interest rates and the time to maturity on investments. A yield curve is simply a graph plotting the yields on a specified security (e.g., T-bills or bank CDs) on the vertical axis, with the maturity of each instrument on the horizontal axis.

Yield curves take many shapes, and seldom remain stable. Most of the time, however, the yield curve rises from the left to the right, as interest rates are higher on longer-term maturities. Such an upsweeping or ascending yield curve is often called a normal yield curve (see Exhibit 9-2).

Exhibit 9-3
Inverted Yield Curve

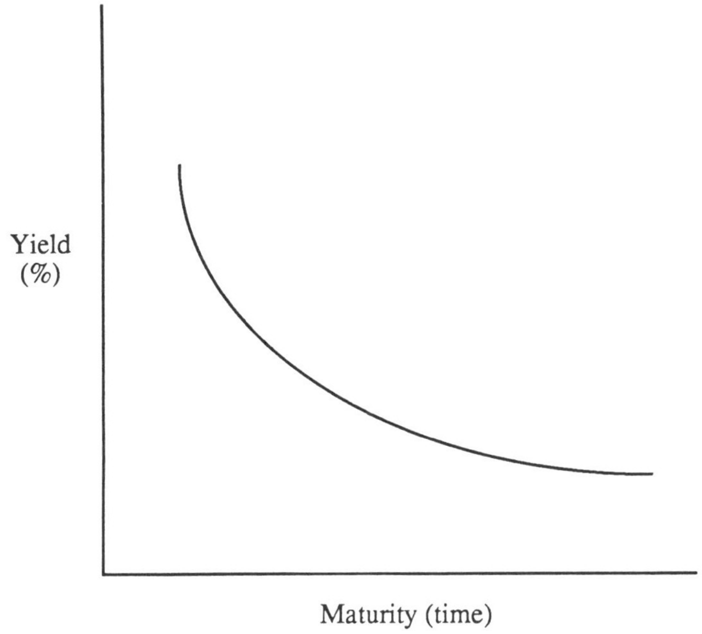

In periods of high interest rates usually associated with the peak of a business cycle, the yield curve may invert (see Exhibit 9-3). When this happens, short-term rates exceed long-term rates. Usually, this configuration reflects investors' expectations that high interest rates will not last forever, and a recession will probably drive interest rates lower.

The yield curve should be a smooth continuous line that flattens out as maturities lengthen. Whenever a specific security lies above the rest of the curve, it usually represents a buying opportunity—or an aberration.

Experienced public investors learn to study the yield curve and find maturities that offer the best relative value. With flat yield curves (or segments) the general rule is to select shorter maturities; with steep curves, longer maturities may offer better investment values.[4]

[4] Yield curve analysis is the process of studying the yield/maturity relationship between various maturities, to determine how much interest rates must change before an investor will be better (or worse) off by investing for the longer term. Specific yield curve analysis methodologies are shown in *Investing Public Funds* by Girard Miller and *Money Market Calculations: Yields, Break-Evens and Arbitrage* by Marcia Stigum.

Investment Safekeeping

Prudent public investors avoid several risks by arranging for their investment securities to be held by an independent third party—somebody different from the bank, dealer or investment company who sells securities to you. Although dealers and local bankers may attempt to discourage you from implementing sound safekeeping practices because it raises their costs, it is important that you act to protect the public's interest. The following general guidelines apply to different investment instruments.

Government Securities. Ownership of U.S. Treasury securities and some federal agency securities is recorded by computerized "book entry" on the records of a Federal Reserve Bank. Your custodian bank usually will be listed on the Fed's book entry system, with your ownership shown as "customer account" or "trust account." Local governments generally cannot have their own name shown on the book-entry system. Therefore, it is very important that ownership be placed with an independent party—either a financial institution other than the one acting as seller, or possibly in the trust department of a local bank (provided there is a written trust agreement). A written safekeeping confirmation should be provided for each security held by the custodian.

Repo Collateral. Securities purchased under a repurchase agreement should also be delivered to an independent custodian or a bank trust department, subject to a written safekeeping/custodial agreement. Governmental investors should avoid "hold in custody" repos, in which the dealer or bank holds the collateral with no segregation and independent verification to protect the customer.

Deposit Collateral. To protect public deposits, some states require each bank to segregate government securities. Collateral usually can be transferred to a Federal Reserve Bank or to a third-party bank, which protects the entity against financial failure. "Pool" collateral usually is discouraged unless it is supervised directly by a state agency.

Mutual Funds. Most mutual funds employ independent bank custodians for their portfolio safekeeping. Before investing in a money market mutual fund or a short-term government bond mutual fund, investors should verify (1) whether the portfolio is held by an independent custodian, (2) whether the fund requires delivery vs. payment in its portfolio transactions, and (3) whether the fund purchases insurance against fraud, embezzlement and computer errors. These protections are offered by many mutual funds and should not be overlooked.

Active vs. Passive Management

One of the most important managerial decisions facing the finance officer in a small government is the issue of management style and strategy. The amount of time and effort devoted to the investment function varies between jurisdictions, depending on numerous factors such as overall staffing levels, organizational structure, and the size and complexity of the portfolio. Some local governments employ active portfolio management strategies and devote substantial resources to the investment function. Most, however, adopt generally passive investment strategies designed to minimize administrative expenses while obtaining market-average rates of return and incurring minimal risks. These decisions historically have been made by individual finance officials, but some local governing bodies are making conscious policy decisions regarding the overall portfolio management style.

The Case for Passive Management

Most local government finance officers conduct numerous activities, including accounting, budgeting, risk management, debt finance, retirement administration, payroll, and purchasing. The finance director and other staff members wear many hats. Nobody is able to devote full time to the investment function, and it is doubtful that improved portfolio performance would justify the additional expense of devoting a full-time person to such an area of responsibility. Even then, the costs of training, equipping and maintaining such an employee often outstrip the financial capabilities of a local government.

In fact, some jurisdictions have discovered to their chagrin that having made the investment in equipping and training a professional investment official, the successful employee quickly acquires experience and is recruited by the private sector for a higher-paying job. Thus, the ability to attract and retain professional investment talent may be more likely to occur in larger jurisdictions.

Many portfolio theorists believe that it is generally impossible to outsmart the market. For every buyer there is a seller, and in matters of market timing and credit risk analysis, somebody must be wrong. Accordingly, there seem to be relatively few opportunities for local governments to detect obvious opportunities to achieve above-market rates of return on investment. If this is the case, then policymakers must ask whether they can warrant the expenditure of public funds when attempting to attain constantly elusive portfolio returns. Further, most local governments lack the equipment and resources needed to operate an active investment portfolio management program. Access to the minute-by-minute changes in the various markets is available generally only to larger jurisdictions that can afford the expense of Telerate and other electronic data services. Being remote from the central markets in New York and Chicago, most local governments learn of breaking financial news only after it has happened and after the markets have already adjusted to new price levels. Accordingly, many finance directors have concluded that they must be price takers, not market makers.

Most local governments also operate relatively smaller portfolios of less than $20 million. Such portfolios generally are difficult to diversify sufficiently to absorb higher credit risk, and also are too small to facilitate the larger trading blocks of capital needed to obtain efficient market pricing. Accordingly, a passive portfolio management strategy that seeks to obtain reasonable rates of return with a modest investment of staff time may be preferable.

Some of the passive management strategies that can be employed by a local government include:

Passive Technique #1: Create a Liquidity Pool. After safety, liquidity is the second most important investment objective of public officials. Particularly for smaller governments, the risk of being caught short on cash to pay bills is unacceptable. Therefore, most cash management programs begin with a liquidity pool. This can be created in various ways, including the use of repos, money market funds, state investment pools or Treasury bills.

The disadvantage of a liquidity pool is that it may detract from yield. By trading yield for unneeded liquidity, less interest income may be obtained than desired. Thus, a liquidity pool generally should comprise only part of the overall portfolio, albeit a key, core element.

Passive Technique #2: Cover the Next Disbursement. Beginning cash managers usually learn quickly that the easiest way to sleep at night is to invest incoming funds to match the next "uncovered" disbursement. Thus, tax receipts might be invested to mature on the biweekly payroll date due in six weeks, because the next two already have been covered. By moving funds out into slightly longer maturities, better investment returns generally are realized. Fortunately, most local government cash disbursements are highly predictable, so this strategy can help improve returns.

Passive Technique #3: Invest to the Maximum Term under the Cash Budget. This technique goes beyond #2 by stretching out maturities when the cash budget shows that future incoming cash receipts can be used to cover upcoming disbursements. For example, instead of investing cash to mature in the middle of the next tax collection cycle, it might be possible to extend maturities further because incoming cash will provide ample liquidity for the payroll and disbursements that fall due during tax collection season. If the yield curve is positive and rates are stable, this approach should produce higher returns on long-term investments. Of course if rates rise dramatically, shorter maturities will outperform this approach.

Passive Technique #4: Maintain Constant Maturity. Some portfolio managers prefer to maintain a portion of their portfolio in liquid instruments (e.g., T-bills and money market funds) to meet cash claims, and invest the bulk of their assets in a given maturity range, such as the one-year T-bill. Periodically, the instruments are sold and proceeds reinvested for a longer term in order to maintain a constant maturity. For example, a new year-bill might be purchased each month. *Public Investor's* year-bill index has illustrated the success of this approach over the years. Only when rates rise dramatically, as they have in 1987 and 1988, does the rolling constant maturity portfolio underperform a shorter-term portfolio. One disadvantage: this is not a buy-and-hold strategy, and may be hard to explain. Also, marketable securities whose yields may be less than other buy-and-hold instruments must be purchased.

Pooling of assets permits diversification, allows liquidity and achieves economies of scale. State and local government investment pools offer cash managers in many states the benefits of large portfolio returns. In one-third of the states, mutual funds are legal investments for some local governments. Checkwriting privileges are offered by many of these funds, which typically compete well against repos, T-bills and short-term bank CDs. Smaller investors particularly benefit from these vehicles. The disadvantage: liquidity may not always be needed and a higher return may be available in term instruments. Nothing can beat these instruments, however, for diversification.

The Case for Active Portfolio Management

Despite inherent limitations, some small local governments may be able to generate consistent above average portfolio returns on their cash management funds. Although such instances ordinarily are exceptions, superior talent may exist in some jurisdictions and a few local entities may be able to afford the resources needed to properly equip the operation. Further, it may be possible that a limited active management strategy can be implemented for a portion of the portfolio, while leaving much of the operation in a passive mode. Such a mixed strategy also offers opportunities.

Examples of active portfolio management strategies that warrant consideration by small government officials include:

Active Strategy #1: Take Credit Risks for Yield. Despite the old admonition about safety and liquidity before yield, some investors deliberately and sometimes prudently trade safety to obtain better yields. "Riskier" instruments, such as unguaranteed federal agency securities, uncollateralized bank CDs and commercial paper, occupy the extreme end of the money market risk spectrum, and therefore offer higher yields. In a large, diversified portfolio, such credit risks can be controlled, thus producing significantly higher returns. Large government portfolios, local government investment pools and money market funds all provide the size and diversification needed to ensure such protection. For smaller investors, however, the risks associated with default cannot be controlled, and the staff effort needed to properly research and document prudent decision making may exceed the return on the investment. The problem: E.S.M. Government Securities was the classic case history—defaults do occur.

Active Strategy #2: Ride the Yield Curve. During a business cycle recovery and expansion, interest rates on longer maturities typically exceed those on shorter maturities. Some cash managers seek to enhance returns by riding the yield curve. They buy longer maturities in anticipation of selling them later at the same or a lower interest rate. If their strategy works, the total return during the holding period will exceed the interest rate on shorter-term securities. The risk: rising rates. Research has shown that over time, interest rates usually have risen during periods dominated by rising (normal) yield curves. Hence, the market often already has anticipated higher rates and this strategy proves to be more mythical than real.

Active Strategy #3: Spreads and Swaps. Market imperfections occasionally do arise, and public investors' objectives and tax circumstances may give them opportunities to "arbitrage" the market by swapping out of one instrument into another for a better total return. Too often, however, the swaps proposed to local investors by dealers involve greater risks, less marketability or other problems that may be overlooked by the public officials. Extensive time, effort and documentation are needed for a successful swap program—and large portfolios usually are needed. Always ask, "Why wouldn't the dealer take this trade himself if it's such a great idea?"

Be wary of the smoke and mirrors that have been displayed under the name of "horizon analysis" and "swap analysis" printouts. Cautious investors should read Homer and Liebowitz's *Inside the Yield Book* before stepping into this arena, and plan to make a major time commitment. Also, do not be afraid to ask the dealer what the markup is!

Active Strategy #4: Special Situations. Sometimes a good deal does come along. For example, a group of taxable investors may elect to exit the Treasury securities market, leaving good values to non-taxable investors. Sometimes dealers will make concessions to clean out odd lots from their inventories. New, untested securities may carry a yield premium as the market gains experience. Beware, however, of the special deal that involves extraordinary risks or high dealer profits. More junk has been sold under the label of "special situations" than have truly investment-grade securities.

Active Strategy #5: Market Timing. No single investment topic generates debate as much as market timing. On the average, it is impossible for the majority of investors to be successful market timers, because for every buyer there is a seller. Somebody has to be wrong about the direction of interest rates. Academic research has dismissed technical analysis and asserts that the market is essentially a random walk. Nonetheless, interest rates clearly do move in general trends, so it seems plausible that trend-oriented market timing could be a successful strategy. *Public Investor* has published moving average charts for some time now, with good success in identifying the dominant rate trend and trend-reversal points. Other systems have been developed by speculators to assist in the market timing game, although none shows reliable track records when tested independently.

Due to market volatility, a strong emotional constitution is needed to be a successful short-term market timer. Further, the local government environment (a goldfish bowl containing political sharks) hardly is suitable for admitting error—which every successful market timer must do from time to time.

Active Strategy #6: Hire an External Manager. The newest trend in public-sector active management strategies is external management. The private sector has recognized the vast pool of assets held by local governments and has begun marketing its management expertise. For local governments that believe that full-time professionals can outperform a part-time or inexperienced portfolio manager, the cost of hiring an external manager may be unimportant. For others, the comfort factor is worth a price.

Major issues are how to select and control the external manager. Recent successes in a bull bond market should not be confused with skill, so public officials also should study a manager's performance during bear markets, such as the June 1986–December 1988 time interval. Then comes the problem of measuring performance and evaluating comparative performance once a contract has been signed.

Notwithstanding the problems of measurement, a case can be made that full-time market professionals should be able to produce better results through active management than their part-time public-sector counterparts who generally lack facilities, resources and experience.

What's Right for You?

Public investment officers and policymakers should devote some time to a review of their investment capabilities, constraints and objectives. Only by analyzing the environment and the potential returns can public investors decide which approaches are best for them. Usually, a combination of two or three will provide the best comfort and the best long-term returns on the public's dollar.

Summary

The management of short-term investments is one of the most challenging aspects of local government cash management. Prudent cash managers should become familiar with the performance and risk characteristics of the various investment instruments legally allowed in their jurisdiction. Proper safekeeping procedures and other precautionary measures should be put into place. Depending on the size of the portfolio, the complexity of operations, the size of the staff and other local factors, various active and passive investment management strategies should be researched and considered. In the final analysis, however, cash managers should be mindful of the "SLY" priority of investment objectives: Safety and Liquidity *always* come before Yield.

Investing Bond Proceeds

by Girard Miller

An increasingly complex topic in public cash management is the investment of proceeds received from the issuance of tax-exempt bonds and notes. Special laws and regulations apply to these funds, sometimes causing cash managers to adopt specialized practices.

Different Laws and Indenture Restrictions. Some states have enacted special legislation to govern investments of bond proceeds. These statutes generally have been drafted either to protect bondholders or to expedite financing alternatives. To protect bondholders, some states have enacted restrictive lists of permissible investments so that statewide bond ratings could not be jeopardized by foolish investments. Elsewhere, however, a permissive approach applies: several states permit considerably more latitude in the investments of bond proceeds than with general operating cash. The rationale behind the latter, permissive statutes is that bond counsel, underwriters, fiscal advisors, and rating agencies provide considerable input and restrictions into the investment program, so that prudence is assured by their involvement.

Permissive state laws might not apply to a specific debt issue if restrictive covenants are written into the governing bond resolution. An example would be resolution language requiring that investments be made only in U.S. government securities, collateralized bank CDs or AAA/AA-rated money market securities. Thus, the public cash manager should always verify legal authority first before embarking on a radically different investment program. Where possible, efforts should also be made to persuade bond counsel to write resolutions with the maximum legal flexibility permitted under the law.

Safety is Definitely First. Investment losses are always difficult to accept, but nothing jeopardizes bond ratings and invites repressive legislative backlash as quickly as investment losses involving bond proceeds. Following the losses of several bond issuers who had invested in E.S.M. Government Securities in 1984, both of the major national bond rating agencies instituted programs to examine local investment policies and practices. Uncollateralized debt instruments are particularly disliked by most professionals associated with the investment of bond proceeds.

Basics of the Arbitrage Law. An important, complex aspect of investing bond proceeds is compliance with federal laws governing the arbitrage of tax-exempt debt issuance.

Arbitrage is generally understood to be the process of trading in two markets to make a profit on the price spread. In currencies and precious metals markets, this is accomplished by executing simultaneous offsetting transactions on different exchanges to capture market price discrepancies. In public finance, arbitrage means the investment of low-yielding tax-exempt bond proceeds in higher-yielding taxable securities to earn a profit. If this practice were allowed on an unlimited basis, tax-exempt debt might ultimately be issued in such massive amounts that municipal interest rates could eventually exceed the yields on default-free Treasury bills and bonds.

To control this potential for abuse, Congress has enacted statutes that impose certain limitations on investment activities of tax-exempt issuers. Although local governments have objected to the various statutes and ensuing Treasury arbitrage regulations over the years, most public officials have agreed that certain limitations are in fact necessary to prevent transactions created solely for the purpose of arbitrage.

Until 1986, the Treasury controlled arbitrage activity through three rules. First, an issuer was required to begin spending tax-exempt proceeds within six months and exercise "due diligence" in making progress toward completion. Second, within three years, 85 percent of the debt-financed funds were to be spent for the project unless unforeseen problems arose. Lastly, short-term borrowing was limited to the maximum anticipated cumulative cash flow deficit projected for the next 13 months. Failure to comply with any or all of these requirements could result in revocation of the issuer's tax exemption.

In 1986, Congress enacted the Tax Reform Act, which went much further than ever before in specifying additional limits on arbitrage activity. The law's arbitrage rebate regulations usually restrict the flexibility of municipal issuers to earn and retain arbitrage interest on bond proceeds. First, it sets a six-month period for spending tax-exempt debt proceeds if arbitrage profits are to be kept. Second, those issues which expend greater than 95 percent of their funds within six months generally are exempt from the requirement to rebate excess investment income (arbitrage profits) to Treasury. Finally, for financing beyond six months, the entire excess of investment income over borrowing costs, including the rebate amount earned in the first six months, generally must be refunded.

Safe Harbors. Bond issuers may avoid rebate and potential penalties through certain exceptions to the general arbitrage rules, sometimes called "safe harbors." The only safe harbors from these new rebate requirements are investments in tax-exempt securities, mutual funds or special Treasury securities whose yields are restricted by formula.[1] Issuers who sell less than $5 million in a single calendar year (including their subordinate entities' debt) also are exempt from rebate requirements, although the pre-1986 law still applies to their debt.

The Arbitrage Speed Trap

Bond issuers are required to rebate to the federal government any excess earnings from investment of their bond proceeds if these investments are not granted "safe harbor." Excess earnings are defined generally as the amount by which investment income exceeds the bond yield (net borrowing cost). For rebate calculation purposes, the bond yield reflects the net yield to initial investors (the public), which often is less than the original yield at the bond sale because it is reduced by the underwriter's spread. Finance officials have dubbed this "net" bond yield as "the arbitrage speed limit"—once investments exceed the earnings limit, they become subject to the penalties of the arbitrage speed trap.

Many bond issuers have come to realize that once they have entered the arbitrage speed trap, their investment objectives change. For investment portfolios whose yields exceed the arbitrage speed limit, factors like safety, liquidity, convenience, and administrative cost reduction become the foremost objectives, because Uncle Sam will capture all investment yields exceeding the bond yield.

Arbitrage Compliance Strategies. To cope with federal regulations in this area, public cash managers typically have resorted to the following strategies:

[1]Investments in tax-exempt bonds subject to the alternative minimum tax (AMT) are not granted a "safe harbor," however.

1. *Think Small.* The 1986 statute allowed a small issuer exemption from arbitrage rebate requirements. If the issuer sells $5 million or less each calendar year, no rebate is required. To avoid rebate, some entities have financed their projects by issuing two sets of bonds in succeeding years. As long as money is spent within three years, the small issuer faces no arbitrage problem. One negative aspect of this strategy is that issuance costs are doubled; if an earnings surplus cannot be generated to offset the extra legal, advisory and advertising fees, this strategy is wasteful.
2. *Blowout.* Some issuers borrow only for short time intervals or prepay expenses from other cash sources to ensure that 95 percent of proceeds will indeed be spent within six months. This is called "blowing out" the proceeds, so that excess arbitrage earnings can be retained by the issuer.
3. *The Arbitrage Fairy.* Some bond issuers steadfastly continue to conduct "business as usual," maximizing their earnings within the normal limits of prudence. Hoping that somehow, someday, the courts or the Congress will repeal the rebate provisions of the 1986 Tax Reform Act, these investors are probably wasting precious staff time amassing substantial earnings surpluses that will eventually be remitted to the federal government.
4. *The Lucky Devils.* A small but significant number of tax-exempt debt issuers have found ways to invest in tax-exempt securities or tax-exempt money market mutual funds to avoid arbitrage rebate. Generally, these issuers are large AAA or AA-rated borrowers with excellent standing in the markets, and low borrowing costs. By investing bond proceeds in tax-exempt securities, they have been able to earn a positive spread and avoid the rebate and reporting requirements.

   Unfortunately, most state laws still require amendments to make this strategy viable. GFOA's model investment legislation and 1987 policy statements provide guidance to public officials seeking to implement this strategy. A final caution to investors considering use of this strategy—portfolios generally cannot include bonds subject to the alternative minimum tax.
5. *The Ostrich Strategy.* In some states and localities, a political decision has been made that a rebate simply will not be paid to the federal government—just as a matter of principle. To accomplish this, money is invested in the open market at competitive rates in securities that under-yield the issuer's bonds. For example, one state cash manager with relatively low borrowing costs has invested in short-term U.S. Treasury bills that pay less than the state's borrowing rate. Unfortunately, this strategy is economically inefficient and might even become impossible to accomplish if interest rates rise after the bonds or notes are sold. The federal government could also prohibit use of this strategy.

   Some public officials have reportedly sought to achieve artificially low interest rates through "sweetheart deals," by leaving money uninvested or by informing bidders on investment contracts that the bids will be rejected if rates exceed the borrower's bond yield. Such practices are likely to invite future inspection by Treasury Department auditors who will be responsible for assuring compliance with "prohibited transactions" rules.
6. *If You Can't Lick 'Em, Join 'Em.* Some issuers may choose to invest in the Treasury Department's State and Local Government Series (SLGS, or "Slugs") instruments. These yield-restricted U.S. Treasury bonds and notes assure compliance with the arbitrage laws, although sometimes at the cost of lost flexibility and interest income.

7. *Big Brother Programs.* Several states have designed special investment programs for their localities. Small governments should enquire with their state officials regarding the availability of such special programs. Simplicity and economies of scale may be available to participants in statewide arbitrage investment programs.
8. *The Dumb-Like-a-Fox Strategy.* Years ago, the administrative behaviorist Herbert Simon coined the term "maxi-min" to describe decision makers who maximize gains and minimize losses. In the upside-down world of arbitrage rebate investing, some issuers have likewise learned that certain investments may not pay the highest possible rate, but they exceed the issuer's bond yield and permit the governmental entity to minimize direct expenditures for recordkeeping rebate calculation and filings with the federal government.

   An example of such a strategy is the use of money market mutual funds, possibly supplemented by a few buy-and-hold government securities, to produce a portfolio yield that exceeds the borrower's bond yield. Some mutual fund companies provide arbitrage recordkeeping and statement services for the entire portfolio as a client service, thus eliminating the need for the bond issuer to absorb such costs.

How to Develop an Arbitrage Investment Program

Although the details of a small government's arbitrage investment program may vary with each issue, the following checklist is a good place to start in designing your program.

1. *Consult with Advisors and Bond Counsel.* Your fiscal advisor and bond counsel should be able to suggest strategies and warn you of pitfalls to avoid. Either the advisor or the bond counsel may also calculate the bond yield "speed limit" for you.
2. *Explore Tax-exempt Securities.* This strategy usually does not work for small bond issuers, but it should not be overlooked. If you can profitably invest in qualified tax-exempt securities, the investment returns need not be rebated to the federal government.
3. *Determine How You Will Perform Rebate Calculations.* Will you purchase specialized software such as GFOA's Arbicalc package? Or will you retain an independent third party such as a fiscal advisor, bond counsel or CPA firm, to perform the calculations? Make sure that your records are kept in a format suitable for arbitrage rebate calculations.
4. *Explore Alternative Investment Instruments.* Some investment instruments can be subjected to public bidding, such as "flexible repurchase agreements" and bank investment contracts. These instruments may offer a constant interest rate. Alternatively, some money market mutual funds offer shareholder recordkeeping and reporting systems which simplify rebate calculations and minimize administrative costs. One or both of these alternative investment instruments may help simplify your work, maximize retainable income and minimize rebate reporting expenses.
5. *Do Not Commingle Bond Proceeds with Operating Cash.* You might be accused of subsidizing your operating funds with investment income derived from bond proceeds, and your rebate calculations will become much more complicated.
6. *Obtain the Most Recent Copy of Arbitrage Rebate and Investment Regulations* issued by the U.S. Treasury Department. The first set of regulations

were published in early 1989, proscribing acceptable arbitrage calculation methodologies. Certain investment procedures are expected to be addressed in a second set of regulations to be released late in 1989.

7. *Educate and Legislate.* Bond issuers in states that lack flexible investment authority may find it necessary to educate their legislators about the need for investment legislation that addresses current conditions. Public officials should continue their efforts to obtain relief from the costly burden of the federal government's arbitrage laws.

10

PERFORMANCE EVALUATION AND REPORTING

by Anthony T. Logalbo

Performance evaluation and reporting is an essential, but often overlooked, capstone to the cash management activity. Performance reporting which is restricted to measurement of dollar return and yield is incomplete. A complete evaluative tool must be designed to measure the achievement of all cash management objectives. The reporting system ideally should answer the following questions:

- Legal compliance: has the cash management activity been conducted in accordance with applicable statutory restrictions?
- Market risk: has the return been realized within policy constraints designed to protect the entity from lost opportunities due to interest rate movement?
- Credit risk: has the return been realized within policy constraints governing the placement of funds in secure instruments and institutions in order to protect capital?
- Liquidity risk: has the return been realized through mechanisms structured in relationship to the entity's particular cash flow patterns, so as to insure that cash is available to meet disbursement requirements without forfeiture of interest earnings potential?

These questions address the central issue of cash management performance evaluation—"compared to what?" Concern with relative performance has grown commensurate with the rise in interest rates over the last decade and, thus, with the importance of interest earnings as a source of financing for public expenditures.

The degree of effort and attention devoted in recent years to improving the cash management activity has generally not extended to the evaluation and reporting component. Prior to the inflation-induced surge of short-term interest rates in the 1978–80 period, the relative significance of interest earnings to the budget did not, in most cases, justify extensive evaluative effort. Now, however, even though interest rates have declined from the extraordinary levels of 1980–81, the real rate of return compared to inflation is historically high and the budget impact of investment earnings is sufficient to warrant the attention of elected officials and the general public.

Growing awareness of investment earnings potential has led to expansion of legal investment authority, greater interest in written investment policies and, in some instances, imprudent activities which have demonstrated that market and credit risks have not been fully understood. Performance evaluation is an essential part of the cash management routine and a formal performance report should be regarded as a required element in fulfilling the public cash manager's stewardship obligation.

Reporting the results of cash management efforts has, for many jurisdictions, been limited to a simple statement of cash-basis or accrual-basis interest revenue. Sometimes this is accompanied by a calculation of yield for the reporting period. Little guidance has been available to assist public cash managers in the development of more comprehensive reporting systems. The restrictive view of the treasurer as the custodian of cash has given way to the realization that the cash management activity can be a major producer of government revenues. Similarly, the idea that reporting consists solely of dollar earnings and yield must be broadened to reflect the goals and standards set forth in written investment policies with performance evaluated in accordance with safety, liquidity and yield objectives.

Earlier chapters have been concerned with improving cash management results through attention to fundamental administrative elements and policies. This chapter discusses the concepts and key elements of communicating those results while focusing on the purposes and uses of performance reporting and the development of a performance report.

Purposes and Uses of Performance Reporting

Cash management is a time-consuming activity. Performance reporting adds an additional commitment of time at the end of the process. Since time is often scarcer than money, the reasons for allocating time to performance reporting must be strong and clearly understood. Some of these reasons are discussed in the following paragraphs.

Public Relations/Stewardship

Finance officers have few "good news" stories to tell. Usually, the finance area gets public attention when there is bad news. Cash management performance is a continuing "good news" message and one which can be conveyed as having a direct impact on the taxpayer's pocketbook. Certainly, one is not likely to see a headline "Treasurer meets liquidity objective"; the media are more likely to focus on the "dollar value" or "equivalent tax rate" message. Still, the public can be given a sense of the care, prudence and success with which its dollars have been put to work while in the temporary custody of the public treasury.

In a more fundamental sense, the absence of a meaningful performance report inhibits the public's right to hold managers accountable for results. Performance reporting completes the cash manager's stewardship responsibilities. A well-designed performance report also establishes an important communications link with local elected officials. It enables the finance officer to demonstrate that the treasury operation is a significant "profit center." As with tax enforcement, this argument can only be taken as far as the law of diminishing returns allows; but it can help the finance functions to avert curtailment in periods of general cutbacks if there is a demonstrated history of staff effort leading to revenue production.

Legal and Policy Compliance

Performance reporting is a vehicle for monitoring and demonstrating compliance with adopted investment policies and/or statutory requirements. Investment activity may be guided or constrained by considerations of safety and liquidity in the following ways:

- Type of permitted investment: the reporting system should be able to demonstrate that only permitted investment vehicles have been utilized and that required security has been obtained where applicable.
- Concentration by type: the reporting system should convey the allocation of the portfolio among allowed investment types. Applicable laws or internal policies may restrict the use of any single investment type by dollar value or portfolio proportion.
- Concentration by institution: as a means of controlling credit risk, the portfolio may be restricted either by dollar value or proportion placed with any single financial institution.
- Limitation by institution: applicable laws or internal policies may restrict the dollar value placed with any single institution in relationship to some financial characteristic of the institution (rather than an arbitrary proportion of the portfolio).
- Term of investment: applicable laws or internal policies may place limits, either absolute or in proportion to the portfolio size, on the amount which may be invested at or longer than specified terms as a means of controlling liquidity and market risk.

A performance reporting system which addresses and portrays these compliance issues is a form of insurance against loss of public funds. The existence of an investment policy, while necessary, may not be a sufficient barricade.[1]

Tactical and Strategic Modifications

A performance reporting routine serves to keep the cash manager self-informed about the nature of the market. At any given level of acceptable risk, the general situation is that higher yields are realized from longer maturities. Within legal or policy constraints, and subject to cash flow projections, the cash manager often has some latitude to lengthen or shorten maturities and to move into or out of

[1]For more information on portfolio diversification and the development of an investment policy, see Chapter 8.

investment types. The difficulty arises in trying to determine when and in what direction to move. Constant monitoring through a performance reporting mechanism affords a considerably more reliable and comprehensible basis for making such decisions.

Revenue Forecasting

Budget makers sometimes lapse into incremental thinking. They are inclined to assume that the cash manager can produce a little more each year. Cash managers know that investment income is a tempestuous revenue source, subject to volatile factors not under the cash manager's control. A performance reporting routine can serve to bring these two disciplines together by keeping all parties abreast of actual results and the underlying reasons for the results. The budget maker's desire to predict higher revenue and the cash manager's inclination to assume that interest rates and cash availability will decline can be tempered through a reporting system which leads to more informed projections of future revenue.

Verification of Transactions

The performance reporting process serves as a vehicle for verifying transactions both internally and externally. Typically, the internal accounting system will record interest receipts from maturing investments on a cash basis until the year-end entries are made to record interest earnings accrued but not yet received. The periodic performance report, which must be based on accrued earnings for consistency, can be utilized to reconcile the difference between earnings accrued and received at any point. This serves two purposes. First, it catches any internal posting errors. Second, it verifies that all earnings have in fact been received. It is not uncommon for a financial institution to miscalculate interest paid at maturity or to fail to make payment exactly on the maturity date. If undetected, these can be costly discrepancies.

Relating Results to a Benchmark

Finally, the performance reporting process is a measuring device. It is supposed to answer the question—"compared to what?" A report which does not include a valid benchmark comparison misses the point of the effort. Users of the report need to have some shorthand way of judging the effectiveness of the cash management activity. The cash manager needs a benchmark as an indication of what alternative strategies may be required due to changing conditions. Selection of an appropriate benchmark will be related to the goals, objectives and constraints set forth in the written investment policy.

Developing a Performance Report

The remainder of this chapter discusses the development of a performance evaluation and reporting capacity. Although the basic concepts and elements introduced can be used by all governments in the development of their own performance evaluation and reporting system, cash managers in small governments will find them of most value. Cash managers interested in developing a performance report should use the following as a guide.

Reporting Principles

Just a few ideas are important in developing the reporting component of a cash management system:

- it must be simple and speak plainly to the intended audience with information which is, at least interesting, if not also useful;
- it must be produced on a timely basis with no greater allocation of effort than its worth to the overall objectives;
- it must portray the relationship of performance to the elements of the investment policy and objectives;
- the degree to which investment goals, legal restrictions and risk control policies have been attained should be readily discernible by the report user; and
- it must be honest, reporting without distortion unfavorable as well as favorable results.

Establishing a Benchmark

As noted above, it is very important that investment performance be compared with a suitable benchmark measure in order to evaluate the effectiveness of the cash management program. An appropriate performance benchmark will have the following characteristics:

- it will be available, reliable and logically related to the jurisdiction's permitted investments;
- it will be either a direct investment alternative or a representative surrogate for investments which could be made directly (e.g., an index);
- it will behave consistently through a market cycle, validly representing the relevant sector of the money market; and
- it will share the characteristics of the portfolio with respect to legal constraints and investment policy compliance.

No benchmark will be perfect, but a useful benchmark will permit the cash manager and the report user to reach clear and accurate conclusions. Within the characteristics described, the following types of benchmarks might be selected:

- *Local Government Investment Pool (LGIP).* A number of states now operate these pooled funds which function as short-term money market funds. Typically, they offer a high degree of liquidity. This benchmark is appropriate for a short-term portfolio with an average maturity similar to the LGIP or where the yield-objective is expressed in relation to the LGIP yield. The premise is that the LGIP is an alternative investment whose yield should at least be matched.
- *Treasury Bill Rate.* This data is continuously available, reliable and representative of the market. A benchmark could be derived from a single instrument (e.g., the 90-day rate) matching the average maturity objective of the

portfolio or on a weighted basis of several rates (e.g., 50 percent on a 30-day rate, 50 percent on a 90-day rate) deemed to reflect the characteristic maturity ratios of the portfolio.

- *CD or other Market Ratios.* In contrast to Treasury bills, other money market instruments may reflect local area conditions more representative of actual opportunities for the local portfolio. As with T-bills, a benchmark can be constructed on a single or blended basis. Generally, a single rate benchmark will be satisfactory for a portfolio of short average maturity (e.g., 90 days or less) and a blended rate benchmark will be more valid for a portfolio of longer average maturity since interest rate movement will become more important in evaluating yield performance. After all, the entire portfolio cannot be redeemed and reinvested every month.

For portfolios operating with a significant proportion of assets invested for terms of one year or more, a more elaborate approach to finding a valid benchmark may be required. It may be just as useful, however, to use a very straightforward benchmark such as Donoghue's money market index and state the investment yield-objective as some factor of this index. The premise would be that the extra effort and risk involved in utilizing longer-term instruments must be justified by achieving an acceptable yield above the short-term market.

The process of selecting a benchmark should not become a barrier. The purpose of the benchmark is not to find fault with the cash manager, but rather, over the course of time, to indicate whether the pattern of investment decisions is achieving a desired and effective result *or* what changes might be made to improve results. For the vast majority of entities with small to modest portfolios, the simplest benchmark consistently applied and reported will suffice and attention to the production of cash (speeding up collections and slowing down disbursements) will prove to be a more lucrative endeavor than squeezing a few more basis points out of the portfolio.

Reporting Elements

The structure of the report ought to be straightforward, built up in a manner which permits the user to proceed from general overview to documentation at whatever level of detail may be appropriate. A thorough report will include:

- a brief narrative statement of results for the reporting period, discussing changes in market conditions, the impact of cash flows, actions taken by the cash manager, and key numbers which provide a quick picture of results and progress toward or attainment of investment goals;
- an overview tabulation of the portfolio describing allocations by investment categories and earnings results;
- detailed listings of investments supporting the overview table; and
- charts and/or graphs depicting results.

Examples from Walnut, California and Concord, Massachusetts illustrate these elements. Exhibits 10-1 (Concord) and 10-2 (Walnut) portray the portfolio overview, using similar ideas but with differing emphasis.

Exhibit 10-1
Cash Management Record
Town of Concord
May 1988

Table 1
Investment Performance: General Funds

	Average Daily Balance	Percent of Total	Interest Earned	Yield
Certificates of Deposit	$7,550,000	58.79%	$46,565.07	7.26%
NOW accounts	615,323	4.79	3,198.86	6.12
MMDT	2,726,081	21.23	15,604.01	6.74
Money market accounts	1,944,067	15.14	11,163.27	6.76
Other	---	---	---	---
Subtotal	$ 12,835,471	99.96%	$ 76,531.21	7.02%
Checking accounts	5,764	0.04		
TOTAL	$ 12,841,235	100.00%		

Interest Earned: Pooled Funds

This Month	Fiscal Year to Date	Prior Fiscal Year (11 Months)	Rate of Return on TOTAL CASH This Month	Rate of Return on TOTAL CASH Last Month
$ 76,531.21	$ 661,487.94	$ 506,240.83	7.02%	6.98%

Prior Year Comparison

	1987	1988	Dollar Difference	Percentage Difference
Average daily balance:	$ 13,415,687	$ 12,841,235	$ (574,452)	(4.3%)
Interest earned:	74,596	76,531	1,935	+2.6%

	1987	1988
Rate of return on total cash:	6.55%	7.02%
MMDT rate of return:	6.32	6.74
Ratio - Town + MMDT rate:	1.036	1.042

The top half of the Concord exhibit fulfills the same purpose as the Walnut exhibit; both examples show:

- total invested position; Concord shows this on a daily average basis while Walnut shows this as of the report date;
- allocation by percent of the portfolio among the various investment types (MMDT and Local Agency Investment funds are, respectively, the LGIPs of

Exhibit 10-2
Investment Portfolio Summary

City of Walnut
Investment Portfolio as of April 30, 1987

	Cost	Percent	Average Days to Maturity	Yield
S & L certificates of deposit	$ 6,039,000	45.87%	381	7.465%*
Local agency investment funds	4,500,000	34.18	—	7.044*
Federal/Agency issues	698,768	5.31	5,670	8.411*
Negotiable certificates of deposit	—	0.00	—	—
Bankers acceptances	1,629,898	12.38	36	6.434*
Commercial paper	297,506	2.26	36	6.434*
Repurchase agreements	—	0.00	—	—
Passbook savings	10	0.00	—	5.127*
Total investment portfolio	$13,165,182	100.00%**		

1985-86 actual interest income	$ 862,912
1986-87 budgeted interest income	$ 770,000
Actual year-to-date interest income	$ 687,587
Percent of interest received to date	89.30%
1986-87 estimated interest income	$ 793,500
City weighted average rate of return	7.22%

* All averages are weighted

** May not add due to rounding

Massachusetts and California administered by the state treasurers in both instances); and

- interest earned; Concord reports this by investment type for the period while Walnut shows this as a year-to-date amount compared to the prior year, the budget and a revised budget estimate (Concord's report does somewhat the same thing in the middle of exhibit 10-1).

These two examples then depart somewhat, based upon the particular circumstances of their legal authority, cash flow characteristics and investment approaches. As Walnut uses longer-term investment instruments, "average days to maturity" becomes an important focal point in its performance report. Concord's cash flow characteristics and legal constraints cause it to operate much more as a very short-term money market fund. Therefore, its report, in the bottom portion of Exhibit 10-1, focuses attention on a comparison of results against a benchmark of the State LGIP performance.

Neither of these exhibits warrant being copied automatically. They suit the investment environment which they seek to depict.

Exhibits 10-3 and 10-4 portray the investment logs which support the overview tables. Only the certificate of deposit (CD) section is shown in this extract. In each example, a weighted average return is computed and shown on the portfolio summary. In the Concord example, the average daily CD balance is the sum of (cost × days of interest) for all CDs divided by the number of days in the month. The yield for the month is then computed using the basic formula:

$$\text{Interest} = \text{Principal} \times \text{rate} \times \text{time}$$

Solving for the rate, expressed on an annualized basis, this is: $r = \frac{i}{p} \times \frac{T}{t}$.

Where: i = interest earned;
p = principal value of investments;
T = the number of days in the year; and,
t = the number of days in the month.[2]

Referring to the data from Exhibit 10-3:

$$r = \frac{\$46{,}565.07}{7{,}550{,}000} \times \frac{365}{31} = 7.26\%$$

The Walnut example instead calculates the weighted average rate of the holdings as of the end of the reporting period and the yield to maturity. Strictly, this is not the same as portfolio return, but again the construction of the reporting format is suited to particular circumstances and the presence of longer-term securities in this portfolio can make yield to maturity a more appropriate measurement.

A Note on Measuring Portfolio Return

The simplest measurement of portfolio return is interest earnings divided by average daily cash balances. Market movements after the purchase are not reflected in this measurement, however. For a portfolio of very short average maturity managed with a "passive" strategy in which securities are held to maturity, this kind of measurement is reasonable. It will not, however, reflect what might have been achieved if interest rate movement had been anticipated with perfect accuracy.

A different approach—the "mark-to-market" method—can be used for evaluating portfolio performance or determining the current value of a portfolio. True measurement of portfolio return would require the recognition of realized and

[2]While a particular instrument may utilize a 360-day year to calculate interest, the portfolio is earning interest every day of the year and thus 365 or 366 days should be used for the purpose of measuring portfolio return.

Exhibit 10-3
General Fund
Short-Term Investment Roll and Interest Earned
Town of Concord
May, 1988

Investment Type	Date of Purchase	Date of Maturity	Cost	Days of Interest	Amount	Rate	Source
CD	12/2	6/1	$ 200,000	31	$ 1,290.98	7.60%	First Bank
	2/23	5/31	500,000	30	3,124.99	7.50	Second Bank
	3/1	6/15	250,000	31	1,582.29	7.35	Third Bank
	3/8	6/7	400,000	31	2,412.05	7.10	Fourth Bank
	3/10	6/14	100,000	31	607.26	7.15	Fifth Bank
	3/15	6/21	$ 400,000	31	$ 2,497.22	7.25%	Second Bank
	3/15	6/14	100,000	31	573.29	6.75	Sixth Bank
	3/21	7/12	500,000	31	3,229.17	7.50	Third Bank
	3/29	6/28	100,000	31	607.26	7.15	Seventh Bank
	4/15	8/4	500,000	31	3,143.06	7.30	Second Bank
	4/12	7/19	$ 300,000	31	$ 1,885.83	7.30%	Second Bank
	4/22	8/9	1,000,000	31	6,174.17	7.17	Third Bank
	4/22	7/26	1,000,000	31	5,984.72	6.95	Eighth Bank
	4/29	8/29	1,000,000	31	6,113.89	7.10	Ninth Bank
	4/29	8/9	1,200,000	31	7,233.33	7.00	Eighth Bank
	5/31	9/13	500,000	1	105.56	7.60	Second Bank
					$ 46,565.07		

unrealized gains and losses in each period, the process referred to as "marking to market." This is accomplished by calculating the portfolio's return based upon the market value of the securities at the beginning of the period. While marking to market requires the use of a complicated series of calculations, the basic formula for marking to market and determining total return is the following:

$$\text{Total Return} = \frac{\text{Sum of Accrued Interest} + \text{Changes in Portfolio Value}}{\text{Beginning Market Value of Portfolio} + \text{Price of Investments Purchased During Period}}$$

The principal advantage of marking to market is that it reflects both interest earned and changes in portfolio value. Critics of the method claim that it is too erratic, that it fails to reflect true portfolio yield, and that market changes are not important unless an asset is to be sold.

Exhibit 10-4
Example List of Certificates of Deposit
City of Walnut
Investment Portfolio as of April 30, 1987

Description	Cost	Rate	Yield	Purchase Date	Maturity Date	Days to Maturity at Purchase	Days to Maturity
*** S&L***							
First S&L	100,000	7.500%	7.900%	09-May-86	11-May-87	367	11
Second S&L	96,000	6.300	6.300	17-April-87	18-May-87	31	18
Third S&L	50,000	7.500	7.500	19-May-86	19-May-87	365	19
•	•	•	•	•	•	•	•
•	•	•	•	•	•	•	•
•	•	•	•	•	•	•	•
Ultimate S&L	100,000	7.500	8.839	17-May-83	15-Sept-90	2,678	1,234
	6,039,000	7.368%	7.465%			594	381

Given the amount of time and resources it takes to mark to market on a frequent basis, this method is generally used only by those who actively trade portfolio assets. For governments with very short (90 days or less) passive portfolios, validity of the portfolio performance statistics can be established by relationship to a well-chosen benchmark comparison. In a period of rising rates, a money market fund benchmark would, for example, also rise. Comparison of the benchmark with the static portfolio return would reveal the same "opportunity loss" as the mark-to-market approach, without the potentially alarming presentation of a negative rate of return.[3]

Summary

The limiting view of the treasurer as the custodian of cash has given way to the realization that the cash management activity can be a major producer of government revenues. Similarly, the idea that reporting consists solely of dollar earnings and yield must be broadened to reflect the goals and standards set forth in written investment policies with performance evaluated in accordance with safety, liquidity and yield objectives. The development of a performance evaluation and reporting capacity that encompasses these goals and objectives can lead to a greater understanding of the cash management process and an improved cash management program.

[3]Those with a need to develop more elaborate and technically correct approaches to calculating portfolio yield should refer to Marcia Stigum's *Money Market Calculations: Yields, Break-Evens and Arbitrage* (Homewood, IL: Dow Jones-Irwin Inc., 1981).

11

SHORT-TERM BORROWING: STRATEGIES AND ISSUES FOR SMALL GOVERNMENTS

by Ian J. Allan

Short-term borrowing is frequently an important component of an effective cash management program. It is generally used to finance temporary cash flow deficits and enable governments to meet budgeted expenditures, such as payrolls, prior to the receipt of current revenues. Short-term borrowing is also used, under certain circumstances, as temporary financing for long-term capital improvement projects. In some instances, borrowing has been used as a means to earn additional interest income for a government through arbitrage investing.

The ability of governments to borrow in the short term is restricted by law and by other factors, such as local policies regarding debt issuance. State and local laws and local debt policies generally specify who can borrow, how much can be borrowed, from whom money can be borrowed, and what types of debt can be issued. Federal laws and regulations, such as those governing the earning of arbitrage interest, also act as constraints upon a government's ability to finance temporary cash deficits. These statutes, regulations and local charters provide the framework for short-term government borrowing.

The ability of governments to engage in short-term borrowing is also dependent upon access to the credit markets. Access to these markets is not guaranteed and depends on a number of factors, including:

- the creditworthiness of the issuer;
- a demonstrated record of performance in the credit markets, based upon the prior issuance of debt;
- a favorable market environment, with stable interest rates; and
- the ability and experience of management in implementing a financing plan.

Small governments with healthy fund balances to cover operating expenditures or those that rely strictly on permanent bond financing to provide monies for their capital projects may never have the need to borrow funds in the short term. A large number, however, will need to borrow funds in the short-term credit markets. Those engaging in short-term borrowing need to be sensitive to the fact that too much short-term debt can lead to fiscal problems. Therefore, when governments find it necessary to issue short-term debt, it should be for a specified time period and only when the revenues to repay the debt are assured. Furthermore, short-term borrowing for operating purposes should always be repaid by the end of the fiscal year in which the funds were borrowed.

The focus of this chapter will be on the short-term financing of a government's temporary operating deficits and the development of a short-term borrowing capacity. Cash managers faced with temporary cash deficits should be concerned with covering the anticipated shortfall with temporary financing while keeping interest and other borrowing costs to a minimum. Several aspects of short-term borrowing will be examined in this chapter, including: short-term credit markets and debt instruments, cash forecasting, borrowing strategies, arbitrage issues, and evaluating short-term debt.

Short-term Credit Markets and Debt Instruments

Credit Markets

The amount of short-term tax-exempt debt issued annually is substantial. Publicly offered tax-exempt note financing alone amounted to $15.5 billion in 1987.[1] Considering that a large proportion of short-term debt is placed directly with commercial banks and that statistical data on these issuances are not readily available, the total amount of such borrowing is probably far in excess of that figure.

Prior to engaging in any activity involving commercial banks or other elements of the credit markets, governments should develop a policy that contains coherent, practical guidelines for dealing with those entities. For example, governments, as part of their banking services agreement, could make arrangements with their local depository banks for a line of credit to cover temporary cash needs.[2]

Cash managers seeking short-term financing can obtain it from three places:

- local banks;
- regional and national credit markets; and
- state liquidity pools.

Local commercial banks are by far the primary source of funds for a government's short-term financing of temporary cash flow deficits. Generally, the simplest and easiest transaction for a government is the direct bank loan.[3] Interest rates charged by local banks are usually somewhat higher than those offered in the regional and national credit markets, however.

---

[1]Source: *The Daily Bond Buyer.*

[2]The GFOA book, *Banking Relations: A Guide for Government,* offers guidance in this area. See Chapter 5 for more information on bank credit services.

[3]Whether a jurisdiction pays taxable or tax-exempt rates on such loans (or other debt issuance) depends on the use of the proceeds and bank demand for tax-exempt obligations (a function of the bank's particular tax situation). Small governments should thoroughly explore the tax-exempt options available to them prior to issuing any taxable debt obligations. It should also be noted that small

Credit markets such as regional and national banks, investment banks, and underwriters of municipal debt provide other sources of financing for local governments. These markets offer access to tax-exempt note financing, usually at lower interest costs than that of direct bank loans. By issuing tax-exempt notes, small governments can demonstrate to citizens and rating agencies the government's creditworthiness and ability to access financial markets broader than the local commercial bank. An additional advantage to using the credit markets is that interest rates obtained there can be readily compared to those received by other local governments on their short-term debt.

A recent development in state and local government finance is the liquidity pool. Liquidity pools are ordinarily operated by an entity of state government which issues long- or short-term debt and makes the proceeds available to local governments to assist them with their short-term borrowing needs.[4] Because states can issue larger amounts of debt, and generally have better credit ratings than local governments, borrowing costs can be reduced and borrowing procedures simplified. In addition, there is no need to pay to have local debt rated.

Debt Instruments

Governments faced with temporary cash deficits have a number of options available to them. Each should be evaluated in terms of its costs and benefits, including the length of time required to issue securities and receive funds. Other short-term debt instruments, such as tax-exempt commercial paper, have a place in the short-term debt market, but may not be cost-effective or practical for small governments to utilize. Consequently, they have not been included here. The major short-term financing options available to and feasible for small governments are described below.

Bank Loans. Bank loans are the most commonly used instrument for short-term financing by small governments. Interest rates paid by governments have generally been lower than the prime lending rate charged by banks to their best customers, due primarily to the tax-exempt status of most loans made to governments. These rates are slightly higher than those for tax-exempt note financing, which is the result of limited competition. Interest costs for bank loans vary widely with governments considered to be good credit risks and/or good bank customers often getting more advantageous rates.[5] Cash managers are advised to shop around

---

governments which issue less than $10 million annually may pay lower rates due to the preferred tax status of their obligations.

[4]Michigan and Indiana are two of the states with this type of short-term borrowing mechanism. Cash managers should check with their state government to see if such a program is available and to learn more about eligibility, procedures, and terms of the loans.

[5]The Tax Reform Act of 1986 altered the tax situation of many banks, making bank ownership of tax-exempt securities, including loans, less desirable. Since banks have been major purchasers of tax-exempt debt, these changes may place upward pressure on interest rates paid by governments. For more information on this subject see the GFOA publication *Tax-Exempts and Tax Reform: Assessing the Consequences of the Tax Reform Act of 1986 for the Municipal Securities Market,* by John E. Petersen.

for the best rates, and to keep negotiation on a professional basis.[6]

Bank loans are often the simplest and easiest to use, with no requirements for the preparation of formal disclosure documents or public announcement as is required for the issuance of short-term tax-exempt notes. In some states, for technical purposes, loans may be called tax anticipation notes (TANs), revenue anticipation notes (RANs), or bond anticipation notes (BANs).[7] Terms for direct bank loans are often quite flexible, and can easily be renegotiated.[8]

Tax-exempt Note Financing. For governments that issue short-term debt on a frequent basis or in large quantities, use of the tax-exempt note market may be appropriate. Borrowing costs in this market are generally lower than bank financing, primarily due to greater competition. It can take several months to prepare for a note issue, however. This may not be practical for small governments faced with unstable cash positions. Tax-exempt notes are always issued for a specified period of time, such as six months or a year. There are several options available to those considering the use of tax-exempt note financing to cover short-term operating needs, including:

- Tax anticipation notes (TANs): issued in anticipation of a government collecting revenues from taxes. For example, a government may experience temporary cash shortages, necessitating short-term borrowing, prior to the receipt of a large amount of property tax revenue at mid-year.
- Revenue anticipation notes (RANs): almost identical to TANs, but are issued in anticipation of a government receiving non-tax revenues.[9]
- Tax and revenue anticipation notes (TRANs): a combination of tax and revenue anticipation notes, with similar characteristics.
- Grant anticipation notes (GANs): issued by governments in anticipation of the receipt of federal or state grant funds. Because the grant is the security behind the notes, GANs should be issued only when the issuer has a firm commitment that the grant will be made. In issuing GANs, the government must be aware of the fact that it, not the granting agency, is solely responsible for repayment of principal and interest on the notes. Failure to receive anticipated grant revenues does not eliminate or diminish a government's responsibility to its noteholders.

Liquidity Pools. These pools are designed to provide local governments with a source of short-term financing that is both cheaper and easier to obtain than conventional short-term financing. This can be done through the issuance of short- and long-term debt instruments by a state entity. Because states generally have better credit ratings than local governments, interest costs are usually lower than

---

[6]Maintaining "distance" from bankers is important in order to avoid the appearance of conflicts of interest and to make decisions that are not biased by personal considerations.

[7]BANs are issued by governments in anticipation of permanent financing for capital improvement projects.

[8]See Chapters 5 and 6 for more information on banking relations.

[9]In some cases RANs may be issued in anticipation of the receipt of a mix of tax and non-tax revenues.

those which local governments would normally receive. Liquidity pools are very similar in concept to local government investment pools and state bond banks.

While local governments of all types can benefit from the use of liquidity pool financing, the primary borrowers have been local school districts. In fact, many liquidity pools have been formed for the purpose of financing the short-term borrowing needs of such government entities.[10] This situation can be expected to change however, as more and more general-purpose governments become aware of the benefits of this type of short-term financing, and additional liquidity pools are created to serve their needs.

Cash Forecasting

The development of an accurate cash forecast is essential to the development of a program of short-term financing and the efficient operation of government. Accurate cash forecasts can provide the cash manager with advance warning of cash deficits which occur when expenditures exceed revenues and cash on hand, giving the cash manager valuable time to arrange short-term financing. Cash forecasts are also necessary to obtain a credit rating on tax-exempt note issues and to ensure compliance with federal arbitrage laws.[11]

Cash forecasting involves the projection of anticipated receipts, disbursements and cash balances over a certain period of time, typically a year. Cash forecasts can identify the timing, size and length of cash deficits, and revenues for the repayment of principal and interest. The key to developing an accurate cash forecast is to determine the timing of cash receipts and disbursements.

Exhibit 11-1 depicts the cash forecast for Sometown, USA, initially shown in Chapter 7. For much of the fiscal year Sometown has a positive cash position, but it experiences a temporary cash deficit of approximately $1 million in October. Because the cash manager has taken the time to develop a cash forecast, the government can make plans to finance the deficit well in advance of its occurrence.

Borrowing Strategies

Once the characteristics of a cash deficit are known, the cash manager should evaluate the options for financing that deficit. The options available to small governments will include direct bank loans, tax-exempt note financing, and the use of state liquidity pools. Each must be evaluated in terms of their costs and benefits to the government, which will vary depending on the circumstances. Usually this will mean the selection of the option with the lowest interest cost;

---

[10]Many school districts have uneven cash flows due to their dependence on two sources of revenue—local property taxes and state aid. Because uneven cash flows have led to cash flow deficits and short-term borrowing on a large scale, several states have formed liquidity pools to assist their local school districts.

[11]See Chapter 7 for a detailed discussion of cash forecasting.

Exhibit 11-1
Annual Cash Forecast—FY 19X9
Sometown, USA

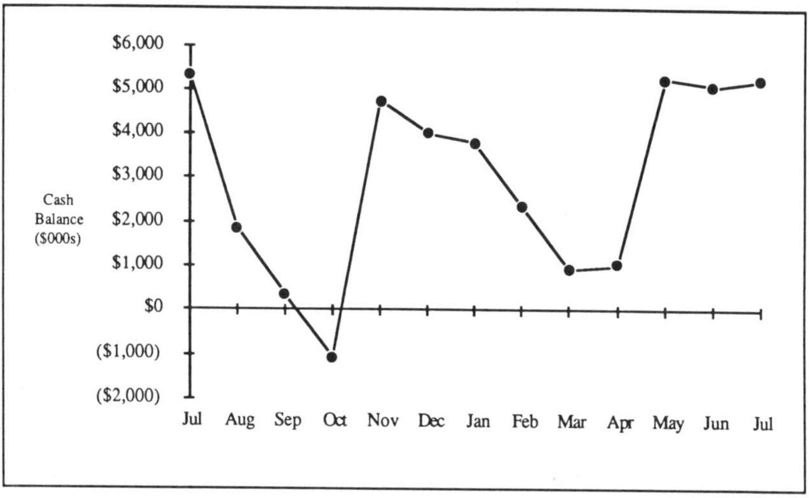

however, borrowing options that entail little or no issuance costs or allow easier access to the credit markets, although at higher interest costs, should also be considered. For example, bank loans generally carry higher interest rates than tax-exempt notes and liquidity pool financing, but are usually the easiest to arrange.

The cost of borrowing (transaction and interest costs) is dependent not only on the type of financing used, but on circumstances in the financial markets. The shape of the yield curve (positive, flat or inverted) represents the relationship between short- and long-term interest rates.[12] Historically, the yield curve for tax-exempt municipal obligations has been upward sloping, with governments paying lower interest rates on short-term securities.[13] Again, there may be a tradeoff between shorter-term instruments and those with longer maturities with higher borrowing costs, easier availability, and greater certainty of debt service requirements.

Once the costs and benefits of the available financing options have been delineated, a strategy can be developed to deal with the deficit. Cash managers faced with short-term borrowing needs can generally engage in two strategies to meet their cash requirements:

---

[12]See Chapter 9 for more information on the yield curve.

[13]This situation may not hold true in the future, however, given changes in the federal tax code resulting from passage of the Tax Reform Act of 1986. These changes have altered the tax situation of commercial banks and other holders of tax-exempt municipal obligations, depressing demand for such securities and causing municipal issuers to look to taxable obligations to finance public/private activities in particular.

Exhibit 11-2
Lump-Sum Strategy

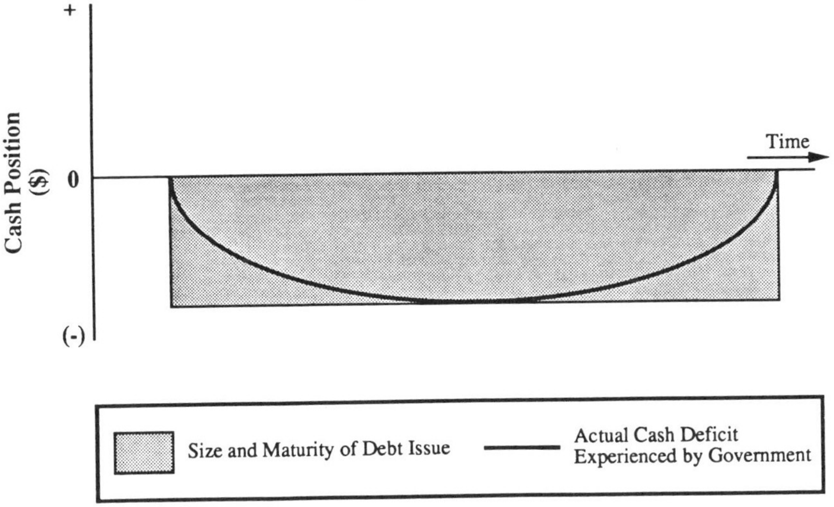

- lump sum financing; and
- as-needed financing.

Both are subject to the restraints imposed by the Tax Reform Act of 1986 and applicable state and local laws and debt policies. Of particular concern is the arbitrage rebate rule which requires governments to rebate to the federal government arbitrage interest earnings from the investment of tax-exempt bond or note proceeds in higher-yielding taxable securities. (See the section on arbitrage issues for a list of exceptions.) This requirement can set the parameters for the size, timing and maturity of short-term debt issued.

Lump-sum Financing. Under this strategy, the cash manager borrows the entire amount needed to cover the deficit prior to its occurrence and retires the debt after the deficit has passed and sufficient revenues become available. Use of this strategy is cost-effective if interest rates are going up. In addition, the administrative costs associated with a single debt issuance are generally lower than those for multiple financings. Issuing debt on a single occasion can also minimize the risk of poor market timing. Exhibit 11-2 illustrates this type of strategy.

As-needed Financing. Under this strategy governments borrow only as much money as is needed to cover immediate expenditures. This approach can minimize borrowing and possibly result in lower borrowing costs when interest rates are falling. If not handled properly, however, the transaction costs associated with this approach could be quite high. Also, if interest rates increase rather than decline, the cost of borrowing will increase as well. There are at least two ways governments can finance deficits on an as-needed basis. The first is known as staged financing, while the other involves the periodic rollover of debt.

Exhibit 11-3
Staged Borrowing Strategy

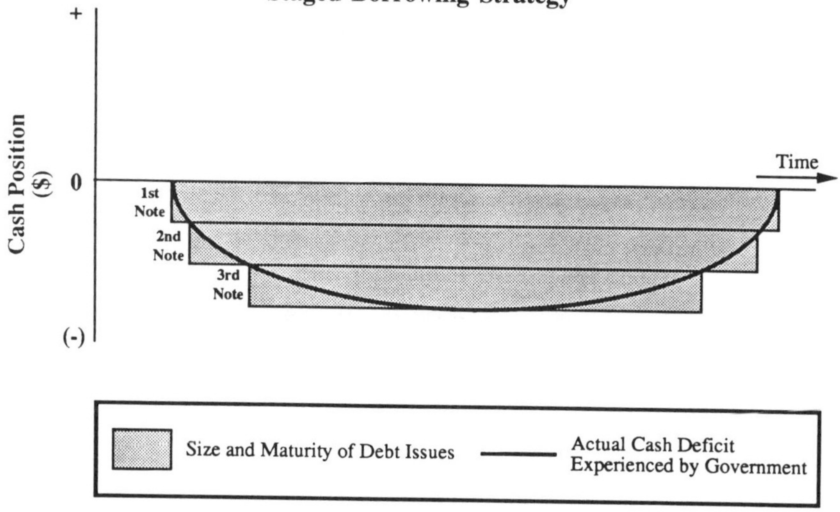

Staged financing occurs when a government borrows the required amount each month (or other time period) throughout the course of the deficit cycle. Monies are borrowed only as needed and for the period needed. Exhibit 11-3 depicts such a strategy, in this case involving tax-exempt note financing. For the purposes of compliance with the federal arbitrage law, such successive financings may be treated as a single financing, and, therefore, would not allow governments to circumvent the six-month arbitrage rebate rule. (See the section on arbitrage issues for further information.)

Debt rollover, on the other hand, occurs when a government issues an initial amount of debt and then reissues the debt on a monthly (or other time period) basis to the extent that it is required. The best example of this type of financing is provided by the federal government and its refinancing of the national debt. Exhibit 11-4 illustrates such a financing strategy.

Arbitrage Issues

For many years governments have had the ability to earn arbitrage interest income from the reinvestment of tax-exempt bond and note proceeds in higher yielding, taxable investments. Monies earned in this manner have been used to offset borrowing costs, reduce the amount of debt issued, and decrease the burden on taxpayers.

Since 1969 federal laws have sought to curb the ability of state and local government to engage in arbitrage investment activities. For example, arbitrage investment restrictions were applied to the proceeds of tax and revenue anticipation

Exhibit 11-4
Debt Rollover Strategy

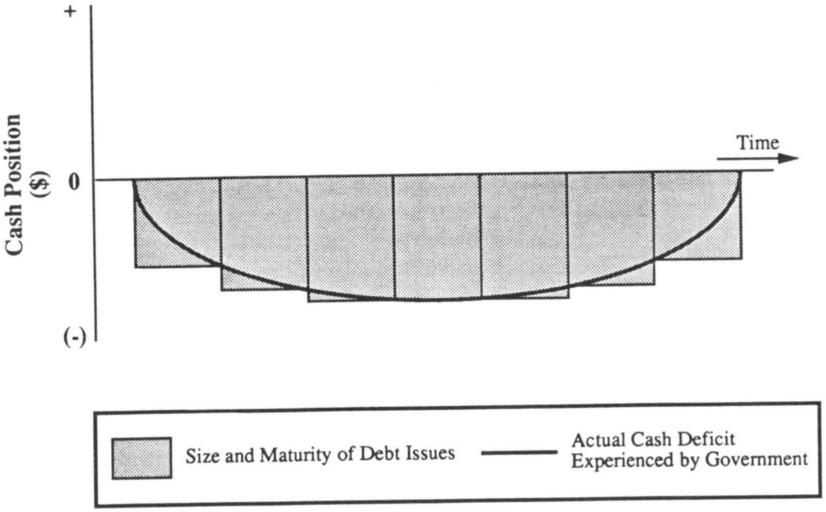

notes that were not spent within 13 months, and the size of the issue was restricted to the "maximum anticipated cumulative cash flow deficit" plus the next month's expenditures. Until recently these laws have not seriously hindered the ability of governments to increase investment earnings through the practice of interest rate arbitrage. In fact, many governments counted on earning arbitrage profits from the investment of proceeds of short-term debt instruments to supplement tax and non-tax revenues. Today, governments of all sizes are generally prevented from pursuing this sort of investment strategy by the Tax Reform Act of 1986.

The Tax Reform Act of 1986 placed practical constraints on the size and maturities of short-term debt issued by governments to finance temporary cash deficits. While still allowing governments to finance these deficits, the new law restricts the earning of arbitrage interest profits on the proceeds of tax-exempt notes issued to finance them. Generally speaking, if the proceeds of a tax-exempt note issue are invested in taxable nonpurpose obligations, such as certificates of deposit, with a materially higher yield than that on the note, the law calls for the rebate of arbitrage interest earnings to the U.S. Treasury.[14] Exception to the rebate rule is allowed under the following conditions:

- the entire proceeds (except for a small amount) are spent within six months of the receipt of the bond or note proceeds;

[14]Nonpurpose obligations include investment securities such as U.S. Treasury bonds, corporate bonds, certificates of deposit issued by banks or other financial institutions, or any other "investment-type property."

- proceeds are invested in tax-exempt municipal bonds that are not subject to the alternative minimum tax (AMT) or Treasury securities of the State and Local Government Series (SLGS);[15]
- total financing by a governmental unit in a calendar year is not expected to exceed $5 million; or
- the obligations are tax and revenue anticipation notes (TRANs) where the cumulative cash flow deficit exceeds 90 percent of the proceeds of the issue within six months of the issuance.

Unlimited arbitrage can be earned on the investment of debt proceeds so long as governments stay within these boundaries and those imposed by prior federal law and regulation. Practically speaking, this still leaves room for small governments to earn arbitrage interest on the proceeds of their short-term debt issues. For example, as Exhibit 11-5 illustrates, most governments issue less than $5 million in debt each year. This means that so long as total short- and long-term debt issuance is restricted to $5 million or less, these governments can continue to profit from arbitrage investing. Governments can also earn arbitrage interest over the shorter six-month time period.[16]

Evaluating Short-term Debt

Most of the short-term debt issued by small governments is unrated because much of it is in the form of direct bank loans. On those occasions when cash managers deem it appropriate to issue short-term debt in the form of tax-exempt notes, however, this debt will most likely be evaluated by one or both of the major credit rating agencies: Moody's Investors Service and Standard & Poor's.[17]

As with other types of credit analysis, note analysts attempt to measure the ability of a government to make timely repayments of principal and interest to noteholders. In evaluating short-term debt the rating agencies generally take the following into consideration:

- security pledged;
- cash flow; and
- management capabilities.[18]

Credit concerns focus on the security pledge behind the note issue. The rating analysts want to be sure that sufficient revenues will be available when the note comes due. In order to ascertain this, rating analysts will examine several things,

---

[15]Municipal bonds issued for "private activities" (other than qualified 501(c)(3) bonds), such as those for industrial development, are subject to the alternative minimum tax (AMT).

[16]See Chapter 9 for a more detailed discussion of investing bond and note proceeds.

[17]In some cases, the cost of having credit rated is a factor in whether such an analysis is performed. In other cases, tax-exempt notes may be purchased by local banks that do not require a formal credit rating.

[18]Both major rating agencies provide detailed information on the criteria used in the evaluation of short-term debt obligations and make this information available to interested parties. Moody's Investors Service publishes *Moody's on Municipals: An Introduction to Issuing Debt,* and *The Appraisal of Municipal Credit Risk;* while Standard & Poor's publishes *Credit Overview: Municipal Ratings.*

Exhibit 11-5
Total 1987 Municipal Debt Issuances:
Percentage Distribution by Issue Size
Total Number of Issues and Total Dollar Amount Issued

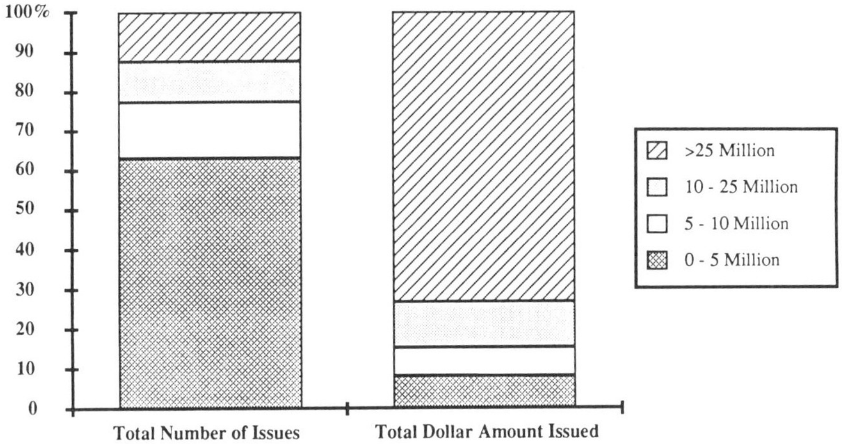

Source: Government Finance Research Center

including: whether revenues are pledged towards the repayment of the note, when funds can be set aside for repayment, and the lien position of the note. Generally speaking, the stronger the legal pledge a government makes towards repayment of principal and interest on a note, the better the credit rating.

Analysts also evaluate cash flow, and make a determination as to the relative ability of a government to obtain on a timely basis the revenues pledged to note repayment. This is a very critical component of note evaluation, and an accurate cash forecast is an important factor in the rating process. In addition to the fiscal year cash forecast, historical and projected cash flows will be examined.

The capability of the government to perform cash management and other finance functions is also part of the evaluation of a short-term financing. Rating analysts will evaluate the government's financial operations, investment policies and management, and the planning that has gone into the sale of the debt issue.

While there are similarities between the rating agencies' evaluation of short-term debt obligations, there are fundamental differences between the two. For example, Standard & Poor's links its short-term note ratings to a government's long-term bond ratings, whereas Moody's believes there is no "automatic or direct correlation" between the two. Cash managers should take this difference into account when seeking a rating on their short-term debt.

An important issue for governments engaged in short-term borrowing is the effect that such borrowing has on creditworthiness. Long-term debt ratings may be jeopardized by governments engaging in too much short-term borrowing.

Governments that borrow on an increasingly frequent basis or that borrow increasingly larger amounts of funds in the short-term credit markets may be perceived by the rating agencies as being in financial difficulty. Historically, this has been a fairly accurate predictor of fiscal weakness.

Summary

The development of a short-term borrowing capacity can be an important component of an effective cash management program. For many governments, the ability to finance temporary cash flow deficits through short-term borrowing will be crucial to their successful operation. The issuance of short-term debt has become a more complex task, with stricter federal laws and regulations regarding the earning of arbitrage interest. Cash managers should also be sensitive to the fact that misuses of short-term borrowing can lead to fiscal difficulties.

12

CASH MANAGEMENT TECHNOLOGY

by W. Paul Zorn

Successful cash management has two major objectives: the maximization of available cash, and the maximization of investment yield. These objectives are interrelated. Available cash can best be maximized when investments are managed prudently to earn market yields. Investment yield can best be maximized when cash receipts and disbursements are managed to increase the amount and duration of investable funds.

Achieving these objectives involves a complicated series of decisions and transactions that require accurate forecasts of the jurisdiction's cash position, up-to-date records on current investments, daily information concerning the investment markets, and extensive knowledge regarding a bewildering variety of arcane calculations designed, it seems, to confuse rather than enlighten most investors.

In this hectic environment, computer technology is regarded as a potential solution to many of the problems facing cash managers. The ability of computers to organize and analyze information, to maintain current records, to quickly perform complicated calculations, and to communicate almost instantaneously with other computers has brought them to the forefront of modern finance. Furthermore, the rapidly advancing power of today's microcomputers, coupled with the falling prices of computer hardware, has made the automation of many cash management functions possible for smaller jurisdictions.

Computer technology, however, has not been altogether a good thing. While alleviating much of the drudgery of cash management, computers have also increased the speed and complexity of investment transactions. Furthermore, automation has also added a new wrinkle to the daily life of cash managers: the problem of deciding how to automate their cash management systems.

The purpose of this chapter is to provide public officials with useful information regarding the application of current microcomputer technology to cash management. It begins by reviewing some of the advantages and disadvantages of automating cash management. It goes on to describe the functional requirements of an ideal cash management system, and the steps that should be taken when acquiring cash management software. The chapter concludes with a brief discussion of some of the recent changes in computer technology and their implications for cash management.

The Advantages and Disadvantages of Automation

Simply stated, cash management involves a series of tasks that are performed to ensure that the monies received by the government are put to the best possible use before they are disbursed. This involves estimating the amount of funds that are available for investment on a given day, comparing the bids on different investments to obtain the highest yields, maintaining a data base on investment purchases and sales, recording and accumulating the interest received on investments, and evaluating the performance of the portfolio. In addition, cash managers must be able to present this information in a way that is clear and useful to others.

One of the major problems faced by cash managers with manual systems is that the collection of this information, the development of investment reports, and the calculation of investment yields is complex and cumbersome, requiring a great deal of time and effort. While it would be useful for cash managers to spend more of their time analyzing the market and exploring new investment opportunities, many are constrained by the time that they must spend on the clerical aspects of their jobs. In addition, some finance officers are able to spend only a portion of their time on the cash management function, and so have even less time to analyze investments.

The Advantages to Automating Cash Management

As noted above, there are substantial advantages to automating cash management. Computer software can improve management efficiency by providing important and useful information faster, more accurately, and with less effort than could be done using a manual system. This, in turn, can produce additional revenues by helping cash managers:

- forecast cash to help maximize yield;
- invest a higher percent of idle cash;
- pool cash from different funds for investment;
- evaluate investment performance; and
- manage the costs of banking services.

In addition, the information maintained by the computer regarding cash and investment transactions can provide a detailed audit trail when reconciled with bank records, dealer confirmations, and trust department reports.

The Disadvantages to Automating Cash Management

However, there are potential disadvantages to automating cash management. First, the software user may be relegating certain important decisions to a "black box." Unless the user is familiar with the equations used by the software and is comfortable with interpreting their results, he or she is relying on someone else's logic.

Second, unless it is very well designed, computer software usually involves some loss of flexibility. Since input screens, calculations, and report formats are fixed in software's code, it is usually difficult for the user to improvise. The need for a new report may require reprogramming the software or involve the manual compilation of the required information.

Functional Requirements of Cash Management Software

Regardless of whether the software is developed internally or externally, cash managers must first analyze the tasks or functions that they want the software to perform. This analysis, sometimes called a "needs analysis" or a "functional requirements analysis," is probably the most important single step in the acquisition of any piece of software. For the purpose of specifying the functional requirements of cash management software, these tasks can be aggregated into six major categories:

- cash forecasting;
- cash position management;
- investment management;
- debt management;
- bank management; and
- telecommunications.

Each of these functions is described below. The discussion that follows is intended to outline an "ideal" cash management system, and is not intended to provide strict standards for evaluating cash management software. Only the most expensive treasury management workstations today perform all of the functions discussed below. Furthermore, many cash managers may not want their software to perform all of these functions.

Cash Forecasting

The cash forecast helps cash managers estimate the timing and amount of the jurisdiction's receipts and disbursements. This information, in turn, can be used to improve investment yields. Cash managers who know how much cash will be available for investment, when it will be available, and how long it will be available can carefully plan the denominations and maturities of their investments. Thus, given an upward-sloping yield curve, higher-yielding securities can be purchased for longer terms without substantially endangering the jurisdiction's liquidity. Cash forecasting can also help cash managers plan short-term borrowing by estimating the amount and timing of required funds.[1]

Three types of reports may be useful to cash managers in preparing and evaluating the cash forecast. These are:

---

[1]See Chapter 7 for more information on cash forecasting.

- the historical detail report;
- the detailed cash forecast; and
- the summary cash forecast.

Historical Detail. Cash forecasts make the greatest contribution to a cash management program when they are based on historical experience, supplemented by informed judgment about future events. Historical details of receipts and disbursements allow cash managers to see past cash flow patterns and to make inferences about current and future cash flows. To highlight these patterns, historical details should show actual amounts, average amounts, and the percent distribution of receipts and disbursements for specified periods (weekly, monthly, quarterly) over a three- to five-year span.

Detailed Cash Forecast. Periodically, cash forecasts should be compared to actual receipts and disbursements in order to judge the accuracy of the forecasts and adjust the investment strategy. To assist with this task, the software should provide detailed cash forecasts that compare actual and forecast amounts for specific receipts and disbursements. In so doing, the difference between the actual and forecast amounts should be calculated and shown.

Summary Cash Forecast. The summary cash forecast presents a single, summary picture of the amount of cash that is available for investment (or will have to be borrowed), when it is available, and for how long. This information might best be summarized through the use of a graph or chart.

Cash Position Management

The purpose of cash position management is to track cash transactions by maintaining records of bank balances, daily receipts and disbursements, investment income, debt payments, and compensating balances. This information is used to manage cash flows, meet bank compensation requirements, and project the amount of investable cash at the end of the day. In addition, this information can be used to revise the cash forecasts.

Three reports may be useful to the cash manager for carrying out this function. They are:

- the cash balance report;
- the cash transaction listing; and
- the cash worksheet.

Cash Balance Report. The cash balance report tracks current ledger and collected balances by bank account and by fund. This report also provides summary information regarding total deposits and withdrawals, and end-of-day cash balances for each fund and bank account.

Cash Transaction Listing. This report provides a listing of individual cash transactions (e.g., deposits and withdrawals) by fund and bank account for a period selected by the user. It can be used to check bank transactions and to aid in account reconciliation.

Cash Worksheet. The cash worksheet provides cash managers with current information on bank account balances, total daily receipts and disbursements, maturing investments and debt, bank target balances, and the amount that can be invested or must be borrowed that day. In a sense, the cash worksheet lies at the heart of cash management, since it ties together current information about receipts, disbursements, and investable cash for a specific day.

Investment Management

The goal of investment management is to maximize the income earned on cash invested in short-term, low-risk securities. Generally, these securities include U.S. Treasury and agency obligations, bank certificates of deposit, commercial paper, and other money market instruments. To accomplish this goal, cash managers must be able to track what investments have been purchased, how long they will be held, and how much they will yield. In addition, cash managers should be able to obtain information on the distribution of their investments by investment type, broker, maturity, and fund.

In order to allow flexibility in the selection of investments, cash management software should be able to track a wide variety of investments, including:

- U.S. Treasury obligations;
- U.S. agency obligations;
- certificates of deposit;
- bankers' acceptances;
- commercial paper;
- repurchase agreements;
- money market funds; and
- time deposits.

The following five reports would be helpful to cash managers as they manage investments:

Investment Transaction Listing. This listing reports the three essential investment transactions: the purchase of an investment, its sale, and the receipt of interest. The listing should include the terms of the transaction (e.g., price, rate, yield, settlement date, maturity date, interest accrued and paid, and the amortized discount and premium, if applicable), and where the security is held for safekeeping.

Investment Maturity Listing. It is generally agreed that public-sector investments should be planned so that invested funds are not required before maturity. A listing of the maturity dates and amounts of current investments is useful to help managers see the cash flows that result from their current investments, and to plan the maturities of future investments.

Investment Earnings Report. This report presents the actual interest income, the accrued interest, and the effective yield for each investment as of a specific date.

Portfolio Performance Report. This report is used to evaluate the performance of the different types of securities in the portfolio, and of the portfolio as a whole. It shows the weighted yield for each investment type, and the weighted yield of the portfolio as of a specified date.

Pooled Interest Allocation Report. This report is used to allocate the interest earned by the individual funds contributing to a pooled investment account.

Debt Management

Although the issuance of long-term municipal debt is generally not considered to be a function of cash management, the issuance of short-term debt and the payment of principal and interest on long-term bonds are often tasks that are performed by the cash manager. Consequently, cash managers who have these responsibilities should be aware of the timing and amounts of debt service payments, and should track the costs of issuing short-term debt.[2]

Cash management software can help local officials by maintaining an inventory of outstanding long- and short-term debt, providing a calendar for debt service payments, and calculating the costs of short-term loans. Information can be passed to the cash manager through the following reports:

Inventory of Outstanding Debt. This report records the amount borrowed, the borrowing date, the maturity date, the interest rate, issuer, broker, type of debt.

Debt Service Payment Schedule. This report shows the payment dates and the amount of interest and principal to be paid over a period specified by the user.

Debt Position Report. This report shows the amount of debt outstanding as of a certain date, and the effective yield of the debt for each instrument and for the debt portfolio as a whole.

Bank Management

The general purpose of the bank management function is to maintain efficient banking relationships by making full use of bank services at the lowest possible cost. This requires tracking the use of bank services, analyzing the costs of these services, and maintaining the proper level of compensating balances with the bank. Software designed to aid in bank management can do so through the following reports:

Bank Service Analysis. This report analyzes the use and costs of banking services by tracking the volume of transactions and the unit costs of services per bank. Given this information, it also calculates the balances required to compensate the bank for these services.

Target Balance Report. This report compares target and actual bank balances, and calculates the adjustment necessary to achieve the target balance by month-end.

Bank Index. This "electronic rolodex file" keeps track of individual bank accounts, including approved signers, their authorized limits, and names and addresses of the banks and contact persons.

Telecommunications

Even before the development of computers, telecommunications played an important role in cash management. Cash managers "telecommunicated" each time

---

[2]See Chapter 11 for more information on short-term debt issuance.

they called their banks to obtain information about cash balances or to initiate wire transfers.

With the advent of computers, the role of telecommunications in cash management has become more formal. To reduce the time spent contacting banks for information, cash management workstations may contain modules that automatically dial the banks' computers and obtain balance and transaction information. In addition, the workstations may have the ability to make electronic fund transfers. Given this, there are two general telecommunications submodules that may be of interest to cash managers:

- automated bank balance reporting; and
- automated fund transfers.

Automated Bank Balance Reporting. This submodule provides the telecommunications commands to obtain and consolidate bank account information. The cash manager chooses the time for the computer to call each bank's computer, retrieve and store information, and call the next bank.

Fund Transfers. This submodule can be used by the cash manager to initiate the electronic transfer of funds, or it can be set to automatically transfer funds (e.g., for an automatic transfer of funds to the payroll account). If such a submodule is offered, however, it is vitally important that it contain security codes, with different levels of access for different users.

Additional Software Requirements

The previous section described the functional requirements of software pertaining to cash management. This section presents additional requirements that are applicable to any software system. The following items constitute some of the criteria to consider when evaluating the general aspects of the software. These criteria include:

- user-friendliness;
- integration;
- flexibility;
- storage requirements;
- security;
- system backup;
- software support;
- training; and
- documentation.

The priority given to these criteria will vary with the needs of the user, so the order that they are presented here is not meant to reflect their importance. However, each should be given due consideration when evaluating the software. The criteria are discussed in more detail below:

User-Friendliness. This is clearly an important aspect of any software. The software should be easy to use, and generally this has meant that it is menu-driven. It should also feature help screens, and intelligible error messages.

Integration. Software integration allows information entered through one module to be automatically shared by other modules. Integration is important because it eliminates the time and potential errors involved in rekeying information.

Flexibility. Theoretically, all software should provide information in exactly the format that the user wants. Practically, however, unless you develop your own software, this is not possible. Although most software developers will customize reports (for a price), most off-the-shelf software will require the user to make some concessions to format. Some software is more flexible than others, however, and will allow users to create their own reports.

Storage. Storage requirements constitute a double-edged sword. On the one hand, software that maintains detailed, historical records of all transactions provides useful information to the cash manager. On the other hand, the amount of memory required to keep these records grows with the volume and detail of the transactions, and may outgrow available memory. Some of the larger treasury workstations now recommend that users have at least 20 megabytes to run their systems.

Security. System security is especially important for workstations with telecommunications facilities. Access to wire transfer routines should be restricted to authorized personnel, and the software should contain security codes that restrict access. The software should also maintain detailed records of all fund transfers in a file that cannot be altered by the user.

Backup. Because computer breakdowns occur even with the best precautions, all active files should be copied frequently and stored in a separate location. To facilitate this, the software should contain a backup utility that allows users to copy the current version of all data files at the end of the day.

Software Support. Once the software had been purchased, it is important that the vendor continue to support it. In the words of one software consultant: "You can live with an average product that is superiorly supported. You cannot live with a superior product that is poorly supported." Software support should take a variety of forms, including the vendor's response to customer inquiries, their promptness to fix any "bugs" in the system, and their willingness to update the software to make use of new technologies.

Training. Training is an important aspect of software support, and is indispensable for full application of the software, especially of the complex treasury workstations. Many vendors offer on site training. This is expensive to the vendors, however, and the costs will be passed down to the customer. It would be wise to include training costs in your assessment of the total software costs.

Documentation. After training, the manuals supplied with the software are likely to be the users primary source of information about the software. To be most useful, the documentation should be clearly written, complete, up-to-date, and comprehensible to all software users. In addition, since the documentation will be frequently used to answer specific questions relating to commands or functions, it should include a detailed index.

Acquiring Cash Management Software

After deciding what your cash management software needs to do, the next step is to decide how you are going to acquire it.

Methods for Acquiring Software

Essentially there are three methods for acquiring cash management software:

- internal development;
- external development; and
- hybrid (internal/external) development.

Internal development involves the design and programming of the software by the jurisdiction's staff. This can be the development of simple spreadsheets by internal staff, or it can be a full blown effort by the treasury, accounting, and data processing departments working together. Either way, internal development requires that the jurisdiction's staff be used in all phases of the software's design, coding, and testing.

External development involves design and programming by an outside developer, either through the purchase of an "off-the-shelf" package, or by hiring a developer to produce software to the jurisdiction's specifications. Hybrid development involves the joint design and programming of cash management software by one or several jurisdictions and an outside developer. Each of these methods for acquiring software will be discussed in more detail later in this chapter.

General Steps in Acquiring Software

Regardless of how the software is acquired, there are four major steps, or tasks, that the jurisdiction should be prepared to undertake. These are:

- needs definition;
- software selection;
- system evaluation; and
- system implementation.

Although the subtasks that make up each of these major tasks will be different depending on whether the software is developed internally or externally, the major tasks will be the same for either method of acquisition.

Task 1—Needs Definition. As noted above, this is the most important phase of software acquisition. Although the above section on functional requirements tried to indicate some of the major areas where software can assist cash managers, the specific needs of each jurisdiction will be different. These needs must be laid out in detail by the jurisdiction before any further steps can take place.

The more specific cash managers can be in their definition of needs, the better off they will be when developing or selecting the software. The current cash management system provides the best source of information on the jurisdiction's current needs. All documents relating to the cash management function should be examined, and all procedures outlined. In doing this, special attention should be paid to current reports. Are they as useful as they could be? If not, how might they be improved?

It should be noted again that all of the functional requirements laid out above are only available on very expensive treasury workstation systems. These systems sell for as much as $60,000 and require dedicated personal computers. Consequently, it is also important at this stage to distinguish between needs and wants, i.e., which reports and files you absolutely need in order to function, and which reports and files you would like to have, but can do without.

Task 2—Software Selection. The next step in software acquisition is to decide what type of software or software language will serve as the basis for your system. This is different from selecting the software package itself. This step is important because different types of software are designed for different purposes, and each has its own advantages and disadvantages. Basically, there are three types of software that can be used for cash management: spreadsheet programs, database systems, and treasury workstations.

Spreadsheet Programs. Spreadsheet programs such as Lotus 1-2-3 and Supercalc are relatively inexpensive and easy to use. They provide excellent computational functions and their tables and graphs provide useful tools for cash management. The major disadvantage of spreadsheet programs, however, is that they are relatively inflexible data managers. The addition or deletion of data records is cumbersome, and requires the operator to be very familiar with the file structure and layout. Efforts to make the programs more user-friendly through the addition of menus and "macros" (i.e., commands embedded in the spreadsheet that serve to automate some of the spreadsheet functions) can quickly become cumbersome to program.

Database Systems. Database systems, such as dBase III+, are generally more expensive than spreadsheets and, initially, may be more difficult to learn. They can be used, however, to create interactive, menu-based programs that allow inexperienced users to easily add, delete, modify, sort, recall, and display cash management data. Furthermore, because database software contains a programming language of its own, database systems are capable of powerful data manipulations.

Some of the earlier disadvantages of database systems have been overcome by improvements in programming technology. The speed of database calculations can be substantially improved through the use of "compilers" (i.e., programs that translate the slower source code into quickly executable machine code). In addition, some database software now offers graphic capabilities that rival those of spreadsheet software.

Treasury Workstations. Treasury workstations are the most sophisticated of the automated cash management systems. The workstations usually have telecommunications capability with banks, and the capacity to consolidate cash position information from the banks' balance reports. Often the workstations allow the user to automate wire transfers and wire confirmation letters as well.

Workstations also offer integration in a way that is not practical with spreadsheets or database programs. The workstations are written in compiled computer languages, and so run much faster than many other programs.

A major disadvantage of treasury workstations is that they are expensive, with initial costs as high as $60,000. In addition, managers must rely on the vendors for training and support, which can also be expensive.

Task 3—System Evaluation. The single most important criteria for evaluating a piece of software is whether it does what you need it to do. The best way to determine this is to use the software with real data, and test it to see if it performs the way you want it to perform. If the software is developed internally, this should be easy. If it is developed externally, this will be more or less difficult depending on whether you are having the software developed for you, or whether you are purchasing off-the-shelf software.

If you are purchasing off-the-shelf software, and the developer is reluctant to let you have it on a trial basis, then ask for a demonstration. Often, software developers will demonstrate their software at trade fairs or conferences and can tell you when the next demonstration will be in your area.

Task 4—System Implementation. The final major task involved in software acquisition is the implementation of the system. This involves everything from installing the software on your computer to replacing the prior system. This is probably the most frustrating of the tasks, since it provides a true test of the system.

A variety of problems are commonly experienced at this stage of the acquisition process. Software that works well with low or moderate quantities of data may be overwhelmed by larger amounts. The software may not allow for sufficient growth in the volume of data. Training and documentation may be inadequate. The vendor may not provide adequate support during installation.

Many of the problems commonly experienced at this stage can be avoided by paying careful attention to the first three tasks. If user needs are well defined and future growth is incorporated into the plan, then there should be no trouble with the software's application. If the system and vendor are properly evaluated, there should be no trouble with software installation, support, or training.

Guidelines for Internal Software Development

While it would be impossible to provide a detailed discussion of software design and development within the confines of this chapter, there are a few general principles that should be pointed out in any discussion of software development.

Guideline 1—Develop a Plan. Computer programming, even at the spreadsheet level, requires that the programmer know what information will be obtained from the program (output), what information will be entered into the program (input), what information must be stored by the program (files and databases), and what calculations must be performed. Combining all of this in a program or series of programs requires that a detailed plan be developed before anyone even begins to program. As an audit consideration, it would be useful to plan development of the software so that the system can be brought on-line near the start of the fiscal year.

The usual process for designing a computer program begins with the output. Since the whole point of the computer program is to provide information, the starting point in programming is to determine what information will be provided.

This is done by specifying the reports (both paper "hard copy" and output screens) that the program will provide.

The next step is to determine what output information can be calculated by the program and what information must be entered by the user. Formulas must be found for all of the calculations, and these formulas should be documented. In addition, benchmark results for the calculations should be collected to be used later for testing the program. The benchmark results must be arrived at independently of the program.

The last major step in designing the program is to determine what information must be entered by the user and how the information should be stored. The input screens and menus should be made as easy as possible for the user, and require only the information that cannot be calculated by the program. Duplicate entry of information should also be avoided both in the input screens and the databases.

Guideline 2—Stick to the Plan. One can waste a lot of time programming for contingencies that lie outside the boundaries of the plan. For example, it is not necessary to have a routine that calculates yield to maturity for coupon securities if the jurisdiction only invests in Treasury bills. It may be nice to have this in the future but, for now, it's not required. This is why it is important to determine what you absolutely need before anyone does any programming.

Guideline 3—Plan to Expand. Although this may sound like a contradiction of Guideline 2, it actually helps one to stay with the plan. No software is likely to meet all of your needs. Changing political concerns and investment markets will undoubtedly require changes in the software. While it is impossible to anticipate all of these changes, one can go a long way by thinking carefully about how one is likely to operate in the future. By leaving room in the software for this expansion, one is less likely to try to incorporate it into the current version. Thus, one is more likely to complete the current version on schedule.

Guidelines for External Development or Acquisition

Step 1—Develop Your Request for Proposal. The request for proposal (RFP) is typically used to obtain information from vendors in a way that enhances competition and implies no commitment to buy. In developing your RFP it is important to state your current and future software needs upfront, and to describe hardware and software that you currently use and plan to use.

Vendors should be requested to respond in a standard manner, possibly by filling in a matrix. This will facilitate comparisons among vendors later in the purchasing process. It is also important to obtain a complete set of sample reports and screen layouts, so that you can get a sense of how much vendor customization would be required.

Step 2—Evaluate the Responses. In evaluating RFP responses, note their completeness and the speed with which vendors reply. Review the responses to make sure that the proposed software satisfies your needs. Weigh each of the software requirements in light of its importance to your cash management goals, and score the vendors' responses according to these weights. Select only as many of the top vendors as you are willing to have present their product.

Step 3—Vendor Presentation. Require that the top vendors demonstrate their product. This will allow you to see the software in action, and give you a sense of its ease of use. Before the presentation, identify any areas of concern that you had with the vendor's RFP, and prepare a check list of the things that you want to see the software do. A good demonstration should cover all of the activities of a typical day, starting from bank balance retrieval and ending with system backup. During the demonstration, bring in people from other areas (accounting, auditing, etc.) who will have contact with the software.

After the presentations, reexamine the RFPs and the presentation checklists. Be careful to assess all of the costs of the software, including any additional required hardware, the cost of updates and vendor support, the cost of in-house support (including clerical data entry), and any time-sharing costs that are required.

Step 4—Check Vendor References. Obtain the names of at least two current customers who come from jurisdictions similar to yours, and who are likely to have similar software requirements. Call them and ask about the product, its service and support, and if they would buy the product again.

New Technologies

Computers themselves are new technologies. Personal computers have only been around for a decade, and only been widely used during the last five years. Even so, changes in the computer field continue to happen, and new technologies appear almost daily.

During the past two years, the computational and storage capabilities have increased tremendously. The advent of new "32-bit" chips (both the Motorola 68000 series and the Intel 80386 series) have dramatically expanded the horizons on what personal computers can do. These chips allow computers to process substantially more information, faster, than could be done by personal computers only a few years ago.

In addition, computer memory is expanding rapidly. Disk storage space is increasing and the costs of hard disk storage are falling rapidly. Two years ago, 20 megabyte hard disks were the rage. Now hard disks can hold more than 100 megabytes. Random access memory (RAM) is also increasing. Add-on memory boards can expand random access memory to as much as 16 megabytes on some machines. These revolutions in computer technology have put today's personal computers on a par with yesterday's minicomputers.

Summary

Given the increasing speed and complexity of investments, and the falling costs of computers, it is very likely that computers and computer software will become essential tools for cash management. Properly designed, computer software can reduce the time spent tracking and reporting cash flows and investment yields, and thus provide additional time for investment planning and analysis. However, it is important to remain in control of this environment. While reducing the drudgery of management, computers must not be allowed to abrogate the responsibilities of management.

BIBLIOGRAPHY

Considerations for Governments in Collateralizing Public Deposits (Chicago, IL: Government Finance Officers Association, 1987).

Considerations for Governments in Developing a Master Repurchase Agreement, Second edition (Chicago, IL: Government Finance Officers Association, 1988).

Cook, Timothy Q. and Summers, Bruce J. *Instruments of the Money Market,* Sixth Edition (Richmond, VA: Federal Reserve Bank of Richmond, 1986).

Glossary of Municipal Securities Terms (Washington, D.C.: Municipal Securities Rulemaking Board, 1985).

Governmental Accounting, Auditing and Financial Reporting (Chicago, IL: Government Finance Officers Association, 1988).

Guild, Nathaniel B. *The Public Money Manager's Handbook* (Chicago, IL: Crain Books, 1981).

Hagin, Robert. *The Dow Jones-Irwin Guide to Modern Portfolio Theory* (Homewood, IL: Dow Jones-Irwin, 1980).

Handbook of Securities of the United States Government and Federal Agencies (New York, NY: First Boston Corporation, 1988).

Harrell, Rhett D. *Banking Relations: A Guide for Government* (Chicago, IL: Government Finance Officers Association, 1986).

Homer, Sidney and Leibowitz, Martin L. *Inside the Yield Book* (Englewood Cliffs, NJ: Prentice-Hall, Inc., 1972).

Kaufman, George G. *The U.S. Financial System: Money, Markets and Institutions* (Englewood Cliffs, NJ: Prentice-Hall, Inc., 1986).

Miller, Girard. *Investing Public Funds* (Chicago, IL: Government Finance Officers Association, 1986).

Miller, Girard. *Selecting Financial Services for Government* (Chicago, IL: Government Finance Officers Association, 1984).

Model Investment Legislation for State and Local Governments (Chicago, IL: Government Finance Officers Association, 1984).

Norris, Donald F. *Microcomputers and Local Government,* Second edition (Washington, D.C.: International City Management Association, 1986).

Patitucci, Frank M. and Lichtenstein, Michael H. *Improving Cash Management in Local Government: A Comprehensive Approach* (Chicago, IL: Municipal Finance Officers Association, 1977).

Petersen, John E. *Tax-Exempts and Tax Reform: Assessing the Consequences of the Tax Reform Act of 1986 for the Municipal Securities Market* (Chicago, IL: Government Finance Officers Association and the Academy for State and Local Government, 1987).

A Treasury Management Handbook for Small Cities and Other Governmental Units (Chicago, IL: Municipal Finance Officers Association, 1978).

Stigum, Marcia. *Money Market Calculations: Yields, Break-Evens, and Arbitrage.* (Homewood, IL: Dow Jones-Irwin, 1981).

Stigum, Marcia. *The Money Market,* Revised edition (Homewood, IL: Dow Jones-Irwin, 1983).

Stigum, Marcia and Fabozzi, Frank. *The Money Market and the Bond Market* (Homewood, IL: Dow Jones-Irwin, 1986).

ABOUT THE AUTHORS

Ian J. Allan is a Manager with the Government Finance Officers Association's Government Finance Research Center in Washington, D.C. His current work includes research and consulting projects in the areas of cash management, taxation, and financial capability. Prior to joining the Government Finance Research Center, he worked for the City of Chicago's Office of Budget and Management. Mr. Allan holds a Master of Public Administration degree from the Maxwell School of Citizenship and Public Affairs at Syracuse University, and a Bachelor of Public Affairs degree from Wayne State University.

David R. Bean is a Senior Manager with Ernst & Whinney in Chicago, Illinois. Before joining Ernst & Whinney, he was director of the Government Finance Officers Association's Technical Services Center. In addition, he formerly served as a director of the National Council on Governmental Accounting. Mr. Bean is a co-author of the 1988 *Governmental Accounting, Auditing and Financial Reporting,* and was the editor of *GAAFR Review* for five years. He obtained his government experience working for the State of Illinois as both coordinator for the Comptroller's Uniform Statewide Accounting System and as deputy director of the state's Generally Accepted Accounting Principles (GAAP) Project. He is a certified public accountant in Illinois, and a member of the Illinois CPA Society's Governmental Accounting Committee—Section on Local Government. Mr. Bean holds a Bachelor of Science degree in accountancy from Illinois State University.

Andrea Daroca is the Director of Finance and General Services and City Treasurer of the City of Santa Clarita, California, and is responsible for direction of the accounting, data processing, purchasing, business licenses and building services departments. She is a member of the Government Finance Officers Association, California Society of Municipal Finance Officers, and California Municipal Treasurers Association, of which she is a member of the Professional and Technical Standards Committee. She is also a member of the GFOA's Task Force on Economic Development and is the author of several articles on government finance and administration. She holds a bachelor's degree in accounting from the University of New Orleans and is currently completing studies toward a Master of Public Administration degree at California State University, Long Beach.

Frank P. Daroca is Associate Professor of Accounting at Loyola Marymount University, Los Angeles, California. His previous teaching experience includes Illinois State University and the University of Southern California. He is a certified public accountant and previously served in that capacity and as controller in private industry. Mr. Daroca is a member of the American Institute of CPAs, the American Accounting Association and the Decision Sciences Institute. He is active in continuing professional education programs and is the author of articles in both academic and professional journals. He holds a doctorate in accounting from the University of Illinois as well as bachelor's and master's degrees from the University of New Orleans.

Paul R. Ferm is Senior Vice President for Federal Government Banking at the Citizens and Southern National Bank in Atlanta, Georgia. Through Mr. Ferm's department, C&S provides a full range of cash management services to various federal departments and agencies, including the U.S. Treasury. Prior to assuming his current responsibilities, he headed a department providing deposit, cash management, and loan services to state and local governments. Mr. Ferm has more than 14 years' experience in providing banking and cash management services to government units at the federal, state, and local levels. He currently serves as an advisor to the GFOA's Committee on Cash Management, and is a member of the National Corporate Cash Management Association, the Municipal Treasurer's Association, and the Association of Government Accountants. Mr. Ferm holds a Bachelor of Arts degree from the University of Minnesota. His graduate work includes studies at the Public Finance Institute of the University of Michigan.

Rhett D. Harrell is a certified public accountant, licensed in Georgia and Florida. He currently is a Client Service Manager in the Public Sector Group of Touche Ross & Co. in Atlanta, Georgia. He has more than thirteen years' experience in public accounting and consulting, specializing in state and local governments. He is the author of the GFOA publication, *Banking Relations: A Guide for Government* (1986), now in its second edition. Mr. Harrell currently serves as an advisor to GFOA's Committee on Cash Management. He also co-developed and teaches GFOA's seminar on "Money Market Management" course. Mr. Harrell holds a bachelor's degree in accounting from Florida State University and is completing graduate studies in business administration.

Bonnie R. Kraft is the Management Services Director for the City of Gresham, Oregon. In that capacity she directs five divisions: Financial Operations, Financial Planning and Control, Human Resources, Data Processing, and Recorder. Previously, she held the positions of Treasurer and Finance Director with the City. She is a member of the executive board of the Government Finance Officers Association, and past chair of the GFOA's Committee on Cash Management. She is also a board member of the Oregon Municipal Finance Officers Association; serves on the Oregon State Treasurer's Short Term Fund Board; and is a member of the Metropolitan Service District Investment Advisory Council. She has authored articles for various finance publications, and has been a speaker at several national and state seminars and conferences. She has a Bachelor of Arts degree in management from Marylhurst College in Portland, Oregon, and is currently enrolled in graduate studies.

Anthony T. Logalbo is the Finance Director and Treasurer of the Town of Concord, Massachusetts, where his current responsibilities include investment of the town's funds. Before assuming his current position he served as the Director of Administrative Services for the Massachusetts Municipal Association, and as an Assistant to the Director of Finance in Oakland, California. Mr. Logalbo holds a Master of Public Administration degree from the Kennedy School of Government at Harvard University, a Master of Science degree in industrial administration from Purdue University, and a Bachelor of Science degree from Rensselaer Polytechnic Institute.

Girard Miller is a Vice President for Government Markets at Fidelity Investments Institutional Services Company in Boston, Massachusetts. His responsibilities include working with Fidelity's clients in the design of prudent portfolios, as well as new product design, legislative and technical support for the public sector, and research assistance to finance officer organizations. He also contributes a monthly investment analysis article to Fidelity's public-sector newsletter, *Investment Exchange.* Previously, Mr. Miller was director of the Technical Services Center of the Government Finance Officers Association in Chicago, Illinois. He also served as director of fiscal services for the City of Southfield, Michigan, and as president of the Michigan MFOA. Mr. Miller founded GFOA's investment newsletter, *Public Investor,* and he is the author of numerous GFOA publications, including *Investing Public Funds,* and *Pension Fund Investing.* Mr. Miller holds a Master of Public Administration degree from the Maxwell School of Citizenship and Public Affairs at Syracuse University, and he holds a master's degree in economics from Wayne State University.

Paul L. Shinn is a Manager at the Government Finance Officers Association's Government Finance Research Center in Washington, D.C. His responsibilities include developing and conducting training programs in public finance, conducting fiscal impact studies, and managing studies on utility financing. His publications include *Staying Financially Healthy* for the Environmental Protection Agency (1989), *Costing and Rate-Setting Workbook for Virginia Water and Sewer Utilities* (1989), and *Touching All the Bases: A Financial Management Handbook for Your Wastewater Treatment Project,* with James C. Joseph and Joseph T. Kelley (1986). Prior to joining the Government Finance Research Center in 1985, Mr. Shinn was Senior Management Analyst and Acting Director of Finance and Administration for Washington County, Oregon; Director of Administrative Services for Lane Transit District, Eugene, Oregon; and General Manager of Rogue Valley Transportation District, Medford, Oregon. He received a bachelor's degree in public administration at the University of Oregon in 1977.

W. Paul Zorn is a Research Principal with the Government Finance Officers Association's Government Finance Research Center in Washington, D.C. While at the GFRC he has modeled federal and state financial mechanisms, conducted studies of state and local government financial capability and condition, and designed software for forecasting urban transportation system finances and assisting in local government cash management. Mr. Zorn has also participated in the development of two software programs: THRIFT (the Transit and Highway Revenue and Improvement Forecasting Templates) produced under contract with the U.S. Department of Transportation, and CashCalc (the GFOA's cash management software). He has experience programming in Lotus 1-2-3, dBase III, BASIC and C. Mr. Zorn obtained his Bachelor of Arts degree from the University of Michigan, and Master of Arts in public policy from the University of Chicago.